Flying Saucers
Over America

Flying Saucers Over America

The UFO Craze of 1947

GORDON ARNOLD

McFarland & Company, Inc., Publishers

Jefferson, North Carolina

ISBN (print) 978–1–4766–8766–7
ISBN (ebook) 978–1–4766–4652–7

LIBRARY OF CONGRESS AND BRITISH LIBRARY
CATALOGUING DATA ARE AVAILABLE

Library of Congress Control Number 2021057573

Front cover image: first daylight photo of—what are they?
Official Coast Guard photograph 5554 (Library of Congress).
Background: document relevant to the inquiry into
Kenneth Arnold's UFO sighting near Mount Rainier
(National Archives/Department of Defense).

Printed in the United States of America

McFarland & Company, Inc., Publishers
Box 611, Jefferson, North Carolina 28640
www.mcfarlandpub.com

Table of Contents

Preface

Unidentified flying objects have been an American obsession for a long time. They have prompted much speculation, and many people have strong beliefs about them. Despite all this attention, however, there is no consensus about what they are, what they mean, or what they represent.

Although some people trace the first UFO sightings back to ancient times, the so-called "modern era" of unidentified flying objects began much more recently. In fact, we can pinpoint its beginnings to a specific date: June 24, 1947. On that fateful day, business owner and amateur pilot Kenneth Arnold (who is no relation) spotted something completely mystifying. Strange lights that moved in astonishing ways appeared in the sky over Mount Rainier that afternoon. This single event lasted just a few minutes, but it was enough to ignite a long-lasting cultural phenomenon.

Unlike many, perhaps most books dealing with flying saucers and UFOs, this volume has no ax to grind. It takes no position about what a person should or should not believe about UFOs, and it does not argue for or against any particular theory. This volume is not an exposé that claims to reveal hidden secrets about the flying saucer sightings. Rather, it was prompted by a simple recognition: something unusual happened in the skies of mid-century America, but the jury is still out regarding what that was. After so much theorizing and so little agreement, perhaps it is time to revisit what we do and do not know about those initial events and rethink whatever conclusions we may have drawn.

Understandably, many people might want to cut to the chase. They may think that surely, after all this time, there must be definitive answers to the many questions about the perplexing UFO sightings of the late 1940s. This impulse is understandable, but it is not as simple as that. There are still many unsettled aspects in the flying saucer story of that

1

time. Indeed, 75 years after the events recounted in this volume, uncertainties and ambiguities continue to cloud the picture.

With that in mind, this book sets out to untangle the beginnings of the modern UFO era. It aims to tell a complicated story straightforwardly to help readers make sense of competing theories and claims. It was written for general readers and students from high school through college who may be looking for background on the subject. It also could serve as a primer to the early days of the modern UFO era or as a different take on that story for those who have learned about it before.

How we think about any topic, especially a controversial topic, matters. Accordingly, this volume encourages readers to consider (or reconsider) their approach to the subject of UFOs. It is a book that invites readers to slow down and take a new look at some very unusual happenings from multiple points of view.

The milestone UFO sightings of the late 1940s also invite us to think about other issues. Indeed, many aspects of the great flying saucer wave raise questions about human behavior and America's social, cultural, and political inclinations. So, as the book sorts through the flying saucer story in the following chapters, readers also will find occasional short digressions. These come in the form of historical and other background discussions that aim to shed light on the events and people at the heart of the main narrative.

Ultimately, the flying saucer story is intrinsically interesting regardless of what a person thinks happened. Because in the end, the UFO phenomenon may be as much about us as it is about strange objects in the sky.

Introduction

A new term—flying saucer—entered the lexicon of the American English language in 1947. Before June that year, no one had ever heard of it. That all changed when odd things started occurring in skies across the nation in the summer of that year. Suddenly, people began reporting strange objects and weird lights in the sky that moved in ways that boggled the imagination. Existing language seemed inadequate to convey the bizarre phenomenon. Into that void, news accounts started calling them "flying saucers." It was a colorful phrase, and it stuck.

There had been somewhat similar reports before, but none had the jarring impact of sightings that seemed to come out of nowhere beginning on June 24, 1947. Starting that day and for a few tumultuous weeks, a wholly unexpected flying saucer craze swept across America. Within just a few weeks, hundreds—possibly thousands—of people claimed they saw unknown objects racing across the sky. Their stories spread like wildfire, but no one was sure what to make of it all. Today, nearly everyone has heard about flying saucers and unidentified flying objects (UFOs). But despite the familiarity of the topic, many people still don't know what to think about it.

Flying saucer sightings in the summer of 1947, including an incident near Roswell, New Mexico, started it all. Those events are now the stuff of legend. Indeed, many accounts, theories, stories, films, and other renditions of these early incidents have appeared over the years. But what precisely happened that summer—or, perhaps more importantly, what people at the time *believed* happened—is still not widely understood. Some people have fixed ideas about those events. Yet, it turns out that many of today's beliefs about the UFO craze of 1947 differ significantly from the original accounts. With this in mind, one of the main projects of this book is to go back to that original time and context to reconstruct a general picture of how things looked in 1947 and why they looked the way they did.

The flying saucer craze of 1947 remains controversial, but one thing is sure. Something out of the ordinary was happening. Flying saucers—whatever they were—captured the public's imagination.

Americans quickly latched onto the colorful term "flying saucer" (or a variant, "flying discs") when they talked about the mysterious lights and objects. (No one called them unidentified flying objects or UFOs at the time. It would be several years before anyone started using that label.)[1] People were not sure what was behind the reports but witness accounts of the strange objects were weird enough and numerous enough to propel the subject to the main stage of American culture.

To some, flying saucers seemed to be little more than a fad. However, the topic immediately resonated with a wide swath of the American public. Within hours of the first report, it seemed that almost everyone wanted to hear about the subject and learn more about it. But no one, not even trusted government officials, seemed entirely sure what the mysterious objects were or how to respond to them. Should people be afraid? Should they expect some shocking new revelation of things previously unknown? Were the flying saucers a joke? No one knew what to believe.

In other circumstances, the 1947 UFO wave might have blown over, and the flurry of reports about them might have faded into history. But that is not what happened. Events from summer were not some quaint, fleeting story. Rather, the flying saucer phenomenon of 1947 served as the foundation for a long-lasting modern obsession that has remained on the stage of public awareness for 75 years, with no signs of disappearing anytime soon.

Over time, public memory of those events has glazed over. Layers of confusion and contradiction have muddied waters that were already far from clear. As the original context has slowly receded into history, what remains is more a set of often-repeated stories and suppositions than a straightforward account.

For three-quarters of a century, the topic has seldom drifted very far from the limelight. A steady stream of new reports—often called "incidents" or "encounters"—has kept the topic in the news media over the years. The subject also provides the entertainment industry with a treasure trove of material for movies, television productions, books, magazines, comics, and more.

While there is no shortage of entrenched opinion and speculation about UFOs, consensus about unexplained aerial phenomena is hard to find. Although some people remain undecided about the topic, many others are confident they fully understand what has been going on.

A U.S. Coast Guard staff member took this photograph of unidentified flying objects flying in a "V" formation near Salem, Massachusetts, in 1952. Numerous photographs allegedly documented the existence of "flying saucers" in the middle of the last century, but most, including this one, were inconclusive (Library of Congress).

Those with the strongest beliefs have largely divided into two main camps: the believers and the skeptics. The believers tend to think that many UFO cases involve spacecraft from other worlds and extraterrestrials. Meanwhile, the skeptics will have none of that. To them, UFOs must have simple, if sometimes obscure, earthly explanations. Talk about space aliens flying over the American heartland or crashing in the desert is ridiculous, they say. In the current situation, the opposing interpretations of the phenomenon could scarcely be more different. Agreement seems nowhere on the horizon. Instead, the warring sides continue to argue about the phenomenon acrimoniously, as they have done for decades.

Shared understandings and agreed-upon conclusions may be hard to find, but no one seriously could doubt the tremendous amount of attention the topic attracts. Many might also agree that the phenomenon reflects something in American culture, even if people do not agree about what that something is. Whatever a person does or does not believe about UFOs, the topic is innately interesting as a historical and cultural phenomenon.

The familiarity of the UFO subject somewhat obscures a simple reality. In the 21st century, nearly everyone comes to the topic with many preconceived ideas. People often approach the issue *thinking* they know what happened to set the UFO saga in motion. But the original story has changed over time. Decades of rumor and speculation have added new layers to the confusion. As a result, it is not always clear which assumptions are based on solid evidence. Consequently, the beginnings of the UFO saga are not always easy to see.

The following chapters explain and explore the basics of what was reported initially and give a picture of what various people thought was happening in the first weeks, months, and years of the "flying saucer" era that began in June 1947. The volume also suggests the relevant context and background to the main events. Flying saucers sightings were big news stories. Many people reacted strongly to news about UFOs, but they also had many other things on their minds. Indeed, this larger context is an integral part of the story.

Because some readers approach any book about this topic with certain presumptions, it is essential to note what this book does *not* attempt. Most importantly, it does not try to tell people what they should think about UFOs. Indeed, the following chapters do not set out to prove one point of view or another. Readers can and should decide for themselves which conclusions make sense to them.

Nor does volume attempt to provide an exhaustive compendium of UFO cases. Numerous famous incidents are explored, as are a few that are less well known. But as an overview, many occurrences are not explicitly discussed. That is a conscious choice. Indeed, the book looks more at the forest than at individual trees, focusing on broad issues and contexts. Settling arguments about one incident or another is beyond its scope or purpose. Instead, the chapters seek only to provide a basic account of events and to offer various ways to think about a controversial and complicated topic. It tries to do so without being drawn into any one side of the polarized debate surrounding the subject.

For a controversial topic such as UFOs, it is essential to ask how we know what we know—or, perhaps more accurately, how we know what we *think* we know. It may seem like an academic question of no importance to an ordinary person. Indeed, the sheer volume of available UFO material may make such questions seem inconsequential. There is so much available that it may seem obvious how we know such things. Yet, it would be a grave error to give in to this impulse and skip these questions. Indeed, failing to consider these issues can seriously undercut our understanding of the topic. And failing to ask such questions can give people a false sense of security about things that may be much less certain than they wish to believe.

Any book about flying saucers and UFOs must grapple with a significant and sometimes difficult question: what source material is sufficiently believable to use in constructing the narrative? This simple question leads to others which can present numerous problems. For example, what sources are even available? How reliable are these sources? And how should they be interpreted? Everyone seriously exploring a nonfiction topic faces similar issues. However, things are significantly complicated by the controversial and contested nature of the UFO topic.

One potential source is obvious. Many government reports, memoranda, press releases, and published interviews have delved into the subject, arguably providing much valuable information. However, not every government declaration will be taken at face value by some people. Indeed, the United States government maintains many secrecy policies, has a history of sometimes being less than candid, and has at times exhibited questionable competence in dealing with troublesome issues. (Look no further than the Vietnam War–era Pentagon Papers for evidence of that.)

Still, it would be a mistake to discount everything that government entities have said about UFOs over the years. In many instances, government source material provides a wealth of beneficial information. The problem for a researcher is how to separate what is valuable and reliable from what is not. For this, traditional historical methods are still quite helpful even though it is always possible that an error of interpretation or fact could make its way past a careful review. Such is the nature of research on such topics.

News reports provide another valuable source of information. And indeed, the flying saucer "craze" of 1947 was thoroughly and widely covered in news sources of the day. However, as with other types of material, it is not enough to simply take a news account at its word. It is crucial to maintain a critical eye when looking at a subject that is both new and incompletely understood—both hallmarks of UFO stories when they first appeared on the scene. Indeed, news reports that rely on first-hand witness statements, second- and third-hand accounts, conjectures (even by "experts"), and the editorial judgments of writers, presenters, and news outfits demand scrutiny. And although many things that appear in the news are pretty much as described, media accounts are often subject to unintentional (and sometimes intentional) bias, as well as to errors of commission and omission.

Source material that was produced substantially after the fact complicates matters even more. While an interval of time between some event and a person's statements about it can give people a chance to survey a topic with a clear set of eyes, the passing of time can also introduce new kinds of issues. Of the many types of materials produced long after events, interviews have the most potential and, ironically, create some of the most challenging problems. On the plus side, over time, there is sometimes an opportunity for new witnesses to come forward or for previous witnesses to have processed events more clearly than may have been possible in the heat of the moment. Their thoughts and recollections have the potential to add newer and more profound ways of understanding past events.

On the downside, however, there is an uncomfortable fact. As cognitive scientists have explained in recent years, memory does not work quite the way most people think it does. It is not a camera, and it is far from perfect. And although people can be completely confident about their memory of some event, their recollections, at times, can still be riddled with errors.

In some instances, for example, the well-observed phenomenon of memory distortion can lead to a person "to incorrectly claim to have encountered a novel object or event."[2] Among other potential complications is the misinformation effect, which can occur when "eyewitness memories are altered via exposure to post-event misinformation."[3] Such issues do not always happen, of course. However, they could add additional complexity when assessing witness statements, especially if they are made long after the fact. And since an understanding of the UFO topic relies heavily on witness statements, some of which are issued many years after the fact, it is a potential problem that must be considered. Such are the challenges that confront anyone hoping to examine the beginnings of the UFO phenomenon with fresh eyes.

UFOs have long baffled some of the world's most eminent people. The difficulty of sorting out what did happen, what might have happened, and what probably did not happen has not been an easy task for anyone. Indeed, the topic has proven to be simultaneously riveting and frustrating, as was already evident more than half a century ago.

⇒ 1 ⇐

Things Seen in the Sky

"Something is seen, but it isn't known what," confessed Carl Jung in 1958.[1] It probably was not the answer the one-time protégé of Sigmund Freud wanted to give. More likely, the eminent psychoanalyst would have preferred a more decisive and convincing response to the question people sometimes asked him in his later years.

Jung had devoted much time and effort searching for some satisfactory response, but a definitive answer was elusive. The truths he had uncovered were partial truths. And as much as he may have wanted to give a more definitive reply, he could not say what people hoped he would say with any certainty. So instead, the famed psychologist accepted that there would be no complete answer to the question. He knew his vague and ambiguous response was unsatisfying, but he could take solace that at least it was honest. He was never able to shed more light on the subject. When Jung died a few years later in 1961, he still had not uncovered a satisfactory answer.

The question that perplexed Jung was surprising and controversial: Was there a "physical reality" to the many reports of unidentified flying objects—UFOs—that had flooded newspaper and media accounts in recent years? Did people see something real—something that natural occurrences could not explain? Or did these reports have psychological origins, as some people thought? Perhaps they resulted from hallucinations or some other trick of the mind.

Jung had been curious about the topic since the 1940s. He thought about the subject for years, squeezing time for collecting information about it into his busy schedule. Yet, his notes and data did not add up to very much. "I must tell you that in spite of the interest," he wrote in a 1954 letter, "I have still not been able to establish an empirical basis sufficient to permit any conclusions to be drawn."[2]

Jung may not have found a satisfactory answer, but it was not a frivolous question, especially given the era. Cold War anxieties and the coming of the Space Age provided a dramatic backdrop to the early years of what is sometimes called the modern UFO era. More than ever, things that were long thought to be impossible no longer seemed so. In the new atomic age, fragile humans had built weapons powerful enough to trigger an apocalypse. At the same time, scientific and technological progress brought human space flight closer to reality. In these years of startling scientific discovery and a new world of possibilities, an abrupt surge in UFO sightings was of more than passing interest.

By the time Jung wrote about UFOs in the late 1950s, the subject of UFOs—"flying saucers" as they were still often called—had thoroughly permeated American culture. For more than a decade, numerous UFO sightings had prompted intense speculation. Multiple accounts and treatments of the topic throughout popular culture had generated widespread interest in this puzzling phenomenon.

The public was unsure of what to think. Public officials did not seem to know what to make of it all, either. Some people took the subject very seriously, but for others, it was nothing more than a diversion from the era's more serious news. Some could not decide one way or the other.

Most mid-century UFO accounts seemed to be cases of mistaken identity. The vast majority of reports could legitimately be explained away as weather balloons, optical effects, misidentified aircraft, or weather phenomena. Some other cases did seem to have psychological origins—accounts of the type that initially interested Carl Jung. Other reports turned out to be hoaxes, the work of tricksters, and practical jokers who enjoyed fooling an unsuspecting public. With so many cases easily classified as mistakes, errors, or misrepresentations, many people concluded that the whole subject of UFOs was much ado about nothing.

Yet, some cases were hard to pin down and remained genuine unknowns. And it was from this last category of reports that UFOs had gained a foothold in American culture.

When a flurry of high-profile sightings emerged in the summer of 1947, UFOs took on a life of their own. Many people seem to have kept an open mind as new cases mounted, but a subset of the American population started taking sides.

In that context, some people became very suspicious. They concluded that the unexplained UFO cases could be evidence of hidden secrets—super-weapons in development, covert enemy reconnaissance, or possibly even evidence of beings from another world. Were these people jumping to conclusions? To some extent, it may seem so. In the context of the late 1940s and 1950s, however, such views were not altogether unexpected.

Given the way UFOs are understood in American culture today, it may seem surprising that at first, very few people thought that the unexplained objects came from anywhere other than earth. Initially, however, even people who regarded UFOs as something sinister believed they were of earthly origin. The most common explanation was that they were probably American or Soviet military secrets.

Yet, even early on, some people thought that could not be right. To them, there was nothing earthly about the reported objects. Instead, these people believed the unexplained UFOs were alien spacecraft. This view took a while to develop and spread, but over time it became a popular hypothesis. Indeed, by 2020, a survey conducted by Ipsos, a French marketing research organization, indicated that more than a quarter of Americans believed extraterrestrials had visited earth.[3]

In the late 1940s, however, this view remained atypical. Most of the public seems to have more or less accepted official views, which stressed mundane earthly explanations, even though people probably were aware of some inconsistencies and unanswered questions. UFOs remained an intriguing, sometimes even entertaining topic of conversation. Maybe something was going on that was not yet known, but the subject hardly seemed to rival more immediate concerns of the day.

Carl Jung took an early interest in UFOs, just as media reports started to escalate in the late 1940s.[4] After gathering information and sifting through it, he wrote, "I'm puzzled to death about these phenomena, because I haven't been able yet to make out with sufficient certainly whether the whole thing is a rumour with concomitant singular and mass hallucination, or a downright fact." Jung was a credible observer who had no particular bias in seeing evidence point one way or the other. To him, the whole matter was a puzzle. Whether myth or reality, he said, "either would be highly interesting."[5]

Time never did fully clarify the true nature of every UFO report, but in the late 1950s, Jung was ready to write his analysis of the subject anyway. He did so in 1958 with a short book called *Flying Saucers: A Modern Myth of Things Seen in the Skies.* Jung still lacked clear-cut answers. So, when he addressed the question of whether UFOs "real" or "fantasy products," his honest answer was "This question is by no means settled yet."[6]

The persistence of unanswered questions did not hamper Jung's investigations, however. Because no matter what they might or might not be, UFOs were deeply fascinating to him from a professional perspective. He had always approached the issue "from the psychological aspect of the phenomenon,"[7] as he said. Still, he realized there could be more to it than that. Following the evidence and looking at things from his perspective as a scholar, he tried to remain impartial.

But in 1958, Jung was also annoyed. The source of his irritation was his belief that many people had come to see him as an outright "saucer-believer,"[8] as someone who had already decided that UFOs represented some new kind of reality. That conclusion, he protested, was "altogether false."[9]

Jung blamed the confusion on an article that United Press International (UPI) had recently circulated. He believed the wire story gave readers the impression he thought UFOs were physical objects that could have traveled from another world.

In a specific way, Jung did think there was something "real" in many UFO sightings. That fact probably added to the confusion. However, what Jung meant by saying "real" was not necessarily what most people thought the term meant. His working hypothesis about UFO reports was that people had seen *something*—that some unknown was the basis for the sightings. But whether what people saw was "something material," or instead something "psychic," he could not and would not say. "Both are realities," he explained, "but of different kinds."[10]

In categorizing physical objects and psychic states as two different kinds of reality, Jung was probably clear to readers who knew about the psychological theories that formed the basis of his life's work. For the lay public, however, the word *reality* was not taken in that nuanced way. Indeed, most people probably thought reality meant physical reality—that the unidentified objects were something a person could touch and had material existence. That was far different from Jung's concept of psychic reality, however. So, when the public read that Jung said UFOs were *real*, they presumed he meant that they were physical objects. And if the objects were physically real but not explainable as the result of earthly creation, some may have concluded Jung thought UFOs had extraterrestrial origins.

Jung's attempt to clarify his position was only partially successful. But if he did not want to cast his lot with the saucer believers, it is also true that he was not ready to completely dismiss the possibility that UFOs were evidence of something as yet unknown. This impartiality displeased many of the people with strong opinions about UFOs. However, Jung's was a scientific approach that discarded possibilities only when there were strong reasons to reject them. When Jung was writing in the late 1950s, some theories about the unexplained UFO cases may have seemed improbable—and in some cases, overly so. However, those ideas could not be completely ruled out at the time. Improbable is not impossible.

Although Jung concluded that there was a psychological dimension to the UFO phenomenon, he did not claim that psychic aspects necessarily told the whole story. Whatever merit the "psychological explanation" possessed did not provide a completely satisfactory answer to the fundamental question. He admitted as much in the final section of his book, in which he said:

> Unfortunately, there are good reasons why the UFOs cannot be disposed of in this simple manner. So far as I know, it remains an established fact, supported by numerous observations, that UFOs have not only been seen visually but have also been picked up on the radar screen and have left photographic traces on the photographic plate.[11]

In the end, Jung recognized the situation for what it was. The psychological explanation could not fully account for all the evidence as it was then understood. Something still seemed to be missing. He accepted that there were unknowns and uncertainties. When he said, "Something is seen, but it isn't known what," he was acknowledging that the UFO phenomenon could only be partially explained.

Undoubtedly, Jung's—or any open-minded inquisitor's—difficulty in fully explaining UFOs was complicated by how deeply the subject penetrated the culture. If not yet urban legends at the time, UFOS at least represented something approaching folk wisdom or received knowledge. Numerous reports had piled up over the years, creating a powerful cultural narrative. Indeed, within a very short time after the flurry of stories in 1947, few people remained unaware of UFOs. And few people did not know of various speculations about them. In very short order, then, the public interpreted UFO sightings in light of what people already knew, or thought they knew, based on previous reports.

However, at first and for a brief time, things were simpler. People had fewer preconceived ideas about the unknown objects, and the subject had not crystallized as a cultural concept. Yet, even at the outset, it was not clear what had happened. And when Jung wrote about the subject in the late 1950s, public memory of the actual events and their contexts were hidden under mountains of imperfect memory and obfuscation. By then, the UFO story had developed a life of its own, with readymade storylines and a cast of purported heroes and villains, of reliable witnesses or fools. The whole thing was taken to be a big mistake, a mass delusion, a sign of extraterrestrial alien contact, or a conspiracy. It all depended on one's point of view.

Initially, however, it was not necessarily any of those things. Flying saucers mostly just needed an explanation. In some respects, UFOs were not even something new. After all, people have long recorded mysterious visions in the skies. But in 1947, the summer of the flying saucers, the situation changed. Perplexing aerial phenomena took on a new urgency as hundreds of UFO sightings generated headlines across the country and worldwide. It was only then that the public took notice as never before, sparking a media frenzy. Events in June of 1947 launched a phenomenon into the national conversation, where it has stayed ever since.

No one could have predicted this outcome as the day began on June 24 of that year. It all started with an ordinary man making a routine trip and looking to make a little extra money. By chance, however, he happened to be in the right place at just the right time to see something extraordinary.

≈ 2 ≈

In Search of a Missing Plane

Reports of mysteries in the skies were nothing new in mid-century America. Accounts of inexplicable aerial phenomena surfaced from time to time throughout the early decades of the 20th century. But although people may have had some general awareness of an odd report here and there, it was hardly a subject that made much of an impression on society. The public did not seriously worry about unexplained aerial phenomena.

The closest Americans came to genuine concern about the subject followed an infamous radio broadcast in 1938 when Orson Welles' dramatic interpretation of *War of the Worlds* created a stir. According to media accounts, many people in the radio audience claimed not to realize that Welles' well-publicized dramatization of the famous H.G. Wells science-fiction novel was fiction. Instead, they thought it was a genuine news report about an actual attack from space. The purported misunderstanding quickly achieved urban-legend status.

The media played up the supposed panic spurred by the radio drama. *The New York Times* even ran a major story about it the following day. An article with the headline "Radio Listeners Panic, Taking War Drama as Fact" reported that Welles' broadcast had erroneously "led thousands to believe that interplanetary conflict had started."[1] Some other newspapers presented the story with even more drama. The headline on the front page of the New York tabloid *Daily News* read "FAKE RADIO 'WAR' STIRS TERROR THROUGH U.S."[2] The all-upper-case headline was printed in type so large that it took up a substantial portion of the page. However newsworthy the story was or was not, editors probably thought it was appropriate for publication in their papers' Halloween edition.

In subsequent years, the "panic" was mythologized in American popular culture.

Many people continue to believe that the incident must have generated a substantial scare. However, recent scholarship suggests that many people did not take Welles' broadcast as literally and seriously as is often alleged. If a real, widespread panic accompanied the broadcast, it seems to have been short-lived and far less pervasive than is commonly thought.[3]

Still, it made a good story in the waning years of the Great Depression. The misconstrued broadcast added to Orson Wells' growing reputation as a rising star in the entertainment business. But it did not cause Americans to fixate on spacecraft and visitors from other worlds. Despite any initial confusion, it was nothing more than a piece of fiction dealing with beings from other planets. That was not anything new. After all, the public had followed the exploits of fictional space heroes such as Flash Gordon, Buck Rogers, and similar science-fiction heroes for years. So, after the initial confusion subsided, Welles' radio adaptation of *War of the Worlds* could easily be understood as part of that pop culture milieu.

There had indeed been more serious reports and news accounts of weird aerial sightings before, and these continued to surface occasionally. Even as World War II raged in the early 1940s, for example, reports of strange observations trickled in. Allied pilots spoke of "foo fighters"—strange lights they saw in the sky. Officially, these were determined to be abnormal atmospheric conditions or unknown experimental aircraft, but they were still considered newsworthy at the time.

After the war, witnesses occasionally claimed they, too, had seen unusual things that they could not fully explain. A few such incidents had even occurred in America during the spring of 1947.

Despite a long history of reports about inexplicable aerial phenomena—the term "unidentified flying object" was coined until the 1950s—the subject never drew sustained public attention. There may have been continuing stories of unusual visions, but these episodes attracted little sustained public interest.

That all changed because of Kenneth Arnold, a 32-year-old business owner who was also a licensed pilot. Married with two children at the time, Arnold was a typical young American of the era. Based in Boise, Idaho, he was a no-nonsense family man. Well-regarded as an upstanding citizen, Arnold was eager to get ahead and devoted much of this time to build his small firefighting equipment company.[4] To help the company grow, he had even purchased a small plane to make it easier for him to make business calls around the region.

On June 24, 1947, Arnold made what started as a routine flight from Chehalis, Washington, en route to Yakima, some 150 miles away. It was a clear day—perfect conditions for taking a trip in his small CallAir A-2 two-seater plane.

As he traveled east, Arnold decided to take a minor detour that might lead to a little extra money. It was a small but fateful decision that put him in the right place at the right time to see something remarkable—something that would prove to be the beginning of a significant sea change in the way the public thought about what we now call UFOs.[5]

Arnold's detour brought him over the Cascade Mountains, not far from majestic Mount Rainier. He was hoping to make a discovery—one that would allow him to collect a reward for information about a tragedy that had unfolded there six months earlier.

On December 10, 1946, a military transport plane took off from San Diego to begin what should have been an uneventful flight. The aircraft was part of a six-plane aerial convoy ferrying Marines to Seattle, 1200 miles to the north. The weather was good, and the skies were clear in southern California that day. There was nothing to suggest that this would be anything other than an ordinary mission.

It was a mundane journey at first, but weather conditions worsened in the trip's final hours. As the convoy neared airspace over Washington state, strong winds and pounding rain created difficult flying conditions.

The Curtiss' R5C-1 model (also called the C-46) aircraft already had earned a bad reputation. It was known to present pilots with all

Mount Rainier, the highest peak in the Cascade mountain range, provided a dramatic setting for the first flying saucer sighting in the modern UFO era in the summer of 1947 (Carol M. Highsmith Archive, Library of Congress).

sorts of challenges. "From first to last, the Commando remained a head-ache," Air Force documents said of the model. "It could be kept flying only at the cost of thousands of extra man-hours for maintenance and modification."[6]

Whether that played into the events that followed is not known. What is known is that the mission ran into serious trouble.

As the storm worsened, four planes in the convoy cut their flights short and diverted to Portland, where they could wait out the storm. Another plane successfully pushed through and touched down safely in Seattle as planned. However, the final aircraft, piloted by Major Robert V. Reilly, was not so lucky.

Reilly checked in with the Civil Aeronautics Administration station in Toledo, Washington, by radio at 4:13 p.m. With abysmal visibility and ice on the wings, he wanted to adjust his flight altitude to bring the air-craft over the cloud cover, where conditions would be better.

At the time, the aircraft appears to have been flying at around 9,000 feet. The plane was easily capable of flying at a much higher altitude, but that model's cabin was unpressurized. That meant that it had to stay much closer to the earth when passengers were in the main compart-ment, as was the case that day. Although usually posing minimal risk, an altitude of 9,000 feet in these dire weather conditions was very low and far from ideal. To make matters worse, the plane was in the vicinity of Mount Rainier, which rises over 14,000 feet.[7]

Ominously, radio communications went silent after Reilly's 4:13 check-in. At about the same time, John C. Preston, who was on the job as a superintendent at Mount Rainier National Park that day, suddenly noticed something concerning. Despite the torrential rain, he detected what he believed was the sound of an aircraft overhead.[8] That seemed odd enough, but then there was silence. This turn of events did not seem as though it could be anything good.

With contact lost and the plane presumed to be missing, officials quickly feared the worst. Bad weather made rescue efforts difficult over the following days. With no results and little hope, officials suspended the search just two weeks later. Winter had closed in on the mountain by this time. There would not be a realistic opportunity to resume any kind of organized search until the spring thaw.

It did not take long for officials to conclude there was no realis-tic chance of finding survivors. The 32 people aboard the plane—a crew of three and 29 Marine passengers—were presumed to have perished. With that, the search formally ended.

At this sad juncture, Marine officials decided they wanted to do right by those who were among the missing and presumed dead. They posted a reward of $5,000 for information that could lead them to the final resting place of the downed plane.

That potential reward motivated Arnold to divert his flight and search for the missing plane on June 24 the following summer. Unfortunately, his luck was not better than the unsuccessful searches that had come before. (The wreckage was not found until weeks later.)

Yet, if Arnold's search for the downed Marine transport proved unsuccessful, it was nonetheless fateful. For as he was scouring the rugged terrain below for some sign of the wreckage, he thought he saw— was *sure* he saw—something unusual and unexpected. It first appeared as a bright flash of light in the distance.

The flash lasted only a moment, and at first, Arnold figured it was nothing more than a reflection from the bright sun that day. He looked for the light source but only saw a DC-4 passenger plane at a moderate distance in the other direction. That, he thought, could not have been the source of the light, so he kept looking.

A few moments later, there was another flash of gleaming light. This time, he got a better look at what seemed to be causing it. In the opposite direction from the DC-4, he spotted nine unknown objects flying in a formation over the mountains some distance away. He could not make out what these objects were, though he later described them as crescent shaped. He also noted that their flight behavior was bizarre and not like anything he had seen before.

Whatever these objects were, they were traveling at a tremendous speed. He estimated a rate of well over 1000 miles per hour. Arnold later said that his first thought was that he had caught a glimpse of some super-secret military aircraft—possibly something no one was supposed to see. But something did not seem right. No publicly known American aircraft had broken the sound barrier (767 miles per hour) at the time, as Arnold knew since he followed aeronautical news.

After the objects disappeared from view, Arnold continued to scan the sky for a while, hoping to get another look. But there was nothing more to see. After a short time, he put his plane back on course and headed for Yakima.

When he landed his plane a while later, Arnold had quite a story to tell. And when he was safely back on *terra firma*, he found people very willing to listen.

According to Arnold's later accounting of the events that day, he first told his story to a manager named Al Baxter and a few other pilots at the airport in Yakima shortly after landing. "I recall that he [Baxter] looked at me in a rather puzzled way but seemed quite positive that I hadn't gone crazy and wasn't seeing things," Arnold would write a few years later.[9]

Arnold was puzzled by what he had seen and wanted to talk about it. However, it was getting late, so he took to the air again and headed to his next stop in Pendleton, Oregon, another 150 miles to the east.

By the time he touched down, news of Arnold's story had already reached his destination. "When I landed at the large airfield at Pendleton," he wrote, "there was quite a group of people to greet me. ... [B]efore very long it seemed everybody around the airfield was listening to the story of my experience."[10]

On the following day, Arnold visited the offices of the *East Oregonian,* the local newspaper. He arrived in the late morning, aiming to find out if anyone at the paper had heard rumors about the military testing aircraft in the area.[11] At this point, Arnold still seems to have been looking for a rational explanation for what he saw. He still thought some type of secret military technology was the most likely answer.

Arnold does not seem to have learned anything new during his visit to the newspaper, but he provided a brief account of what he had seen the previous day while he was there. He told his story to local reporter Bill Bequette, who, along with editor Nolan Skiff, was in the office that day.

Though unclear and something of a mystery, Arnold's eyebrow-raising tale seemed intriguing enough to share with readers. Bequette thought enough of it to type a short item for the paper's evening edition. It ran at the bottom of the front page of the *East Oregonian*'s on June 25 with the headline "Impossible! Maybe, But Seein' Is Believin', Says Flyer."[12]

The article about nine unknown objects in the sky was too short to provide much substance, but it seemed like a good diversion from more serious news. It was the kind of "human interest" item that newspaper readers liked and made a good conversation topic.[13]

If the *East Oregonian* had been the only news outlet to publish Arnold's story, the subsequent flow of events might have been very different. It is possible, perhaps likely, that his story would have remained a local or regional story that made only a fleeting impression on the local population. In that scenario, it very possibly would have faded from public memory when media attention inevitably turned to whatever would be next.

Things did not work out that way, however. Instead, within hours, the story of the nine mysterious objects was picked up by the Associated Press. And once the news service distributed the item nationally and internationally, Arnold's intriguing tale took on an unpredictable life of its own.

$\Longrightarrow$ 3 $\Longleftarrow$

Flashes of Light

Something unusual streaked across the skyline of the Cascade Mountains that June afternoon, the amateur pilot said. But what? Even when Arnold landed and had time to gather his thoughts, he was not sure. His search for answers led him to the offices of the *East Oregonian,* a small newspaper in Pendleton, Oregon. When he arrived late in the morning, he asked the staff if anyone knew anything that could explain what he saw. They did not. From that point, the mystery deepened.

Arnold was at a loss to describe exactly what he saw. He tried in vain to come up with a concrete explanation that fit the details as he recalled them. The Idaho businessman was not the sort of person prone to telling wild stories or making dubious reports about strange visions. Instead, he was an average citizen who simply saw something he did not understand. Now he just wanted to know what it was.

Maybe he witnessed a secret military test flight. That thought occurred to him almost immediately. By the time he visited the *East Oregonian,* he still thought that was a strong possibility. By then, as he later recounted, he had time to make some specific calculations about how fast whatever he saw was moving. By his reckoning, the objects traveled over well 1000 miles per hour, an incredible speed for any known airborne technology in those days.[1] Perhaps, he thought, he inadvertently stumbled across a top-secret test of guided missiles. Of course, that explanation did not square entirely with everything he remembered seeing—especially the erratic flight pattern he thought he detected—but maybe it was that simple, after all.

Another possibility was that Arnold had seen a rocket plane of some kind. Although some discussions of the June 24 sighting claim that no American aircraft was capable of the speeds that Arnold reported, the rocket-plane explanation is not as incredible as it may seem at first glance. At the time, military contractors were working feverishly to develop an ultra-fast plane that could carry a human pilot. The details of

21

that experimental technology may have been classified information, but general awareness that the U.S. military was working toward that goal was not.

Indeed, the military's quest for supersonic aircraft was well known. For example, when readers of *San Jose Evening News* first saw the story of the downed Marine transport—the object of Arnold's search—on the front page of the December 11, 1946, edition, they may have noticed another headline just below it: "Rocket Plane Given Test." That syndicated article, which ran in newspapers across the country, played up America's aeronautic advances. "A new air age was heralded today," reporter Jack Hauptli wrote, "with an official announcement by the United States army that its first rocket plane, the Bell XS-1, has successfully test flown ... in the California desert."[2]

At the time, the much-publicized Bell XS-1 represented a leading technology in the U.S. military's rapidly expanding collection of modern, even futuristic aircraft. Even in 1946, the XS-1 had already been flown at well over 500 miles per hour. That was very fast, but the military had much greater hopes for the rocket plane's full capabilities shortly. Indeed, they aimed to crack the sound barrier by a long shot and to do it soon. In December of 1946, officials publicly boasted that the XS-1 would reach 1700 miles per hour by the following summer, an astonishing speed at the time.[3]

It took a few months longer to reach that goal than officials initially predicted. Chuck Yeager would famously pilot an upgraded version of the aircraft to supersonic speeds on October 14, 1947. In the intervening months, however, the project remained in the public eye.

Interestingly, just three weeks before Arnold's UFO encounter on June 24, test pilot Chalmers Goodlin flew the Bell aircraft for a high-profile Aviation Writers Association event.[4] During the brief demonstration, Goodlin put on quite a show. As the rocket plane streaked high above the onlookers, he fired up the rocket engine. It made a big impression, but it also caused a fire that put the aircraft out of action for two months.[5]

There were no known test flights of the Bell rocket-plane near the Cascades on June 24, the date of Arnold's famous sighting. And there is no evidence to suggest that the Bell XS-1 (or its successor, the Bell X-1) was what Arnold saw. Yet, the press widely reported the military's efforts to break the sound barrier in a futuristic new aircraft. Therefore, it seemed reasonable that Arnold wondered if a plane of this type was what he had seen.

In the hours and days immediately following his mysterious encounter, Arnold was preoccupied with finding this type of rational explanation for it. But his efforts to find a satisfactory answer were complicated. While his memory of the sighting was specific in some ways, it was vague in others.

Arnold was sure he had seen nine objects, which he first noticed due to a bluish flash of light in the distance. He was sure of that much. He was also confident that the objects were traveling at an incredible speed, which he roughly calculated to be over 1000 miles per hour— perhaps as much as 1200 or even 1700 miles per hour. So, these details could be explained by some sort of secret missile or advanced aircraft.

But the objects' motions were odd, too. According to one report, the objects had been "dipping and skimming through the sky."[6] Another reported that Arnold had said they moved "like the tail of a kite."[7] It was not like the motion of ordinary aircraft.

On a more fundamental level, the amateur pilot found it challenging to ascertain the exact shape of the objects he saw. If what he saw was a jet or some rocket-propelled plane, where were the tailfins? If they were there, he had not seen them. Based strictly on what he saw (or thought he saw), the objects' overall shape did not have the silhouette of any aircraft he knew. They were, as he described them, "peculiar looking."

News accounts were inconsistent when reporting Arnold's description of the objects. It is difficult to say whether that was due to Arnold using different wording at different times or to inattentive news writing. In one article, for example, he allegedly compared the objects to "pie pans" while also adding they had a "crescent shaped ... [and] half-moon shaped, oval in the front and convex in the rear."[8]

Even though it is difficult to pin down the exact words Arnold used to describe his encounter, the language that newspapers employed soon crystallized around the term "flying saucers." It was a phrase that Arnold later maintained he had never used.

But if he did not say those exact words, he did use language that was close to it. An early news item about the incident quoted Arnold as saying, "nine saucer-like aircraft flying in formation at 3 p.m."[9] The use of the descriptor "saucer-like" in the *East Oregonian* appears to have led journalists to coin the term "flying saucer."

Most syndicated news stories began using the "flying saucer" label almost immediately, although sometimes "flying disk" was used in its place. For example, *Lodi News-Sentinel*, a newspaper based about 35 miles south of Sacramento, ran a story with the headline "Veteran Pilot Clings to Flying Saucer Story" in its June 27, 1947, edition—just three days after Arnold's encounter. (The first part of the article was composed of syndicated material that was dated June 25.) The story starts

UNCLASS[...]

Pilot K███████████ was flying his plane at an altitude of approximately
9,200 feet. He trimmed out plane in direction of Yakima, Washington
which was almost directly east of his position and sat in his plane observing the sky and the terrain. To the left was a DC-4 and, to his rear
approximately 15 miles distant there was a 14,000 ft elevation. The sky
was clear as crystal. A bright flash suddenly reflected on the plane.
Upon looking to the left and to the north of Mt. Rainier he observed a chain
of 9 peculiar looking craft flying from north to south at approximately
9,500 ft elevation and going seemingly in a definite direction of about 170°.
Thought at first they were jet aircraft but noticed that every few seconds
2 or 3 of them would dip or change their course slightly just enough
to cause the sun to strike them at an angle which reflected brightly on his
plane. As they approached Mt. Rainier he could observe their outlines
against the snow quite plainly, but couldn't find any tails. Clocked speed
and found it to be approximately 150 MPH. Never before had he observed
planes flying so close to mountain tops. They flew directly south to
southeast down the hog's back of a mountain range. Pilot thought they were
at approximately the same elevation as he was. They flew in rather diagonal
chain-like line as if linked together and seemed to hold a definite direction
but swerved in and out of the high mountain peaks. Distance which was almost
at right angles seemed to be between 20 to 25 miles. Thought they were quite
large to be observed at that distance even on a clear day. They seemed
smaller than the DC-4 but he judged their span to be as wide as the further-
est engines on each side of the fuselage of the DC-4 (45 to 50 ft). The chain
seemed to be approximately five miles long.

NOTE: It was the opinion of the agent interviewing Mr. ██████ that
           he saw the "flying discs" In this regard agent further stated
           that if Mr. Arnold could write a report of such a character
           and did not see the objects he was in the wrong business and should
           be engaged in writing Buck Rogers fiction.

           The attached is what ██████████d later produced. See "Fate"
           magazine article by ███████████.

                    Seemed to travel in sidewise position and did not
                    appear to whirl or spin

Side View

Top

UNCLASSIFIED

They seemed longer than wide
thickness being about 1/20
of width

Above and opposite: Investigators at the Army Air Forces (forerunner of the
Air Force) took an early interest in "flying saucers." A sanitized collection
of documents relevant to their inquiry into Kenneth Arnold's UFO sighting near Mount Rainier includes some of the earliest records of the pilot's
description of the objects. The document also contains a small hand drawing (visible in the detail image) of the strange aircraft (National Archives/
Department of Defense).

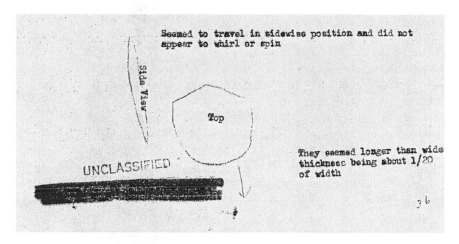

out using language close to Arnold's original words when it says he "clung stoutly to his story that he saw nine, *crescent-shaped* [emphasis added] planes or pilotless missiles fly in formation."[10] Yet, a few paragraphs later, the terminology switches to "flying saucers." The apparent discrepancy between a crescent shape and a saucer is not explained.

Within 72 hours of Arnold's strange sighting and the first news accounts of it, the memorable and colorful "flying saucer" label was being used prominently in publications across the country. People who read about Arnold's encounter often thought he said he had reported seeing "flying saucers," even though he seems not to have used that language at the time.

The precise terminology attributed to Arnold may seem like a minor quibble, but arguably, such details are important. In any case, it was a bone of contention to Arnold, who was generally unhappy about the way his experience was reported in the press. The quick adoption of the "flying saucer" label, which he felt was inaccurate, was a particular sore spot, as he confirmed in an interview with the legendary CBS reporter Edward R. Murrow a few years later.

In a radio interview with Murrow that aired on April 7, 1950, Arnold explained the origin of the " flying saucer" term. "These [unknown aerial] objects more or less fluttered like ... boats on very rough water or very rough air of some type," he told Murrow. "And when I described how they flew, I said that they flew like they take a saucer and throw it across the water. Most of the newspapers misunderstood and misquoted that, too. They said that I said that they were saucer-like; I said that they flew in a saucer-like fashion."[11]

In an understatement worthy of his low-key wit, Murrow replied, "This was a historic misquote."

Decades later, it remains challenging to pinpoint precisely who first used the "flying saucer" label and where it first appeared.[12] Arnold said the term did not originate with him, and there is no compelling reason to presume otherwise. Yet, despite Arnold's insistence that he had not said "flying saucers," the term, and the phenomenon to which it referred, struck a chord with the public.

No matter who said it first, the "flying saucer" label was evidently love at first sight for numerous reporters, editors, and headline writers. Many of them immediately sensed that readers might flock to stories about the mysterious topic. So, they dove into the subject enthusiastically. It is not possible to know whether news people believed that flying saucers were a figment of the imagination, or misidentified aircraft, or unusual natural occurrences, or indeed evidence of some new and potentially otherworldly phenomena. What mattered was flying saucers, whatever they were, appealed to the public, and people wanted to know more.

And so, by the weekend, newspapers in far-flung places across the country were already publishing articles about Arnold's encounter, even as new reports from other sources started to surface, as well.

The editors were right. Mere days of Arnold's fateful flight over the Cascades, the subject had spread like wildfire. The public proved to be thirsty for flying-saucer stories. The unknown objects provided a hot topic of conversation for people across the nation and other countries.

The general public had never heard of Kenneth Arnold before his UFO sighting of June 24, 1947. Had he not decided to search for a missing plane near Mount Rainier, perhaps it would have stayed that way. But it took only a few days after the first publication of Arnold's strange story in the *East Oregonian* for all that to change. After that, Kenneth Arnold, the man who saw something he could not figure out, was famous.

⟹ 4 ⟸

Wildfire

The report of unexplainable objects in the sky near Mount Rainier may have started as a local story in a small-town newspaper. Almost overnight, however, the story made national headlines. As the wire services circulated an account of Kenneth Arnold's experience across the country, newspaper editors in far-flung cities and towns included the amateur pilot's tale in their publications. It provided readers with a diversion from more mundane news, and the subject found a broad audience eager to hear of something new and out of the ordinary.

As the hours and days passed, Kenneth Arnold stuck to his strange story, and public interest in it grew. Many people soon developed opinions about it. A parade of experts, officials, and everyday citizens came up with various explanations for Arnold's peculiar tale. Some of their theories were routine. Others veered into more imaginative territory. The net result was that Arnold, a person who had never been in the public eye before, stayed in the news for days, which turned into weeks. Given the circumstances, perhaps all that hoopla was to be expected.

What may have been far less expected was that many similar reports soon joined Arnold's account. Indeed, within a few days, new stories of equally bizarre and baffling aerial phenomena appeared in newspapers across the nation. The question of what Arnold saw was still far from settled as these additional sightings began to surface.

New accounts of sightings trickled in a few days of Arnold's initial incident. Less than 72 hours after Arnold's encounter, for example, the Associated Press carried a report documenting the experience of 38-year-old Byron Savage, another business traveler with a pilot's license. Savage, too, said that he witnessed something remarkable in the sky. However, in his case, the events occurred several weeks earlier in Oklahoma, more than 1500 miles to the east-southeast of the Cascade Mountains, where Arnold said he saw nine objects.

According to Savage, one late afternoon in mid–May, with "little sunlight in the sky," he noticed "a flat, disc-like object came across the city from just a little east of south."[1] The object did not stay within his view for very long, he said, perhaps only "four or five seconds." That was enough time, however, for him to observe some details about it. "The machine, or whatever it was, was a shiny, silvery color—very big—and was moving at a terrific rate of speed."

Whatever it was, it was unusual, and Savage did not recognize it. There was something else odd thing about it, too. "The funny thing about it was that it made no noise," he reported. "I didn't think it had any kind of internal combustion engine."[2]

Excited to see something so unusual, Savage immediately told his wife about the strange object. She did not share his enthusiasm. He had probably just seen lightning in the distance, she thought. There was perhaps little more to it than that.

Later, Savage also mentioned the incident to a few pilots he knew. But they seemed to agree mostly with his wife and presumed it was a case of mistaken identification.

Facing this disbelief and skepticism when he initially discussed the incident with friends and associates, Savage let the matter drop. "Fear of ridicule kept him quiet,"[3] one news report later explained. After a few days, he seems to have decided not to pursue the case beyond that.

When Kenneth Arnold's sighting made national headlines in late June, however, Savage quickly changed his mind. As of June 26, Arnold's story had only been in circulation for a couple of days. But already, the Idaho-based amateur pilot had become the subject of national speculation and even ridicule. Although the officials who interviewed him later concluded that Arnold was an even-keeled and honest person, his story was very odd. And as often happens when people hear something out of the ordinary, some began to doubt both the story and the witness. Within days, some were ready to cast aspersions. More than a few people assailed Arnold's mental state, reliability, and character overall.

Savage had never heard of Arnold before the newspaper reports. But after the Kansas City resident learned about Arnold and the skepticism directed at his story, he sympathized with Arnold's plight. At that point, Savage decided to go public with his account, apparently with the idea that it would add some credibility to Arnold's report.[4] "I read about that man [Kenneth Arnold] seeing nine of the same things I saw," Savage told a reporter, "and I thought it was only fair to back him up."[5]

The wire services circulated Savage's story just as they had with Arnold's. Whether this new account led very many people to change their minds about Arnold's encounter is difficult to judge. Of those who initially thought that Arnold's report was probably a mistaken identification or hoax, most may not have altered their opinion.

As reports mounted, at least one person changed her mind. Indeed, by the time Savage's account was published, his wife had come around to his way of thinking. She finally concluded that her husband had been right all along when he said he had seen a real, unexplained object in the Oklahoma skies.[6]

If people had previously worried about reporting strange objects in the sky because of what others would think, Arnold's account—and now Savage's and a few others—broke the ice. By the end of the week, more such stories began to surface.

In another instance, a man said he saw "nine of them [saucers] flying in a group, with one a little to one side," according to a story published by the *Chicago Tribune* on June 27.[7]

That same day, the *Portland Oregonian* published a report about a woman in Bremerton, Washington, who said that she also saw mysterious saucers. In fact, she said she had seen them two separate times as they flew over her house.[8]

Meanwhile, 2,000 miles away in Joliet, Illinois, another report indicated that a railroad engineer named Charles Kastl witnessed something unusual. Kastl reported seeing nine "flying pie pans ... going very fast" and racing across the sky to the east.[9]

The pace of new reports quickened. Within days, a few cases turned into many as reports of flying saucers and unexplained aerial visions started to pour in. At first, most sightings were from Western and Midwestern states, such as Washington, Oregon, Idaho, California, Arizona, Colorado, Missouri, and Nebraska. Before long, however, sightings spread geographically.

By Independence Day, which was only a week and a half after Arnold's sighting, reports of unidentified aerial objects were rampant. By then, such incidents were occurring far and wide. On Saturday, July 5, crowds attending several large gatherings in different parts of the country said they saw flying saucers, too. In South Carolina, a newspaper reporter—presumably a reliable observer—said, "a flying saucer passed over Charleston headed east at 7:20 p.m."[10] He was apparently only one of 200 witnesses who saw the same thing.

As more cases started appearing in the media, Arnold's initial sighting remained controversial, and newspapers continued to report about it. After hearing about the story, a United Airlines pilot was highly skeptical, scoffing that he had "never seen anything like that. What that other fellow [Arnold] probably saw was the 'reflection of his own instrument panel,'" he said.[11] Another theory, put forward by a weather bureau official in Portland, speculated that Arnold unknowingly had suffered from "snow blindness."[12] And an astronomer from the University of Oregon reasoned that Arnold's sighting was probably a mistaken impression caused by "persistent vision from reflections on the glass of his plane."[13]

As flying saucer stories spread, new explanations for them appeared, as well. In one instance, a pilot flying over New Mexico reported a "ball of fire with a blue, fiery tail behind it."[14] Harold R. Turner, an officer from a nearby air station, dismissed that sighting as nothing unusual. "Jet airplanes which have circular exhaust pipes that might give the illusion of discs when heated," he said.[15]

It was soon evident that no single answer would clear up questions about the many differing accounts. Although many of the reports had similarities, there were often significant differences in the details. The descriptions and circumstances varied, as did the backgrounds of the people making the reports. Each case presented a unique mix of particulars.

Some sightings later turned out to be clear-cut cases of misidentification, and some were deliberate hoaxes. Other instances, however, proved to be inconclusive and seemed impossible to figure out. It took time for journalists, officials, and other interested parties to sift through the many reports. It was time-consuming to determine which cases warranted close attention and which safely could be set aside.

Whatever was or was not happening in the skies, one thing was becoming apparent. Some public officials, quite understandably, wanted to keep UFO sightings from creating a situation that would get out of hand. They were not about to leave the matter for the public to sort out on their own. So, within days of the first report, sources from various levels of government began to debunk much of the speculation that had appeared in the press. A few dismissed the sightings outright, suggesting they were not substantive or newsworthy.

There is no evidence suggesting overarching coordination of these denials. Those familiar with the complexity of government bureaucracies in the era will not be surprised by this general lack of coordination, which is quite typical. In the sprawling postwar federal government, one department, agency, or office frequently had little idea about what other parts of the government were doing. Add in state and local government offices, and the situation often resulted in mixed messages.

As for the UFO stories that were then new to the scene, reporters were sometimes successful in rounding up officials from different levels of government to provide statements. Some officials presumably did not wish to make any public declarations about the matter, as would be the case about many topics. Of the officials willing to go on the record, however, journalistic accounts read as though the officials making statements knew little more than what they had read in the newspapers.

For all these reasons, official pronouncements were not always consistent in tone or substance. The type of response that an official gave to a reporter's questions seemed to depend on the person being asked, that person's predisposition, and what that person had or had not already heard about the saucers.

In most cases, officials suggested mundane explanations for the odd things seen in the skies. A June 26 newspaper report out of Pendleton, Oregon, quoted not one but two officials regarding the Kenneth Arnold story. According to this item, spokespersons for both the Army and the Civil Aeronautics Administration "expressed skepticism" about the incident.[16]

The Civil Aeronautics Administration source is quoted as saying, "I rather doubt that anything would be traveling that fast."[17] Meanwhile, an Army spokesperson dismissed the report and said that "as far as we know, nothing flies that fast except a V-2 rocket, which travels at 3,500 miles an hour—and that's too fast to be seen." The implication was the whole thing must either have been an illusion or some other kind of mistake.

In the same news item, which the Associated Press circulated, the Army spokesperson also discounted one of the then-prevailing theories about the Arnold incident. That was the speculation that Arnold had seen something secret—that he had seen something real, but it was not something he was supposed to see. The official quickly dismissed that idea outright, stating that the government had not conducted high-velocity tests anywhere near Arnold's alleged encounter near Mount Rainier.[18]

Regardless of official denials, the rapidly escalating number of reports and the growing interest created a situation approaching a flying saucer mania. The sightings were recognized as something out of the ordinary at the time. No matter what they believed or did not believe about the mounting UFO reports, the public seems to have been well aware that it was an odd social phenomenon at the very least.

The public's response to the many reports was wide-ranging. A few people seemed to be afraid, but most seem simply to have been curious. Others were generally suspicious of the whole matter, although suspicious of *what* was hard to say since the entire situation was unclear. Others found the reports amusing, or in some cases, interpreted this as evidence that some of their fellow citizens were gullible dupes. In any case, public reaction to the flying saucer craze ran the gamut of possible intellectual and emotional responses. For the most part, however, few people initially thought the saucers, if they were real, had come from anywhere other than earth.

The extensive attention and speculation made it challenging to make sense of the situation, almost from the start. Indeed, in a press report of June 27, 1947, only a few days after his by-then famous sighting, Kenneth Arnold complained, "Half the people I see look at me as a combination Einstein, Flash Gordon, and screwball. I wonder what my wife back in Idaho thinks."[19]

It had only been a few days, but already Arnold was quite frustrated with the whole situation. Irked by the lack of answers, he said, "This whole thing has gotten out of hand."[20]

⇒ 5 ⇐

Contagion

News of Kenneth Arnold witnessing something mysterious over the Cascades was only the beginning of a tsunami of similar reports in the days and weeks that followed. Before Arnold's incident, very few people reported seeing such things. After his story hit the wire services, however, the floodgates opened. By the end of June 1947, flying saucers, as most of these objects at the time were called regardless of their reported shape, had not only become a topic of conversation. They almost seemed to be a national obsession.

The sharp increase in UFO sightings immediately after Arnold's first report remains puzzling even after decades of reflection and reexamination. Even today, the escalation of the "flying saucer" story from a solitary account to a mass phenomenon that involved hundreds of other witnesses is one of the most intriguing aspects in the entire history of the modern UFO phenomenon. There are multiple ways to think about the 1947 wave of UFO sightings. Yet, despite many efforts and many attempts to explain it away, the exact nature of the sudden uptick in reported sightings remains as perplexing as it did all those years ago.

Indeed, despite decades of speculation, it remains challenging to say precisely what was going on. Did people see real, tangible objects of some sort? Or were these reports due to hoaxes or cases of mistaken identity? There are other possibilities, too. Perhaps, for example, many were the result of a peculiar psychological phenomenon. It was, and is, all very confusing.

In the summer of 1947, many people seemed not to know what to make of Arnold's story or the others piling up. Unsurprisingly, Arnold himself was the subject of much skepticism. He had earned a solid reputation—a conclusion with which government investigators concurred—but his story seemed so bizarre that many questioned his reliability and credibility as a witness. Many other witnesses faced similar skepticism since a simple, rational explanation was hard to find.

Still, the psychological explanation had an allure, and some were already thinking along lines that Jung would adopt about a decade later. So, was the sharp increase in sightings mainly a psychological phenomenon, perhaps a mass delusion of some sort? Although this is possible, it is difficult to say with any certainty. Even if psychological effects were somehow in play, how did that work? Did people see something real? Or did they simply imagine that they saw something?

But it could have been much simpler than that. Maybe many witnesses did see something that they could not quite identify. In some cases, there may have been physical objects to see. However, in instances where witnesses could not precisely identify what they had seen, some people probably were then influenced by what they had already heard about "flying saucers." Said differently, possibly some witnesses, without being fully aware of it, may have fleshed out details that were missing or ambiguous in their memories with information they had heard about before. Thus, it may be worth considering some sort of bandwagon effect was at work in at least some of the increasing number of sightings.

How ideas spread across communities and even whole societies has long interested social scientists. Of particular interest is social contagion, a type of influence that can result in a wide range of imitative behaviors. In a way, this is a complex phenomenon that often operates without people being fully aware of it. In another way, however, it is a simple and often-observed phenomenon: people doing and saying things mostly because other people have already done or said them.

Social contagion often plays a part in a wide array of circumstances, ranging from fads and fashions to panics and crazes. In many instances, contagion spreads only frivolous or insignificant ideas and behaviors. However, it can also be instrumental in proliferating more impactful beliefs and behavior among a social group, large or small. And it can be in play without anyone thinking much about it.

When someone does or says something unusual and others seem to follow, the reason is not always evident to those involved. Thus, it can be difficult to judge whether the common thread is shared, spontaneous experience, on the one hand, or if the imitative behavior is the result of social influence on or imitation (possibly subconscious) of the other.

Could some type of social contagion be why there were so many new UFO sightings after Kenneth Arnold's story became well known? That seems possible. And if so, this suggests that Arnold's account somehow may have influenced other people's interpretations of their own subsequent experiences—especially in cases where the details were not apparent to the witnesses involved.

History provides numerous examples of imitative social behavior.

It is not a new phenomenon, though it is not always easy to understand. One particularly intriguing case emerged in Europe several centuries before the sightings of flying saucers in America in 1947. That earlier case has only tenuous similarities to the wave of UFO sightings after World War II. Still, its distinctiveness and mysterious nature offer food for thought in relation to the later events.

As with the saucer sightings, it remains impossible to know if the much older incident arose from some external physical cause or was rooted in something psychological. However, even without definitive answers, this bewildering historical case illustrates how difficult it can be to find a satisfactory explanation for some types of unusual new social phenomena.

The story dates from the summer of 1518 and involves a woman who lived in Strasbourg near the present-day border between France and Germany. Frau Troffea, as she was called, seems to have been at the center of one of the most unusual cases of possible social contagion to have been documented. In July of that year, she left her home and started to dance uncontrollably in the city streets for no apparent reason.

Unsurprisingly, the sight of a woman randomly dancing in the middle of the road seemed very odd to many townsfolk. Adding to the unusual nature of the incident, it was soon apparent that Frau Troffea had no intention of stopping. Indeed, she continued dancing for hours, which then turned into days. She danced on and on. It was not until she eventually became too exhausted to continue that she finally collapsed.

As time progressed, the situation became increasingly bizarre. When Frau Troffea felt refreshed, she got up and began dancing once again. She continued for days, evidently dancing throughout her waking hours. It was quite a puzzle, and no one knew of any obvious explanation for it.

The situation was already gaining local attention when other townspeople started dancing, too. Soon, what began as an unusual individual behavior morphed into unusual group behavior. Within four or five days, as many as 30 residents joined in the uncontrollable, nonstop dancing—all evidently doing so for no discernible reason.

The dancing continued for days. And as it did, more and more residents joined in. At one point, upwards of 200—some estimates place the number closer to 400—danced along Frau Troffea. They continued doing so incessantly.

City officials concluded the dancing residents must be victims of something they didn't comprehend. They managed to coax the transfixed dancers to move out of the streets and into a side area and waited

Occasional outbreaks of "dancing mania"—sometimes called the dancing plague—were among the most unusual social phenomena in Europe, mainly between the 14th and 17th centuries. This Hendrick Hondius engraving after a 1564 drawing by Pieter Brueghel, the Elder, depicts one such occurrence (Wikimedia Commons).

for something to happen. Local officials hoped the episode would come to some sort of end soon. They figured that eventually, the dancers would become too tired to carry on. It seemed a reasonable approach to a baffling situation.

According to contemporary accounts, several of the people who participated in the dancing eventually died. Their deaths were apparently due to medical issues that occurred as the phenomenon wore on.

Whatever was going on, by September, it came to an abrupt end. The dancing ceased as quickly as it had started. It certainly was an unusual case that defied easy explanation.

This bizarre incident, sometimes called the "dancing plague" or "dancing mania" of 1518, was only one of several similar episodes of spontaneous dancing that broke out in Europe over the years. Medical historian John Waller, who studied the phenomenon intensively, identifies several such incidents along the Rhine and Mosel rivers "beginning as early as the thirteenth century."[1] Thus, people have known about the Strasbourg incident and other cases for centuries since the events were well documented. For just as long, however, experts have struggled to explain what caused them.

From the beginning, some have suggested that the dancers were inflicted by some supernatural force—perhaps demonic possession or some other evil influence. As time passed, however, people offered different reasons.

Over time, many began to see the incident as a medical episode of some sort, perhaps a physical or psychological pathology. Some 19th-century sources concluded the behavior, which they called "tarantism" or "Saint Vitus' dance," was evidence of insanity. One unidentified writer of that era described it as "a wonderful and unheard of disorder… [in which] groups of both sexes … leaped and jumped in choral dances, totally divested of personal volition … by the restless force of this singular malady."[2]

The medicalized interpretation remained a dominant explanation well into the 20th century. But then, some researchers began to blame the epidemic (as it was often called) on the ingestion of a toxin, thus suggesting a definite physical instead of purely psychological cause for the incident. Perhaps, some experts speculated, the dancers had consumed bread that caused a fungal infection. A disease called ergotism can be acquired by eating rye bread contaminated with ergot fungus. Thus, researchers considered it a possible culprit.

Yet, that explanation was not entirely convincing. Ergotism typically presents multiple symptoms, including seizures, which are vaguely consistent with the behavior of the spontaneous dancers. But some aspects of the Strasbourg episode—and similar attacks—did not seem to conform to ergotism's usual symptoms. So, if ergotism was the cause, could it have been another physical sickness at work? That remains possible, though it is difficult to say what this other disorder would be.

Given the lingering questions, medical historian Waller developed a new hypothesis that more squarely located the episode in the realm of social contagion. Specifically, he suggested that the dancing plague episodes could be symptoms of mass psychogenic illness (MPI), sometimes known as epidemic hysteria or mass hysteria.

As researchers M.J. Colligan and L.R. Murphy describe it, MPI is the "collective occurrence of physical symptoms and related beliefs among two or more persons in the absence of an identifiable pathogen."[3] After Waller connected the phenomenon as a potential explanation for the Strasbourg incident, many scholars agreed that it was a strong contender.

In concluding that MPI was the most likely cause of the dance episodes,[4] Waller notes that the people of Strasbourg and other affected cities were "experiencing acute distress" when these occurrences broke out.[5] That context, he suggests, was a key factor and probably contributed to the disorder's emergence.

Waller's argument has been widely accepted, but there are still many unknowns. So, it is not necessarily the last word on the subject. Still, some form of contagion is an explanation worth considering, not only for the mysterious outbreaks of dancing mania five centuries ago but also for the strange rash of UFO reports that emerged immediately after Kenneth Arnold's 1947 UFO sighting.

There are many differences between the dancing plague and the wave of UFO sightings, but the general similarity prompts at least some speculation. Dancing and seeing are not the same things, of course. Nevertheless, in the cases of the dancing plague and the UFO frenzy of 1947—two otherwise disparate occurrences—each episode quickly escalated from a single unexplained incident to a much broader phenomenon drawing many people into the fold. And in both cases, it has proven to be impossible to completely ascertain whether they resulted from an external cause (a toxin in one situation; real flying objects in the other) or social influence.

This is not to say that the many new UFO sightings reported in the wake of Arnold's story were necessarily cases of people influenced by the June 24 encounter. Yet, it seems reasonable to ask if at least some of the many UFO reports could have been affected, perhaps subconsciously, by the extensive media attention.

With newspapers carrying numerous stories and generating widespread public interest, flying saucers were in the national consciousness. As a result, they could easily have come to mind when people saw things in the sky that they otherwise could not readily identify.

Still, it is debatable whether the summer 1947 wave of UFO

sightings can be reduced merely to social influence. It remains a strong possibility and probably even a likelihood for many cases. Other reports, however, did not—and still do not—fit that bill neatly. Those cases require other explanations, which in some instances, have been hard to find.

⇛ 6 ⇚

Visitors from Mars

As sightings of unidentified aerial objects dramatically increased in the summer of 1947, the public's understanding of what was going on did not. Most new cases were as baffling as the first, and Americans remained bewildered as ever. No one seemed to have definite answers.

A newspaper headline from June 29 summed up the confusion: "'Flying Saucers' May Be This or That; Speculation Rife."[1] In the accompanying story, journalist Les Barnard noted that competing claims and subsequent official denials were hard to sort out. Moreover, no single explanation seemed to fit every case or satisfy very many people. The "flying saucers ... are not mirages,"[2] he wrote. But that left many other possibilities, none of which was wholly convincing.

As the number of new cases rose over the following days, mass hysteria remained a popular explanation. Although social contagion may not have applied to every reported sighting, it at least seemed plausible for many of them, especially given the significant uptick in cases that emerged as the days passed. Even some mental health professionals endorsed this explanation.

Dr. Winfred Overholser, then a well-known psychiatrist at St. Elizabeth's Hospital in the nation's capital, believed "national hysteria" was likely behind many sightings. "Scratch the surface," he said, "and you find the same hysteria which predominated during the witchcraft scare."[3] According to published accounts, several others from the medical and scientific communities thought much the same.

That conclusion was far from universal, however. Harry Steckel, another prominent psychiatrist, was openly skeptical of this type of psychological explanation. A distinguished government consultant and professor emeritus of psychiatry at Syracuse University's medical school, he was unequivocal in expressing his views. "They [flying saucers] have been seen by too many people, in too many different places to be dismissed to so lightly," he said. "The element of mass hysteria should not be taken into consideration."[4]

By early July, flying saucers became increasingly difficult to ignore. Given the commotion, Steckel did not entirely rule out social contagion as a contributing factor. However, he did not think this could not explain the phenomenon as a whole.

Flying saucers, a term that had not even been used a few weeks earlier, now appeared on front pages of newspapers, in radio reports, and in everyday conversations around the country. Hundreds, possibly thousands of people, had seen them if news accounts were to be believed. But if the saucers were not the result of some psychological effect, what explanations were left? The leading contenders fell into three broad categories.

The first possibility was that at least some of the sightings could have been the result of natural phenomena. Some so-called flying saucers could have been unusual weather events or rare atmospheric conditions. Or maybe some of the supposed saucers were misidentified meteors burning up as they streaked through the atmosphere. Earl Bouilly of American Airlines thought that hypothesis was reasonable. According to a published account, Bouilly believed that "the earth is never really safe from meteors" and that the so-called flying saucers could have been "meteoric bodies, which are known to fly through space by the millions."[5]

Various other natural occurrences, including rare phenomena such as ball lightning, were also proposed as explanations. This hypothesis, which was suggested in the very early days following Arnold's sighting, would remain popular for some time to come.

The second possibility was one that Arnold himself had suspected from the start: that the flying saucers were unfamiliar or unrecognized human-made objects, possibly aircraft or missiles. The most innocent of such possible cases was that flying saucers were nothing more than weather balloons, or maybe reflections from commercial aircraft in the distance. Since many of the early sightings took place in daylight hours, this appears to have been a reasonable conjecture for some cases.

Of course, there was a more mysterious possibility within the category of human-made objects: technologies that were top-secret military hardware. In that scenario, saucers arguably could have been missiles, new types of jet aircraft, or even rockets. Many people gave very serious thought to this explanation, unnerving as it might be. Indeed, this seems to be what Kenneth Arnold suspected in the first hours after his June 24 sighting.

Officials regularly issued denials of that theory. That was probably to be expected. Even if such conjectures were true, it is hard to imagine that American officials would have agreed to confirm them. After all, this was 1947, a year in which rising Cold War suspicions and anxieties were already exerting a notable influence on society. And within that context, the U.S. government was making a massive effort to develop and deploy new aerospace technologies. Suppose the government had been conducting secret tests of experimental aircraft or missiles that the U.S. military did not want the public to know about. In that case, it seems very unlikely that officials would have been forthcoming with that information.

The government had long since concluded that secrecy was a top priority in the newly christened Atomic Age. And it was already experienced in maintaining secrecy about new technologies, too. The stealth with which the U.S. government had managed to keep the massive Manhattan Project, which created the atomic bomb just a few years earlier, proved that the government was very capable of keeping even massive and far-flung covert programs out of the public eye. In the case of flying saucer sightings, expecting the government to tip its hand if members of the general public had inadvertently seen some of its secret technology would have been unrealistic, even if it were true.

There was also the chance the flying saucer sightings were evidence of something even more ominous—advanced Soviet technology stealthily intruding into American airspace. That, too, almost certainly would have been regarded as classified information. In those days, maintaining secrecy in the face of threats to national security was a paramount concern to government officials. If the U.S. had some secret new technology, officials would have wanted to keep that under wraps. And if the Soviets possessed some new threatening technology, American officials would not have wanted to let on that they were aware of that either.

A third possibility, which most people seemed reluctant to voice initially, was literally out of this world. Perhaps the saucers were interplanetary space vehicles that had come from another planet. At first, many people regarded the extraterrestrial-origin hypothesis with skepticism—even ridicule. Few seemed to take it seriously, and even fewer wanted to be known for having that opinion. But this perspective was not entirely unknown.

Unlike the case in later years, during the very early days of the 1947 wave of sightings, most people seemed to think the extraterrestrial explanation was far-fetched—possibly even evidence that persons drawing such conclusions were not in full possession of their senses. Indeed, only a small number of people initially suspected that these "flying saucers" could be anything other than some yet-to-be-explained earthly

Early UFO witnesses often wondered if what they had spotted was actually some new military technology. One such aircraft was the Bell XS-1 rocket plane, which first flew in American skies in January 1946. It was faster by far than anything then familiar to the American public (National Archives/ NASA).

phenomenon. The vast majority appeared to think the saucers were only misidentified natural phenomena or human-made objects (including secret military hardware of either American or Soviet design). Those seemed both possible and plausible.

Yet, even though other, presumably more staid and ordinary explanations already had been floated in the press, the extraterrestrial hypothesis appeared within hours of Arnold's initial sighting. One of the first published accounts that hint at the extraterrestrial hypothesis appeared on June 27. A story about Arnold's sighting published on that date quoted an unnamed woman who recognized Arnold from media reports. According to the report, a woman entered a café in Pendleton, Oregon, and noticed Arnold. She "took one look at him and then dashed out shrieking, 'There's the man who saw the men from Mars.'"[6]

How much stock to put in such reports is difficult to determine. This type of story offered vivid quotes that made for entertaining newspaper copy. But it is impossible to know how literally a person should take such comments. Moreover, there is no evidence that Arnold believed, at this early date, that he had seen a spaceship from another world. On the contrary, the available evidence strongly suggests that he suspected he had stumbled across some ultra-secret new military technology. Although he seems to have changed his mind later, initially, he was not among those speculating that the flying saucers were visitors from out space.

But no matter. Once publicly aired, the extraterrestrial-aliens hypothesis would take on a life of its own. Some who voiced this view may not have intended it to be considered a serious possibility. In fact, in many situations, the extraterrestrial explanation may have been intended to convey precisely the opposite meaning. Some may have used it presuming it would be understood as a thinly veiled mockery of the very idea it suggested—something so outlandish that merely saying it illustrated how absurd they thought it was.

Yet, although initially few in numbers, the people who embraced this theory perceived no sense of irony or absurdity about it. To them, it was a legitimate possibility. All of them may not have thought it was probable, but the new Atomic Age had shown that many things once thought to be impossible were not as impossible as they once seemed. Speculations that there could be life on other worlds had appeared in popular culture and the news media at times for decades. There was nothing novel about that. And since humankind had recently harnessed the power of the atom and was beginning to unlock the potential of rocketry, why would it necessarily be so absurd to think that other life forms on other worlds might be able to do the same?

So, as a theoretical possibility, the extraterrestrial explanation for flying saucers did not necessarily strike everyone as fanciful and impossible. Improbable? Maybe. But this was an environment in which there were doubts about the more mundane explanations. And none of those other hypotheses was demonstrated to be unquestionably correct.

Many reports were hard to pin down, which added to the uncertainty. They often contained gaps, ambiguities, and uncertainties. Simply put, there were cracks in the usual explanations that were big enough for doubt to seep through. And with the introduction of doubt, there was much opportunity for further speculation.

As speculation ran rampant, it became evident that the rising furor would not fade away anytime soon. The escalating number of new UFO reports varied so much in their details that it was hard to refute even the most unlikely suggestions that people put forward to explain them in many cases. To completely rule out one theory or another was difficult. Although some of the suggested explanations seemed highly unlikely, that was not to say they were impossible.

In the early Atomic Age, people were no longer sure about what was or was not impossible. Science had unlocked many of nature's secrets, and technology had made incredible advances. Things that were unimaginable just a few years previously were now a reality. In that context, formerly bizarre theories—including speculation that the flying saucers could be from outer space—did not necessarily seem as wholly implausible as before. Was this explanation still implausible? Maybe. But that was a long way from impossible.

So, it was hard to completely rule out these speculations, at least in cases where witnesses were generally credible. The facts did not fit neatly with other, more ordinary explanations. Making matters worse, the situation made it difficult to rule anything out definitively. Even the most unusual and atypical theories could not be proved to be impossible. They were not, to use a term associated with philosopher of science Karl Popper, *falsifiable*. And if they were not falsifiable—in other words, if they could not be proven incorrect—they remained technical possibilities.

Popper, who was well-known in mid-century, did not write about UFOs; he was interested in theorizing more generally about what science can and cannot tell people about the world. Yet, he was onto something that would be a vexing problem in sorting out UFO reports in 1947 and years to come. Some things are simply not disprovable. Even if some ideas seem highly improbable, it may never be possible to eliminate them entirely as theoretical possibilities.

When there was no set of explanations for the UFO sightings that could satisfy everyone that summer, this left the door open for continuing speculation. The absence of a compelling narrative with a simple, earthy explanation meant there were plenty of opportunities for some people to devise and push theories of a sometimes-fantastic nature.

In some ways, this is not surprising. Suggesting that flying saucers could be evidence of life on a distant planet fit with the zeitgeist of mid-century America. After all, this was the Atomic Age, a time of astonishing scientific breakthroughs, when the line between possible and impossible no longer seemed clear cut. The universe had many secrets, but now they were starting to be revealed. Many people were reluctant to stick with only the most mundane and ordinary explanations for strange things in the skies in this context. Why not consider other possibilities, even if those would have seemed far-fetched just a few years earlier? The extraterrestrial theory was an uncommon belief in 1947, but over the long term, it attracted many advocates—a development that would turn out to have long-lasting ramifications.

⇒ 7 ⇐

Fever Pitch

Despite widespread interest in the subject, flying saucers hardly dominated the news in the summer of 1947. In fact, it represented only one of many topics competing for the public's attention. More ordinary matters filled most news reports. Local and regional stories continued to flow in and out of daily news reports. National and international concerns also gave Americans much to ponder. Earlier in the year, labor issues often made headlines. That had been the case when a weeks-long telephone workers' strike emerged in April. Labor remained a big story in the months that followed. It dominated headlines again in June when Congress overrode Truman's veto to pass the controversial Taft-Hartley Act.

Another subject unexpectedly made the news just a few days after the flying saucer stories hit American newspapers. On June 29, 1947, only a few days before the nation's annual Independence Day celebrations, Harry Truman made a short but historic trip to the Lincoln Memorial. There he addressed the thousands of attendees who had assembled for the National Association of Colored People's 38th annual conference. Truman was the first sitting president to speak before the renowned civil rights group. His remarks were broadcast on national radio.

"I should like to talk to you briefly about civil rights and human freedom," Truman declared. "It is my deep conviction that we have reached a turning point in the long history of our country's efforts to guarantee freedom and equality to all our citizens. Recent events in the United States and abroad have made us realize that it is more important today than ever before to ensure that all Americans enjoy these rights. When I say all Americans, I mean all Americans."

The president's words were generally well-received, especially within the African American community. That was something of a surprise because few people expected the president to speak explicitly

46

about racial justice issues. An article in the Black-owned *Kansas City Call* newspaper summed up the proceedings. "Truman so strongly denounced race prejudice and discrimination based upon race, creed, color, and national origin," it stated, "that even his enemies were convinced that the Missourian in the White House had left behind him Missouri's tradition of second-class citizenship for Negroes."[1] The civil rights movement was, in some ways, just getting started. However, it already attracted attention, exposing the unhealed wounds and fissures within American society.

At the same time, the nation was also anxiously following developments in the evolving Cold War. On that front, recent news of the massive European Recovery Program, which Secretary of State George Marshall had announced just three weeks earlier, was also a well-covered news topic. Its stated aim was to help a still-ravaged Europe rebuild from the war by promoting "the revival of a working economy in the world so as to permit the emergence of political and social conditions in which free institutions can exist," as Marshall said.[2] Yet, the plan was just as much part of the United States' quest to limit the spread of communism as it was a humanitarian project.

The U.S. news media had these and many topics to cover in the summer of 1947. With many stories of international troubles and domestic worries, in addition to the mundane accounts of routine events, newspapers, and broadcast outlets had much to report. Moreover, everyone knew that the next presidential election loomed. Just 16 months away, the contest was likely to command the news media's attention with political wrangling before long.

Still, summer months are often times when the American public is distracted by other things. The regular ebb and flow of the news cycle in most years—1947 included—historically provides opportunities for human-interest stories and articles featuring unusual or offbeat subjects. In the doldrums and heat of summer days and nights, people often look for a break from the ordinary. The flying saucer stories appearing in newspapers throughout the country provided readers with just this sort of material. It was a break from more mundane or expected news—a novelty, at minimum. Kenneth Arnold's flying saucer story seemed to break the ice.

After this story made the rounds in the media, many similar accounts began to appear, flooding newspaper and radio broadcasts with an unusual and potentially exciting new topic.

There is no disagreement that a vast number of flying saucer reports appeared in the press. But how many? And how many separate incidents did these news reports represent? These seem like simple questions, but they can be surprisingly tricky to answer with certainty. For one thing, there was no mechanism or central authority for systematically collecting the information. There is also no assurance that officials recorded all such information in logbooks or that subsequently, the news media would have published all of them even if they were. Moreover, many sightings probably were never reported to anyone.

For all these reasons, it may be reasonable to conclude that newspapers and other news media did not necessarily tell a complete and unambiguous story. Beyond that, as a highly decentralized realm, the media possessed no systematized way of collecting and organizing the information even if every report had made its way to a newsroom somewhere. It is thus difficult to say how complete, exhaustive, and accurate the flying saucer news accounts really were. Many of these items appear to be journalistically solid in retrospect, but many others are not easy to assess. What emerges from the many news stories is, in many ways, a somewhat hazy and ambiguous picture.

The large number of reports presents other complications, too. The wire services picked up some stories but not others. So, some accounts were broadly distributed, while others drew little attention. Some articles appeared in major newspapers and reached many readers. Others, however, were only published in small-town papers. Many of those reports were and remain obscure.

Further complicating the situation, stories from the wire services were sometimes edited and revised for local use. The edits could lead to slightly different versions of the same incidents, adding a new element of potential obfuscation. As a result, articles that appear to be about different sightings at first glance can turn out to be iterations of a single incident.

Then there is the question of just how many people saw UFOs. Some articles mention multiple witnesses—sometimes numbering in the hundreds. Yet, the sources of those numerical estimates are obscure, and it is unclear whether they should be taken at face value or with a grain of salt.

Considering these types of difficulties, the final word on exactly how many sightings occurred and how many witnesses saw them has yet to be written and never may be determined definitively. Nevertheless, it is beyond doubt that there were many such reports and many such witnesses scattered across the country, whatever the precise numbers.

Despite such uncertainties, one fact, at least, is clear. In the early days of July 1947, flying saucer reports spiked. The public was well aware of this trend at the time, though it is doubtful that anyone knew exactly what that meant.

Some years after, a UFO researcher named Ted Bloecher set out to shed light on this question. In a widely cited study, Bloecher documents hundreds of UFO reports in the month or so following Kenneth Arnold's June 24 incident.[3] In a feat seldom attempted before or since, Bloecher combed through about 140 newspapers from 90 different cities to assemble his detailed account. Whether or not one chooses to believe Bloecher's exact numbers or accept as accurate each case he identifies, he plausibly paints a picture that fits with the generally accepted turn of events. Namely, the number of UFO reports rose markedly in and around the July 4 weekend. And this increase in cases was not merely a small change from the days before; it was a massive departure from what had come earlier. Indeed, in the span of just a few days, there was a deluge of saucer reports unlike anything previously experienced.

In the first days immediately following Arnold's June 24 sighting, Bloecher identifies dozens of published reports about flying saucers in U.S. newspapers. The number he found for given days between June 25 and July 3 varied somewhat but is within a range of 12 to 24 on most days. (Only June 26 and July 3 have slightly higher numbers.)

By Independence Day, however, the number of cases rose sharply. In just two days, July 4 and July 5, there were 160 reports, a massive increase. Then, on July 6 and 7, the numbers skyrocketed even more. Over 300 reported new incidents from at least 37 different states on those two days alone.

According to Bloecher's research, these cases involved hundreds of witnesses, possibly more. What had started in the press as the lone account from an Idaho business owner had turned into a much broader, national phenomenon in less than two weeks.

Yet, as quickly as the saucer reports increased, a sharp drop-off in sightings soon followed. On July 9, the number dropped to about 90, a decrease of more than 45 percent. Then on the following day, the numbers dipped again to only 24 new reports. And the day after that, July 10, there were only ten reports.

The trend continued downward. In the days that followed, additional new reports were few and far between. Whatever had been going on several days earlier appeared to have gone away. It would be some time before anything remotely approaching the scope and scale of the previous days' flying saucer wave would be seen again.

The bulk of sightings appear to have occurred during daylight hours during this period. Some incidents involved lone unidentified objects; others involved more than one. Moreover, the term *flying saucer* was itself ambiguous. People routinely used it to refer to objects that varied widely in size and shape. Overall, then, there were many differences but also some similarities across the many accounts.

Bloecher's study from the early 1960s provides one useful analysis of published flying saucer accounts. However, it was not the first systematic attempt to sort out the mid-century UFO phenomenon.

A few years earlier, in 1955, the Air Technical Intelligence Center (ATIC), a unit of the Air Force, had undertaken an exhaustive analysis of UFO sightings reported since 1947.[4] The compilers of this thorough and meticulously documented study explain the sources of their data, their research procedures, and the results of multiple statistical analyses.

This latter part was a complicated task in the mid–1950s. It involved carefully coding hundreds of reports, mainly in a prose format, into numerical data that could be processed in that era's electronic computer systems. In many cases, what started as narrative correspondence, typed forms, or interview records ended up as a collection of punch cards that could be fed into a computer to be analyzed. By the end of this complex process, the researchers had produced many different ways of looking at the many cases, categorizing them, and statistically interpreting the information they had.

The resulting monograph was prepared for internal use and reads like many government reports. It is dry, dispassionate, bureaucratic. Yet, it appears to be a competent and informative effort and is straightforward in its design and conclusions.

Bloecher's study a few years later would identify hundreds or more UFO sightings in the summer of 1947. The ATIC report, however, included nowhere near that number.[5] The source of this difference probably lies in the procedures used in collecting and recording cases. Bloecher aimed to be exhaustive and relied heavily—almost exclusively—on newspaper and other publicly available accounts, which he tracked down over many years. By contrast, the ATIC report included selected cases based on criteria that the analysts developed. The presumed goal was to be thorough without adding extraneous material.

Despite employing different criteria and strategies for collecting data, the ATIC study reveals similar overall findings as Bloecher. Both show an immediate, though initially modest uptick in flying saucer sightings in the days after June 24. A marked increase came in the early days of July, followed by an equally rapid decrease shortly after that. Although UFOs would remain on cultural, if not physical, radar for some time, the flurry of activity in those weeks in the summer of 1947 represented a fast-moving phenomenon that left as quickly as it came.

There is little disagreement about this overall shape of the summer saucer phenomenon, which interestingly resembles the standard distribution—the well-known "bell curve" found in various phenomena. The most significant difference between the ATIC and Bloecher reports is not in this general shape, but the sheer number of cases involved. Bloecher suggests that in early July, hundreds of sightings occurred in just two days. By contrast, the ATIC report lists only 48 sightings for the entire month of July.

As noted above, significant differences in sources and methods probably account for a large part of the discrepancy. While Bloecher relied heavily on plentiful news accounts, the ATIC researchers took a different approach. Their report identified three primary data sources.[6]

The first consisted of cases obtained through "regular military channels"—in other words, claimed sightings that various military branches were aware of and regarded as significant enough to document.[7]

Their second source came from reports that witnesses and concerned citizens sent directly to the military. Many of the letter-writers, the researchers said, were probably inspired to send their accounts along after a magazine article suggested the idea.[8]

Finally, the authors gleaned data from questionnaires that the researchers sent to a "selected group of the writers of the direct letters." After reviewing the correspondence, usually unsolicited, they had received, the ATIC researchers followed up with the people whose reports warranted, in their view, further study.[9]

As a result of this process, the ATIC study came up with fewer cases than Bloecher would later identify. In the end, however, the absolute number of saucers sightings may not be what is most significant. Numerous studies of varying quality have considered the unusual flying-saucer wave of 1947. The ATIC report and Bloecher's account are only two of them. Yet, there is certainly no credible source that disputes the basic fact that a massive wave of incidents burst onto the scene in late June. Differences of opinion about this wave are primarily about its scale, not that it did occur.

The sudden wave of 1947 sightings would last only a few weeks. After that, flying saucers mostly would fade into the background for a time. Before that happened, however, there were more surprises in store. As the nation celebrated the anniversary of its independence, new puzzles and new explanations about the saucer craze awaited them.

≈ 8 ≈

Looking for Answers

Fireworks were not the only aerial spectacle to catch attention during the Fourth of July weekend in 1947. Regardless of national celebrations or anything else going on, little could compare to the bizarre tales of saucers in the sky. Americans were keenly interested in these stories, but they had many different ideas about what the incidents meant. Many found the sightings to be mainly curiosities. Others were genuinely worried, or they suspected that a hidden threat lurked beneath the headlines. Some mostly seemed amused by the phenomenon.

Regardless of varying public reactions, the reports kept coming. The news media, sensing a topic that the readers and listeners would find compelling, sought answers. They successfully rounded up many accounts and found witnesses and potential experts to offer their opinions and speculations.

But newspaper reporters and radio correspondents were not in a position to know all the relevant facts, let alone what exactly to make of them. So, to find a more authoritative view, they, like the public at large, looked to America's institutions and especially to government. Even within the ranks of officialdom, however, the search for definitive answers would be slow going.

By early July, flying saucer reports drew multiple governmental agencies at the national, state, and local levels. As the news media continued to push the story, authorities at various agencies undertook investigations into the reports that had made their way to their desks. This involved many local and state police departments, aviation officials, the FBI, and even the U.S. military. The upshot was that many people, representing quite different kinds of expertise and experience, were looking into the matter. Unfortunately, some of those investigatory efforts were likely half-hearted. However, at other times, officials diligently examined the accounts they received, aiming to separate fact from fiction.

Regardless of the attention that many authorities devoted to their investigations, one cannot conclude that these efforts were well coordinated. On the contrary, it was almost the opposite. Multiple people in multiple offices investigated saucer reports on a piecemeal, ad hoc basis. Some items were passed along from one agency to another or from one level to another. Others, however, likely languished in files stuffed into desk drawers or on office shelves.

In some cases, witnesses reported what they had seen directly to civil aviation officials. However, that was probably not what first came to mind for most ordinary citizens, especially those outside the aviation community. Instead, local and state police departments were often on the front lines during the great wave of UFO sightings in late June and early July. When people saw something strange or frightening, a call to the local police station was often the first impulse. Yet, as a practical matter, UFO sightings were hardly the types of situations that law enforcement officers were trained to handle. Of course, they could make a note of a sighting and investigate if they thought a crime had been committed. Otherwise, however, there was not much law enforcement could be expected to do.

At the national level, the FBI got involved early, even though little about the flying saucer sightings fit within the type of incidents that traditionally interested them either. FBI agents would sometimes take statements, interview witnesses, and perform other matters related to the reports that crossed their desks. However, many aspects of the UFO sightings were well beyond the FBI's realm of experience and expertise. Moreover, despite their prowess in conducting thorough investigations, the FBI is a criminal investigation body. Thus, it was probably not the best choice for sorting out technical questions about atmospheric conditions, military issues, or other dimensions that might explain many of the sightings.

In the background to the FBI's UFO investigations throughout the early days of the flying saucer wave, the Soviet Union was the elephant in the room. Specifically, in the increasingly tense climate of the growing Cold War, the natural tendency was for U.S. government agencies to take seriously anything remotely perceived as a Soviet military threat. Thus, secret Russian planes or missiles that could clandestinely intrude into U.S. air space would have been grave concerns.

Beyond that, though, was a bigger fear: Was the Soviet Union close to developing an atomic bomb? In 1947, American intelligence officials were well aware that the Soviets desperately wanted to acquire an atom bomb. And no U.S. officials had any doubt about that or about the USSR's ability to marshal significant resources toward that end. What

American officials were less sure of was how far along the Soviet atomic bomb program was. As a later Air Force report concluded, "Determining whether the Soviets were testing nuclear devices was of the highest national priority"[1] at the time.

In reality, it would take another two years before the USSR developed a working atomic. However, in the months leading up to that, the U.S. government tried to keep a low profile as it tried to stay abreast of how well the Soviets were progressing. As the Air Force later concluded, "it demanded the utmost secrecy if the information gained was to be useful."[2]

A military unit called Air Materiel Command (AMC) had been in charge of experimental engineering for the army air services for many years. It oversaw many vital activities related to the U.S Army Air Force (previously called the Army Air Corps, and later the Army Air Service). The unit had a particular interest in research and development. Given its history and mission, it was not surprising that as the flying saucer stories gained notice, the AMC and its Technical Intelligence Division eventually became involved.

The commanding officer of Wright Field, the AMC home base in 1947, was Nathan Twining, a lieutenant general with outstanding credentials. Educated at West Point, Twining was a no-nonsense career soldier and a dedicated Cold Warrior. He was a trusted officer possessing a long and distinguished service record, culminating in service as the Chairman of the Joint Chiefs of Staff during the Eisenhower administration.

Twining originally became involved in military air service shortly after World War I, and he later played an active role in U.S. air operations during World War II. After the latter conflict, as commander of AMC, he was immersed in developing the B-52 bomber, which would become an essential piece of hardware in the nation's defense planning for decades to come.[3]

The B-52 project took up much of Twining's time, but he was also involved in other high-level defense matters. On June 5, 1947, Twining received orders to take a short break from his usual post and report to the Sandia Base in Albuquerque, New Mexico. For three days beginning July 8, he planned to participate in a "Bomb Commanders Course" scheduled at the base home to atomic-warfare-related planning and research.[4] By coincidence, the wave of flying saucer sightings began several days before Twining's departure for New Mexico.

A few days before his scheduled flight, reporters telephoned the AMC office at Wright Field in Dayton, Ohio, asking for more information about the strange aerial incidents. At the time, many people suspected that the saucers could be some type of U.S. military hardware. In a statement to the press, Twining quashed that idea, however. He bluntly told a reporter, "The Air Forces have nothing to compare to the [unidentified aerial] objects."[5]

Twining's comments were brief, noncommittal, and measured. That said, he did not completely close the door on speculations that the saucers could have some very unusual explanation. It is possible, given his background, that he was suspicious. Perhaps the saucers represented some type of new Soviet technology or were part of a secret program elsewhere within the U.S. military unknown to him. If he believed that, however, he certainly did not say so. Instead, he treated the subject in a routine matter consistent with his training and office.

Yet, Twining did seem to think there was something odd about the saucers. That, at least, was the impression he gave when he told a reporter that a "reputable scientist" had witnessed unexplained "semicircular objects in flight."[6] However, if Twining had any other ideas about precisely what was going on, it is unclear what they were. The most he would say publicly was that "anyone seeing the objects in flight or having information" should contact Wright Field.

Twining's minor involvement with the saucer question came near the beginning of what would become the military's long and complicated association with UFO phenomena.[7] The relationship between the U.S. military and UFOs has been hotly debated. Since 1947, UFO researchers sometimes claim the military has had dubious and potentially deceptive motivations in many of these incidents. In some cases, it is now known that military officials were aware of operations and activities they wished to keep under wraps for national security purposes. Beyond that, however, most military documents about UFOs suggest relatively straightforward and noncontroversial (at least superficially) explanations.

In the 1990s, the Air Force conducted an exhaustive review of its own previous UFO investigations. The authors concluded that while certain since-declassified military secrets were in play during the summer of 1947, there was otherwise no government cover-up of the type later popularized in movies and television and by some UFO conspiracy theorists. The paper trail, as they reconstructed it, simply did not lead to a massive government cover-up.[8]

The authors of the Air Force report concluded that the official record, as bureaucratic and byzantine as it sometimes was, did not suggest a massive government conspiracy, which they strongly felt would have been nearly impossible to hide if had it existed. "To believe that such operational and high-level security activity could be conducted solely by relying on unsecured telecommunications or personal contact without creating any records of such activity," they wrote, "certainly stretches the imagination of those who have served in the military who know that paperwork of some kind is necessary to accomplish even emergency, highly classified, or sensitive tasks."[9] There were some secrets, since de-classified, that affected how the public understood the flying saucer incidents, they said. But their view was that if there was once some great mystery, it had long since been cleared up.

But in 1947, there was much confusion. Many military officials seemingly did not fully understand the 1947 wave of flying saucer sightings as it was happening. As a result, uncertainty about it persisted for some time.

One of the Pentagon's most thorough attempts to make sense of the 1947 wave came about eight years later in a retrospective internal analysis of the military's UFO records to that time. In an exhaustive statistical analysis, researchers reviewed the data across many dimensions. Their review provides a snapshot of the 1947 wave overall.

The study takes a close look at such factors as time of day, lighting conditions, viewing angles, and many other details, including information about the witnesses, a group that represented a wide range of occupations, educational levels, and ages.

By the researchers' reckoning, there were 68 sightings in June and July of 1947. However, the bulk of those occurred in early July. To help make sense of these and later sightings, the authors created a systematic classification scheme. (See Table A.)

Table A—Evaluation of All Sightings, June and July, 1947[10]

Balloons	10%
Astronomical phenomena	13%
Aircraft	6%
Light phenomena	1.5 %
Birds	0%
Clouds, dust	0%
Insufficient information	16%
Psychological effects	4.5 %
Unknown	23.5 %
Other	25%

Some of the categories were self-explanatory: balloons, astronomical phenomena, aircraft, light phenomena, birds, clouds, and dust. (In these cases, the researchers concluded that the given report was mistaken identification.) The researchers also established a separate category for what they called "psychological manifestations." It was reserved for cases where "it was well established that the observer had seen something [but] it was also obvious that the sighting had been overdrawn"[11] and also included cases of "religious fanaticism, a desire for publicity, or an over-active imagination."[12]

Based on their review of the data, many incidents fit into one of these relatively straightforward explanations. However, "many" did not mean all. A significant number of cases fell into categories they labeled as "insufficient information," "unknown," or "other." To the researchers' way of thinking, the "insufficient information" classification simply meant "some essential item of information was missing," which made a definitive conclusion impossible. In a related way, they described the "unknown" category as those cases in which investigators lacked enough information to reach a definite conclusion. Lastly, the "other" classification, they said, was for "less frequent, but common objects such as kites, fireworks, flares, rockets, contrails, and meteorological phenomena like small tornadoes."[13]

How people today interpret the 1950s study may largely hinge on what they already believe. The "insufficient data," "unknown," and "other" categories represented more than 60 percent of the cases during the 1947 wave, even by the military's estimation. That leaves a significant degree of uncertainty and ambiguity. Indeed, the numbers provide no clear-cut, irrefutable answers that would end debate about the matter.

People differ in how they look at the cases that defied clear explanation, of course. For some, including the authors of numerous military reports, there is not much to suggest evidence of alien technology or any other highly unusual phenomenon. For others, however, this report, as well as other declarations from officials, has done little to quell gnawing suspicions that some truly history-making secret was and is being suppressed.

In the end, the authors of the 1955 study reached a conclusion that would also have been reasonable in 1947: "It can never be absolutely proven that 'flying saucers' do not exist," they wrote. Yet, they also conclude there was "a complete lack of any evidence consisting of physical matter in the case of a reported unidentified aerial object."[14] That type of reasoning was never going to prove wholly convincing to those who thought the UFOs heralded something much more momentous, however. In early July 1947, that became abundantly clear when a rancher walked into the sheriff's office in Roswell, New Mexico, with an incredible story.

≈ 9 ≈

In from the Ranch

About 100 miles outside of Albuquerque is the remote town of Corona, New Mexico. Far off the beaten path, the sparsely populated community was isolated from the growing hustle and bustle of postwar American life in 1947. It sometimes seemed to be in a world of its own.

The J.B. Foster ranch was southeast of town, where there was plenty of space to raise the cattle and sheep. William "Mac" Brazel managed the property. The 48-year-old man, who lived there with his family, knew it well. His work took him all over the property. He often rode on horseback to make his rounds and keep everything in order.

On June 14, Brazel was on the ranch doing a routine day's work. There was no reason to suspect anything eventful would happen that day. Instead, it all seemed very ordinary. As he went about his work, however, he stumbled across something unexpected. Dispersed over an area roughly the equivalent of two football fields, he spotted that he later described as "bright wreckage." He was not sure what it was, but it did not seem to belong to anything to do with the ranch. According to a later statement, he said it consisted of "rubber strips, tin foil, a rather tough paper, and sticks."[1]

The discovery seemed somewhat odd at the time. Brazel wondered why such things would be in a remote area. But odd or not, he took it in stride. The rancher certainly did not think the debris was strange enough to worry much about it and "did not pay much attention to it" at the time.[2] Whatever it was, it seemed to be something he could deal with later. So, he did not get around to doing anything about it for another two weeks.

At the time of his discovery, Brazel had not heard anything about flying saucers. Despite all the hoopla about the saucers, his life on the remote ranch had insulated him from such talk. Brazel did not own a radio,[3] and the flying discs remained unknown to him. The first he heard of them was apparently around Independence Day when the subject came up in a conversation with a relative.[4] And it was only at that point, days after his discovery, that he wondered if the debris could be connected to the saucer sightings.

Hearing about flying saucer stories was enough to raise a few questions in Brazel's mind. When he learned about the numerous accounts of the unexplained objects, he suspected that he had stumbled across something that could be related to them. He most likely thought the "wreckage" he found several weeks earlier could have had come from military aircraft of some sort. That would have been a reasonable supposition. Over in Roswell, about 80 miles away, there was an active military base. It housed a flight training facility during the war and had recently been the home of the Army Air Force's 509th Heavy Bombardment Group before its reassignment to Fort Worth in early 1946. Maybe what he had found on the ranch was something to do with that military base.

Regardless of his newfound suspicions, Brazel still was not overly concerned. Feeling little sense of urgency, he took no immediate steps to follow up with anyone right away. Making a report would require some inconvenience. Since the ranch had no telephone service, he would need to go somewhere in person to make a report.

If suitable officials had offices in downtown Corona, maybe Brazel would have filed a report right away. But there were no such officials anywhere nearby. So given the circumstances, he decided his story could wait until Monday, July 7. He planned to stop by the sheriff's office in Roswell when he traveled there that day to conduct routine business.[5]

Before Monday came, the rancher seems to have made one more trip to the crash site. This time, he brought his wife, their 14-year-old daughter, and their eight-year-old son along with him. According to a report from the era, the family gathered up "a good sample of the broken materials" and then packed them up for the trip to Roswell.[6]

On Monday, July 7, Brazel finally walked into the sheriff's office in Roswell to tell his story. That set things in motion. It would not be long before Brazel's account of finding unusual wreckage on the ranch spread locally. And soon after that, the news was picked up by the wire services, where it was embellished with additional details, official statements, and speculations.

Brazel's intriguing story first appeared in the local *Roswell Daily Record* newspaper the following day, July 8. With the sensational headline "RAAF Captures Flying Saucer on Ranch in Roswell Region," the article made an incredible, seemingly unambiguous claim. "The intelligence off of the 509th Bombardment group at Roswell Army Air Field," the paper said, had "come into possession of a flying saucer."[7]

In World War II, Roswell, New Mexico, was home to vital military instal-lations, including a major Army Air Force base. Even after the military build-up, however, the surrounding region remained sparsely populated, retaining the remote appearance that Dorothea Lange captured in this pho-tograph from 1938 (Library of Congress).

Although the *Roswell Daily Record* article was written relatively straightforwardly, the description was somewhat vague and there-fore open to broad interpretation. For example, the story said that a "disk was recovered on a ranch in the Roswell vicinity" and that offi-cials already had sent the "instrument" to "higher headquarters."[8] More detailed information was scarce, however. The account explicitly said that "no details of the saucer's construction or its appearance had been revealed."[9] It was the sort of story that provided readers with enough information to spark interest while simultaneously being so nebulous that it was open to highly imaginative speculation.

As news of Brazel's discovery started to spread, he remained unsure about what he found a few weeks earlier. Newspaper readers, how-ever, may have gotten the impression that things were far more certain than they were. According to press accounts, an intelligence officer at the Roswell airbase unambiguously said the military had recovered a real-life flying saucer.[10]

As it was worded, readers could reasonably have come away from the report thinking that there definitely was something tangible, concrete behind the flying saucer stores, after all. Although many sources had speculated that previous saucer reports were illusions or delusions, the report from Roswell seemed to say there was firm evidence to the contrary. Because now the U.S. military spoke of a flying saucer as something quite real. In an era before widespread distrust of government, many probably took this statement at face value.

By the time Brazel's story hit the newspapers, it already had begun a journey that led from one official to others. A day earlier, when Brazel showed up at the sheriff's office, his description of the find immediately seemed beyond the purview of local law enforcement. Sheriff George Wilcox quickly concluded that whatever Brazel had stumbled across, it was not the type of incident that the department usually investigated. Accordingly, Wilcox promptly turned the matter over to officials at the local army airbase. This was sensible, especially since Brazel—and likely Wilcox—probably thought the wreckage might have something to do with the base anyway.

When the story had reached the Roswell Army Air Field, it landed on the desk of Major Jesse A. Marcel, an intelligence officer. He promptly contacted Brazel and arranged to make a trip to the ranch to assess the situation for himself.[11] Marcel and another Roswell officer, Captain Sheridan Cavitt, then rode out to the Foster Ranch to see what was behind all the fuss.[12]

After arriving at the scene, Marcel and Cavitt collected more pieces of the wreckage. This material was added to the artifacts that Brazel had previously gathered with his family.

Marcel then took stock of the physical items now in his possession. The assembled debris consisted of bits of a reflective, lightweight, flexible material, some papery substance, narrow, straw-shaped rods, and pieces of what appeared to be some sort of tape with vaguely geometric markings. Whatever it was, it did not amount to much physically. It would have fit into a large cardboard box, and all together, it weighed only a few pounds.[13]

As he looked at the material, Marcel was hard-pressed to draw any definite conclusions. He made several attempts to piece the debris together so that he could see what it might have looked like before breaking apart in the presumed crash.[14] First, he "tried to make a kite out of it," but that did not work. He kept at it, but according to a contemporary press account, he "could not find any way to put it [the debris] back together so that it would fit."[15] Eventually, he gave up.

Despite close examination of the collected material, Marcel was not sure what he had. Whatever it was, Brazel had insisted that the material was definitely not from a weather balloon. As the rancher told a reporter, he had come across remnants of two such objects on previous occasions. His recent find was not at all like either of those.[16] For his part, Marcel seemed unsure of what to make of it. However, it would soon be out of his hands, both literally and figuratively speaking.

Once it was handed over to the military, the debris was the subject of intense scrutiny. It also became subject to the military's complex and relatively inflexible bureaucracy. Brazel's report prompted a flurry of new activity. The matter that would later be known as the "Roswell incident"—no one called it that at the time—quickly flew up the chain of command.

Upon learning about the discovery on July 7, Roswell Army Air Field's commander, Col. William H. Blanchard, evidently contacted his superior, Brigadier General Roger M. Ramey, at the Eighth Air Force headquarters in Fort Worth, Texas. Ramey, a career officer with an exemplary record of service, promptly instructed Blanchard to turn all the evidence over to headquarters.[17] The thinking seemed to be that headquarters would take it from there.

As ordered, the Roswell base quickly shipped the debris to Fort Worth for analysis. Before personnel in Texas had a chance to examine it, however, new complications entered the picture. By then, Col. Blanchard had concluded that his office should issue some kind of statement to the press about the situation. News of Brazel's story had started to leak into the community almost immediately. As base commander in Roswell, Blanchard probably felt a need to issue some kind of official statement about it. To that end, Blanchard worked with the base's public relations officer, Lieutenant Warren Haught, to develop an official press release.

The official statement Roswell coming out of the Roswell base provided an overall account of the situation as officials understood it. Much of it was relatively ordinary. But the information also included details that were translated into exciting newspaper copy.

As the press reported the situation, the news was dramatic. "The many rumors regarding the flying disks became a reality yesterday," said one account, which added that the Army was "fortunate enough to gain possession of a disk through the cooperation of the local ranchers and the sheriff of Chaves county."[18]

At the time, many people throughout the country were taking flying saucers news very seriously. Even among those who thought the UFO stories probably had mundane explanations, no one could be entirely certain that the sightings were not evidence of some sort of danger. The idea that the saucers were evidence of visitors from another world may have been a minority point of view at the time but worries that the mysterious disks could represent some earthly threat were prevalent.

Since soon after Kenneth Arnold reported unknown aerial objects a few weeks earlier, it was clear that the military was investigating the flying disks with some urgency, and many Americans knew it. On the same day that Brazel walked into the Roswell sheriff's office, for example, newspapers were reporting a completely unrelated story about military planes that "hunted the skies over Pacific Coast states" looking for "the mysterious saucers that have puzzled the entire country."[19]

According to that nationally syndicated story, the flights were "routine." Yet, while part of the motivation for the flights could have been to soothe public anxieties, it also seemed obvious the military was looking for photographic evidence if any existed to be found. To that end, all the P-51 planes involved with the search, the report indicated, were equipped with cameras.[20]

By July 9, it had been just two days since Brazel reported his discovery to authorities, but he already was tired of the whole business. As had happened with Kenneth Arnold only a few weeks earlier, Brazel became exasperated by the questions and speculations. A follow-up story in the *Roswell Daily Record* reported that Brazel was "sorry" he had mentioned the discovery at all. Frustrated by the turn of events, he told a reporter that if he ever found anything else unusual that was short of a "bomb, they are going to have a hard time getting me to say anything about it."[21]

Brazel may have wanted it to go away, but it was too late. His discovery was national news by then. After weeks of reports that veered from wild theorizing to dismissive declarations, there finally seemed to be something concrete to back up the flying saucer tales. People following the reports waited for the military to release more information.

≡ 10 ≡

Center of Attention

When the news broke about a nearby UFO crash, the town of Roswell was thrust into national headlines like never before. It was an unfamiliar and not altogether welcomed development. The city was from a household name at the time, and most of those from outside the area knew very little about it. History-minded people may have recalled that the infamous outlaw Billy the Kid had spent time in the town off and on before his death elsewhere in 1881. Still, otherwise, Roswell had seldom attracted much attention.[1]

World War II had started to change that to some extent. With the new conflict, military officials noticed that the town's remote location, dry weather, and topography—factors that were not necessarily regarded as advantageous in earlier days—could be useful for war-related purposes. Indeed, as the war progressed, Roswell was chosen for two crucial military roles that occasionally drew attention.

Early in the war, authorities briefly considered Roswell as a possible site for one of the controversial Japanese American internment camps constructed after the Pearl Harbor attack. Planners nixed that idea, however, partially due to substantial local opposition, much of which appears to have been racially motivated. After scrapping the internment camp plan, officials came up with a new idea. They selected the town for a new prisoner of war camp,[2] and by late 1942, the facility was up and running.[3]

As the conflict progressed, military officials realized they needed a place to house captured prisoners of war (POWs). Many Americans have largely forgotten about the many POWs who were brought stateside during World War II. Yet, numerous enemy soldiers were captured and transported to the United States for the duration of the conflict. As the number of these POWs rose to nearly half a million, the federal government needed someplace safe to put them. So, it commissioned hundreds of secure facilities across the country for that purpose, one of which was at Roswell.[4]

Like most POW facilities in the United States, the Roswell POW camp did not make the news often, at least not outside the immediate area. In mid–January of 1943, however, a brazen escape made national headlines after three prisoners managed to break out of the camp early one evening.

The situation took a dramatic turn when a civilian fired at the escapees as they tried to steal a car, fatally shooting one of them and wounding another.[5] That incident was reported nationally, briefly thrusting Roswell into the spotlight. Things soon returned to normal, however, and the camp seldom was in the news again.

A new military training facility in town brought Roswell substantially more regular, though less dramatic, attention. Area residents welcomed the new base. When the government announced its construction, the news was hailed as the "biggest thing that ever happened in Roswell."[6] The weather and terrain were perfect for a training facility, especially since air warfare emerged as a crucial element in U.S. military operations.

The new base was extremely active throughout the war for army air forces. The Roswell Air Force Field eventually grew to include seven concrete runways and nine auxiliary landing fields.[7] Pilots and crew members from all across the country trained there throughout the war—a fact that hometown newspapers often publicized.

After the war, the base took on a role of even greater significance when the army's 509th bomb group arrived there. Initially based in Utah, the 509th had shipped out to the small island of Tinian for the last months of the war in the Pacific. Then, when the conflict finally ended, the unit received orders to set up operations in Roswell instead of returning to Utah.

By the time they arrived in New Mexico, the 509th was arguably the most crucial air unit of the United States military. The group's importance stemmed from its origins a few years earlier. Indeed, when they created it in 1944, the military command had a particular mission in mind. Instead of preparing for routine assignments, the 509th trained in B-29 Superfortress bombers for only one purpose: to deliver and drop atomic bombs.

At the time of the 509th's creation, the world-at-large knew nothing of the classified Manhattan Project secretly developing atomic weapons. It was a mammoth undertaking involving thousands of workers at multiple locations. For the most part, the U.S. government was able to keep the project a closely guarded secret. Information about it mainly was doled out on a need-to-know basis, so only when there was a legitimate need were people told about it. During his tenure as vice-president, even Harry Truman was in the dark about it. He only learned about it when he assumed the presidency after Franklin D. Roosevelt's death in the war's final months.

The atomic bomb was developed with the idea that it would be put into action. This meant that high-level military officials began planning to use it as scientists were perfecting the atom bomb. As these plans developed, the 509th was created with this purpose in mind. Subsequently, members of the new 509th learned the intricacies of the specially outfitted B-29s and trained for a future atomic-bomb mission. However, throughout months of training, very few people—including many of those involved—knew precisely what the real purpose of the exercise was.

The European theater of the war had ended in the spring of 1945. However, the Pacific conflict was still ongoing, and Manhattan Project scientists continued to work feverishly on an atomic weapon. In early summer, they succeeded. Then, on July 16, 1945, using the codename of Trinity, the military finally conducted a full test. In a spectacle of sound and fury, an atom bomb exploded at a remote site 200 miles south of Los Alamos, New Mexico, some 200 miles northwest of Roswell.

At the same time, the war in the Pacific dragged on. So, with the new weapon now available, Truman finally decided to use it in a bid to force Japan's surrender. When the word to proceed came down from Truman in early August, the task of carrying out the mission fell to the 509th.

A 509th Superfortress dropped atomic bombs on the city of Hiroshima on August 6. Another was dropped on Nagasaki three days later. To date, these were the only instances in which atomic weapons have ever been used in war.

With its mission in the Pacific completed, the 509th soon relocated to its new home at the Roswell Army Air Field. The elite air group was then the only unit in the world with wartime experience delivering atomic payloads. And at a time when many details about the use of atomic bombs were still highly classified, the 509th was an invaluable military asset. Its continuing postwar importance was demonstrated a few months after arriving in Roswell when it was temporarily deployed to participate in new atomic tests at the Bikini Atoll in the South Pacific.

Uniquely possessing experience and expertise in delivering atomic weapons, the 509th became an essential part of the new Strategic Air Command, initially established in the spring of 1946. Therefore, the bombardment group was a critical component in Cold War defenses. American leaders dearly wanted to keep it that way.

It would be difficult to overstate the extent to which the U.S.

military was determined to retain an American monopoly on atomic weapons for as long as possible. "The bomb," as it was called, gave the United States a decisive edge in the postwar era. It was important not only militarily, but also as a powerful symbol of American might. Officials took any threats, perceived or real, to American atomic superiority gravely. As they saw things, it was not an area for lackadaisical response or half-measures.

Considering the context of Cold War military preparedness and the 509th's connection to the Roswell Army Air Field, it is perhaps not surprising that William Brazel's story of a mysterious flying saucer in the area was more enough to raise red flags for the military brass. The debris the rancher discovered at the Foster ranch was reasonably near the base, and that alone made it worth investigating.

The flying saucer craze was already in high gear in the days leading up to William Brazel filing his report. Brazel initially may not have been unaware of the flying saucer mania that was sweeping the nation by early July, but people in the town of Roswell and the local airbase surely were not. On the contrary, townspeople and officials at the airfield had good access to news about everyday happenings in mainstream society. They had easy access to news reports of the strange lights and unidentified aerial objects.

In an apparent coincidence, only minutes before officials at local military base announced that they were in possession of a flying saucer, a Roswell resident named Dan Wilmot had come forward with a UFO story of his own. Described by a local reporter as "one of the most respectable and reliable citizens in town," Wilmot told the paper that he and his wife had seen "a large glowing object [that] zoomed out of the sky ... at a high rate of speed" a week earlier. He said the entire sighting lasted less than a minute. Despite that brevity, it was enough to make a strong impression. Like many witnesses in those days, the Wilmots were reluctant to report the incident. However, when no one else came forward about it, Dan Wilmot felt that he should do so himself.[8]

When first reported in the *Roswell Daily Record*, the Wilmot sighting was combined with Brazel's case into a single story.[9] This may have given some readers the impression that Roswell was a hotbed of UFO activity. Yet, the two cases did not occur in the same location. Although they were reported in the same article, the two incidents actually had occurred two weeks and many miles apart. The latter point was—and remains—lost on many people, who have presumed that both "Roswell" cases must have happened in Roswell. But while the Wilmots reported they were at their Roswell home when they spotted something, Brazel's find was 80 miles away. There was no compelling reason to conclude that the two cases were necessarily related, but it could have seemed so to readers.

Of the two cases in the initial Roswell newspaper account, Brazel's differed the most from the ongoing flurry of UFO sightings that gripped the nation in the early days of July. Contrastingly, the Wilmot report was, in general, very much like most of the visual accounts that made the rounds in the wave of sightings cresting at the time.

Dan Wilmot saw a "glowing" object that he said was "oval in shape like two inverted saucers ... or like two old type washbowls placed together." He described it as "about 5 feet in size" but its distance into account, "it must have been 15 to 20 feet in diameter, though this was just guess." He thought the object was traveling "between 400 and 500 miles per hour."[10]

Interestingly, Mr. and Mrs. Wilmot disagreed about whether the object or light made any sound. Dan Wilmot said it was silent. However, his wife reported that "she heard a swishing sound for a very short time."[11]

As with many UFO reports in the press, Wilmot's account was specific in some respects but vague in others. For example, Wilmot, although a layperson, reported size, distance, and speed estimates. It is not evident he had any experience making such determinations. The article may have struck some readers as more definitive than it actually was.

Whatever the Wilmots saw in Roswell may never be known. How a person interprets Dan Wilmot's report depends on judgments about the reliability of the witness' initial observations and what one makes of his memory of the event several days later. The subjective component of his report, therefore, is potentially significant.

The Brazel case was very different. Not only were physical items retrieved at the Foster ranch; that evidence was quickly passed along to the United States military. And in 1947, the United States military was perhaps the only outfit on the planet with access to aerospace, scientific, and national security intelligence expertise that was sufficiently advanced enough to make sense of it. So with the Brazel evidence now in the military's possession, the question was, what would they do with it?

⇒ 11 ⇐

About Face

From the beginning, many people doubted Kenneth Arnold and the others who claimed they had witnessed mysterious UFOs. Pedestrian explanations seemed to cover most of the supposed unexplained aerial phenomena. People were letting their imaginations get the best of them or only seeing things that were not there. It was interesting to hear about but probably nothing more than that. It seemed this way to many people, at least.

But the stories coming out of Roswell were very different. Now, military experts—the people who knew America's secrets and were in a position to know many things—confirmed they had recovered a saucer. And if they said the army said so, why would that not be true? In the view of nearly all Americans at the time, the military could be trusted. So, its apparent confirmation of the reality of flying saucers was a game-changer. There seemed little doubt about that—at first.

By the time the public learned about William Brazel's discovery of UFO wreckage, the physical evidence had already been removed from the local airbase. Roswell Army Air Base personnel had shipped it "to higher headquarters" to the Eighth Army Air Force District in Fort Worth, under General Ramey's command.

After the story first broke, the Roswell base had issued its famous press release, stating unequivocally that the Army had come "in possession of a flying saucer." The sensational nature of that claim instantly made it a newsworthy story. Unsurprisingly, the press jumped on the revelation that the military now had a flying saucer in its custody. The news spread quickly over the next few hours.

Brazel's discovery generated intense curiosity across the country. Unintentionally, the army "whipped up a flurry of excitement" about it, according to one wire service report.[1]

But no sooner had the news become a hot topic in the national press than the tide changed. What began as certainty increasingly became

69

doubts. Within hours, it started looking as though Roswell Army Air Field officials might have jumped the gun.

Major Jesse Marcel had done his best to fit the bits and pieces of the wreckage back together before sending everything off to Fort Worth, but he was unsuccessful. That did not mean there was any great mystery behind the find, however. After all, it was not the sort of thing that he typically encountered. All he knew was that it was an unusual situation and that he could not draw any definite conclusions. Thus, even as the wreckage was in transit to Fort Worth, he remained puzzled.

Initial reports never described the recovered material as technologically advanced or as anything that seemed unearthly. Yet, when a *Roswell Daily Record* headline declared, "RAAF captures flying saucer," the story seemed astounding. It gave an impression that was at odds with the far plainer language used in the first descriptions of the material. The actual description used ordinary words such as "tinfoil, paper, tape, and sticks." That all sounded very commonplace on the face of it—nothing at all like what the headline implied.

Aside from it being slightly unusual to find such items on a ranch in the boondocks, nothing was shocking about the collected material, if the reports were accurate. Consider, for example, the tape found among the debris. Later, some UFO writers would claim there was something very mysterious about that material. According to them, cryptic and unfamiliar symbols were printed on the tape, supposedly representing an unearthly language and evidence of an extraterrestrial connection. Yet, the tape was not as mysterious as later claimed if the first published descriptions are any indication. Indeed, the earliest accounts mundanely called it "scotch tape with flowers printed on it."[2] That may have been an odd thing to find at a remote ranch, but it was not necessarily much more than that.

Such details were not what made the Roswell story compelling, however. What attracted the public attention was the statement emanating from the Roswell airbase: the sensational claim that a "flying disc" had been recovered. These simple words added an aura of mystery and intrigue to the whole affair. Worded in a way that gave the appearance of certainty when there were really many unknowns proved to be a consequential judgment, made in haste. It would cause headaches for the military over many years and arguably set a series of conspiratorial and extraterrestrial speculations in motion.

Major Marcel was unable to figure out what the assortment of found materials was, but it was a different story when the items arrived in Fort Worth. Almost immediately upon examining the so-called wreckage, Warrant Officer Irving Newton quickly recognized it. Indeed, he quickly spotted an essential clue. Among the various materials were radar reflectors very similar to those used in high-altitude weather balloons. As a weather officer for the Eighth Army Air Force District, Newton had seen them before.[3]

After receiving Newton's report, Brigadier General Roger Ramey promptly issued a statement that substantially undercut the earlier press release issued in Roswell. Ramey clarified that no witnesses had seen the previously unexplained object airborne. Moreover, given the nature of the material, the wrecked object must have been "flimsy."[4] The most critical part of Ramey's statement, however, directly contradicted previous reports. Without a doubt, Ramey said, base wreckage was "nothing more than a battered Army weather balloon."[5]

Ramey was eager to tamp down the flying saucer story before it went any further. To that end, he appeared on WBAP, a local radio station, on the evening of the very day that the wreckage material arrived in Fort Worth. Ramey's decision to go on a radio program personally, rather than sending a press officer, strongly suggests that he did not want the story to get out of control.

Reiterating that the wreckage was only a "weather balloon," Ramey suggested that the story had been blown out of proportion. "The wreckage is in my office now," he said, "and as far as I can see there is nothing to get excited about."[6] Yet, his strategy—if it was intended as a strategy—to deflate the story before it became a headache for the Army Air Force ended up mostly working.

The Roswell incident had already attracted attention. The addition of a new wrinkle, in which an army official had now spoken at some length, made it an even more engaging story. Indeed, editors at many news outlets, including some that had not paid much attention to earlier UFO sightings, felt compelled to say something about the news out of Roswell.

With the incident apparently debunked, the *New York Times* ran a bylined article with the headline "'Disk' Near Bomb Test Site Is Just a Weather Balloon."[7] Previously, the nation's most well-known paper largely had refrained from printing much of anything about flying saucers. The frenzy generated by the Roswell, however, seemed to be a different situation. The front-page story showed that the paper's editors regarded it as serious news.

The Cold War angle, which lurked beneath the surface in stories about a flying saucer crash in Roswell, was probably the source of the paper's interest in the matter. The headline included the phrase, "near bomb test site," which was a strong indication of that. So, it is possible that the saucer itself did not really interest the editors. Rather, the plausible, though speculative, connection to America's atomic arsenal's security and integrity may have been the deciding factor in the paper mentioning the incident at all.

Across the country, American news media, which had picked up the Roswell story before Ramey's statement, quickly circulated the new explanations. Few seem to question Ramey's version. One typical article now said Roswell wreckage "turned out to be nothing more exciting than a weather balloon."[8] That piece also added a new detail attributed to Warrant Officer Newton: "The object found near Roswell, NM, was a Ray wind target used to determine the direction and velocity of winds at high altitudes…. When rigged up, the apparatus resembles a six-pointed star. It's silvery in appearance and rises in the air like a kite, mounted to a 100-gram balloon."[9]

Ramey's office arranged a now-famous photo opportunity to quell any lingering suspicions about there being more to the story than official communications indicated. When word reached the *Fort Worth Star-Telegram* newspaper about it, the city editor looked around for someone to send over to the base. The regular staff photographers were evidently out of the office at the time, but 21-year-old J. Bond Johnson, who fortuitously owned a Speed Graphic camera, was available.[10]

Johnson drove out to the base and was taken to an office where he would take some photos. An assortment of material said to be from the wreckage was laid out on the floor. It was not particularly impressive and looked a lot like foil material, sticks and tape. In a series of about a half-dozen photos, Johnson posed Ramey, Marcel, and Col. Thomas J. Dubose holding the material while examining it. In these now-famous images, the officers calmly look at the supposed saucer wreckage and are even smiling.[11] The photos have all the appearance of a calm and ordinary show-and-tell session.

The *Star-Telegram* promptly printed a story about the wreckage that included some of Johnson's photographic material. The headline's wording, "' Disk-overy' Near Roswell Identified as Weather Balloon by FWAAF Officer,"[12] made light of the whole affair, implying that there was nothing much of substance behind all the commotion. On the face of it, the story seemingly suggested that officials in Roswell had jumped to conclusions.

Since that time, many aspects of this part of the Roswell story have been closely examined by UFO researchers. For some, the Ramey photos raise specific questions. Indeed, in the eyes of some UFO writers, these photos may not be what they seem. Some have wondered if the material that military officials showed photographer Johnson was indeed what officials said it was. Did the photos show the actual wreckage, or did the images show substituted material intended to fool the public? Was there some sort of government cover-up? There has been much speculation about these and other questions.

For example, in one of Johnson's photos, Ramey is holding a document with a printed message of some sort. Although the original image is blurry, numerous people have attempted to decipher it with the hope

Brig. General Roger Ramey's photograph session for local media, which was held shortly after the purported Roswell incident, was supposed to quell public suspicions that anything unusual had crashed in the desert. However, as time passed, people skeptical of the official explanation began questioning whether the material Ramey displayed (shown in the photograph) was really from the supposed crash site. A small note that Ramey is seen holding in the photographs from the session also sparked much speculation (courtesy Fort Worth Star-Telegram Collection, Special Collections, the University of Texas at Arlington Libraries).

of finding evidence that might confirm or refute some of the speculations. To date, those efforts have been inconclusive. (It may all be for
naught, however, since there would seem to be no compelling reason to
think that Ramey was holding a document with secret information that
would be plainly visible to the press.) The fact that so much interest in
that small detail persists illustrates the passionate appeal that the Roswell case attracts three-quarters of a century later.

At the time, the public seemed quite willing to accept the version
of events that the military issued. Most people presumed that officials
knew what they were talking about. The many news articles that stated
the case involved nothing more than a simple weather balloon quelled
whatever anxieties that the first, more sensational reports generated.
There is scant evidence to suggest that Americans at the time thought
officials were lying to them. That was, after all, an era in which people
believed in their government. The age of widespread public cynicism
was still years in the offing.

In any case, behind the scenes, officials at the Eighth Air Force in
Fort Worth spoke about the Roswell commotion with the FBI at the time.
An internal FBI memorandum marked "Urgent" and dated July 8 documents one conversation. The teletyped memo indicates that "an object
purporting to be a flying disc was recovered near Roswell." It also says,
"the object found resembles a high-altitude weather balloon with a radar
reflector, but that telephonic conversation between their office and
Wright Field had not [illegible crossed-out word] borne out this belief."[13]

The memo went on to say that the material was "being transported
to Wright Field by special plane provided this office because of national
interest in case and fact that National Broadcasting Company, Associated Press, and others attempting to break the story of location of disc
today." The document concludes with the sentence, "No further examination being conducted."[14]

The general public did not know about this memo. Since it was not
made available for public inspection until many years later, it played no
part in swaying ordinary Americans' beliefs one way or the other about
the Roswell case. Yet, like other aspects of the Roswell case, this memorandum clarifies and explains some things while simultaneously raising doubts about others. For example, the document implies that the
FBI saw no reason for further action, a judgment that is stated explicitly.
However, if there were no more to the incident than a weather balloon
going astray, why was the wreckage shipped to Wright Field in Ohio, a
thousand miles away? Were officials truthful about what had happened?
In private, it appears, officials may have thought there could be more to
the story than they let on.

⇒ 12 ⇐

Unknown Knowns

Brigadier General Roger Ramey's official explanation for the flying saucer wreckage discovered at Foster Ranch was straightforward and made sense to many people. It was merely a weather balloon, he declared. There was nothing more to it than that.

Ramey's announcement promptly quieted most concerns about the find, at least for the moment. Some years later, however, new questions would emerge. And when officials finally declassified previously secret information, it became apparent that there may have been more to the story than initially reported. Indeed, like much in the late 1940s, the Roswell incident may have been caught up in the chill of the Cold War. The story begins a few years earlier during the last days of World War II.

The blast that obliterated Hiroshima in 1945 announced the dawn of the Atomic Age. The new weapons had ended the war, or at least that is how most Americans looked at it. But that result came with nightmarish implications. As almost everyone realized, the bomb's tremendous destructive power could bring about apocalyptic consequences if it were to fall into the wrong hands. Now a daunting question confronted the world. Would humankind prove capable of dealing with its terrifying potential?

For the United States, the most immediate answer to this question was obvious. The U.S. would need to be sure that the Soviet Union—America's quickly rising postwar rival—did not acquire an atom bomb of its own. The communist giant, which had been America's uneasy ally during World War II, now represented a grave threat, not only to world peace but to the very survival of democratic societies everywhere. The Soviets had long wanted to export communist revolutions across the globe. If it were to gain access to atomic weapons, the USSR would be better positioned than ever to help make that happen.

Fear that the Soviets could soon acquire the atom bomb cast a long shadow over the weeks of UFO reports that gathered steam after

Kenneth Arnold's sighting in June. The possibility that UFO sightings had something to do with the U.S. military or the Soviets was a frequent concern. Unsurprisingly, perhaps, the two topics—UFOs and atomic fears—overlapped in public consciousness. At the time, few people feared the flying saucer episodes had anything to do with extraterrestrial visitations. However, the possibility that the objects pointed to a new Soviet threat, potentially atomic, was another matter.

American defense leaders were as concerned as the general public. Accordingly, they developed strategies to closely monitor atomic developments in the USSR, searching for even the slightest hint that America's Cold War rival was making progress on a bomb of its own.

No one could have been surprised at America's intense scrutiny of the Soviet weapons program. Yet even though Washington's interest in Soviet developments was well known, many of the specifics of American surveillance and intelligence operations in this area were not. Most efforts to keep tabs on Soviet bomb development were closely guarded secrets. So, while people generally knew the American government was keeping an eye on what its Cold War enemy was doing, very few people in or out of government knew precisely how the United States was doing it. The goal was widely known. The methods were not.

Enter Project Mogul, a highly classified program designed to gather evidence clandestinely if the USSR ever conducted atomic tests. Dr. W. Maurice Ewing dreamed up the plan. He was a Columbia University professor affiliated with the prestigious Woods Hole Oceanographic Institution in Falmouth, Massachusetts. During the war, Ewing had investigated how sound could move across great distances in the ocean. Based on this earlier work, he "theorized that since sound waves generated by explosions could be carried by currents deep within the ocean, they might be similarly transmitted within a sound channel in the upper atmosphere,"[1] as an Air Force researcher later explained it.

The idea appealed to military intelligence leaders. Cold War conditions made it difficult to get intelligence agents anywhere near potential Soviet test sites. However, Ewing's research suggested that it might be possible to develop a way to detect such tests at a very long range. The thought was to send "low-frequency acoustic detection" apparatuses to a very high altitude where the devices would have the best chance of collecting evidence. And the best way to do that at the time was to use specially rigged balloons, similar in most respects to the standard weather balloons that were routinely used for meteorological purposes.[2]

The Army Air Forces put the long-range "listening" plan into action under the codename Project Mogul. In addition to Dr. Ewing, the group they created to implement the program included Dr. Athelstan F.

Spilhaus of New York University and several other scientific and military experts.[3] The entire affair was shrouded in secrecy at an extreme level. According to a later Air Force description, the program used cloak-and-dagger methods, including "secluded laboratories, code words, maximum security clearances, and strictest enforcement of need-to-know rules."[4]

After the group started working, it did not take long to put Mogul into operation. The science behind it had been developing for some months. The project's implementation was relatively straightforward at a technical level, especially since much of it could be done by adapting existing technologies and procedures.

Columbia University, Ewing's home institution, developed the sensors for Mogul under a special contract. Meanwhile, the job of creating a "constant altitude" device that could "remain at a 'specified altitude'" was farmed out to specialists at New York University's College of Engineering Research Division.[5]

Efforts to keep the program a secret can hardly be overstated. Even the project's codename, Mogul, was classified information.[6] Indeed, Charles B. Moore, a New York University project engineer working on it at the time, apparently did not know he was involved in anything called "Mogul" until Air Force investigators interview him much later.[7]

Officials subjected the entire program to a regimen they called "compartmentation." It was an "attempt to limit unauthorized disclosure" and to make sure "each participating entity received only enough information necessary to accomplish its assigned tasks." In practice, this meant that "only a small circle of Air Force officers received the intimate details that linked together" the whole project and its aims.[8] That meant the people in the field who carried out the various parts of the project had no idea what the program aimed to do. And of course, the public knew none of this in the 1940s, either. Project Mogul remained classified for many years.

Between 1947 and 1950, the Mogul program included more than 100 launches scattered across various areas. According to later Air Force explanations of the Mogul program, officials tried to shield the project from public view as much as possible. The Air Force's 1994 investigation adds:

> Nevertheless, while the nature of the project remained shrouded in secrecy, some of its operations obviously could not. The deployment of giant trains of balloons—over thirty research balloons and experimental sensors strung together and stretching over 600 feet—could be neither disguised nor hidden from the general public. Moreover, operational necessity required that these balloons be launched during daylight hours. It is not surprising that

these balloons were often mistaken for UFOs. In fact, MOGUL recovery crews often listened to broadcasts of UFO reports to assist them in their tracking operations.[9]

This background might have been helpful for people searching for answers to the Roswell investigation in 1947. However, as a top-secret Cold War project, even meager details of the Mogul program did not come to light until it was declassified two decades later. By then, the so-called Roswell incident had passed into history.

Mogul's relevance to William Brazel's discovery on Foster Ranch is this: Based on the known and verified circumstances, Brazel's unknown wreckage was very possibly material from a Project Mogul test flight. Indeed, the Air Force's 1994 re-examination of Roswell suggests that what was initially described as a "flying saucer" wreckage may not have been parts of an ordinary weather balloon as Gen. Ramey at the time. Instead, the wreckage may have been from a Mogul device.

In their 1994 reassessment of the Roswell episode, Air Force researchers recognized the factor that most likely led to the initial confusion at the Roswell base. The report states:

> Although members of the 509th possessed high-level clearances, they were not privy to the existence of MOGUL; their job was to deliver nuclear weapons, not to detect them. The unusual combination of experimental equipment did not encourage easy identification [and] that undoubtedly left some members of the 509th with unanswered questions.[10]

In a study of the Mogul project, James Michael Young, an Air Force historian, further suggests that it was "one particular [Mogul] flight, launch #4 on June 4, 1947, [that] captured the public's attention when a local rancher recovered the balloon debris."[11]

Personnel on duty at the Roswell Army Air Field that day in 1947 lacked information about Mogul. So, they may not have been in a good position to make a clear identification about what, exactly, they had recovered. It appears to be a clear case of kicking an issue upstairs where people more in the know could deal with it. For the Fort Worth command to want the material sent to them was, in other words, a relatively typical standard operating procedure. Sprawling bureaucracies regularly treat common issues at a low level, sending matters up the chain of command when something is less than routine.

The Roswell case, in this respect, was not unusual. It was not necessarily a sign that officials believed anything was seriously amiss or an enormous problem. Instead, it seems to have been a routine case of forwarding atypical material to a level with more expertise designated to deal with it. It was what the system was designed to do.

However, if sending the wreckage to Fort Worth was a routine matter, the subsequent transfer of the material from Fort Worth to Wright Field may look more suspicious, at least on the surface. Why, after all, send the wreckage to yet another base when it had already been explained? But that decision was almost certainly rooted in bureaucratic standard operating procedures of the time, too. The Air Materiel Command at Wright Field was the entity charged with gathering aeronautic research of many kinds. Whatever it was, exactly, the Foster Ranch material appeared to be relevant to the Air Materiel Command's broad mission. It was logical for Fort Worth to ship the collected material to Wright Field. There was nothing particularly suspicious or unusual about the decision to do so.

However, all of this said, the most perplexing part of the Roswell story is not related to the wreckage itself. Instead, it was the decision by Roswell Army Air Field officials to identify the material as a "flying saucer" so quickly. The authors of the 1994 Air Force report were as puzzled by that as anyone. "Research failed to locate any documented evidence as to why that statement was made,"[12] they wrote. "Additionally," they added, "it seems that there was an overreaction by Colonel Blanchard and Major Marcel in originally reporting that a 'flying disc' had been recovered when, at the time, nobody knew for sure that the term even meant, since it had only been in use for a couple of weeks."[13]

≈ 13 ≈

Down the Rabbit Hole

In another moment down went Alice after it, never once considering how in the world she was to get out again.

The rabbit-hole went straight on like a tunnel for some way, and then dipped suddenly down, so suddenly that Alice had not a moment to think about stopping herself before she found herself falling down a very deep well.

—Lewis Carroll, *Alice's Adventures in Wonderland* (1865)

Precisely why officials at Roswell Army Air Field used the term "flying saucer" when they announced the recovery of nearby wreckage in July of 1947 is unknown. It was an interesting choice, to say the least. The term has just come into use at the time, and it did not yet refer to any one thing. It certainly did not conjure up images of extraterrestrial aliens, at least not in the minds of most people taking UFO reports seriously. Instead, people thought the "saucers" might be optical illusions, simple misidentifications, or possibly some secret new aerospace technology. If Americans harbored any significant concerns about the presumed objects, it was primarily because of the growing Cold War. The nation's sense of anxiety was related mainly to perceived Soviet threats. The extraterrestrial-alien possibility, which later generations would instantly associate with Roswell, did not emerge as a common interpretation until years later.

As time passed, the Roswell episode eventually prompted mountains of analyses, conjectures, and re-examinations. Indeed, the Roswell incident eventually earned a prominent place in popular culture, where it is often presented as a foundational episode in the UFO phenomenon, which has evolved substantially since the summer of 1947.

Over the past 75 years, the Roswell story has grown and morphed so much that, in some ways, modern versions of it are hardly recognizable compared to the first reports in 1947. Ever since the 1980s, when popular books and television shows about Roswell spurred renewed interest in the case, media representations of the Roswell story have almost always included details and allegations markedly different from accounts in 1947.

The possible involvement of Project Mogul—a program the government did not declassify until years after the actual events—was one new wrinkle to the story when it was finally revealed many years after the fact. Although the Mogul explanation was not universally accepted, many UFO community members (though not all of them) took it as a plausible explanation.[1] In some ways, it was possibly one of the least controversial additions to the 1947 accounts, at least for many people.

From military and government perspectives, the Roswell incident was (and remains) a non-event. They presume that the continuing brouhaha over the event is due to a misidentification, fabrication, or the conflating of stories from different times and places. Indeed, for many years after 1947, the Roswell episode was treated mostly this way, even by the gradually growing number of people who later came to associate "flying saucers" and other unexplained aerial phenomena as evidence of visitations from another planet.

In the 1940s and for quite a while afterward, however, the crashed-balloon explanation made sense. After Gen. Ramey's clarification, it appeared that Roswell represented nothing more than a brief misunderstanding that was readily sorted out. For the most part, people forgot about Roswell. It remained little more than a distant memory for many years—a situation that would not substantially change until about 1980.

There seems to be little reason to doubt the military's general outline of events as issued various times over the years. However, some details about the Ramey press event have attracted doubters.

After a possible connection between Roswell and Project Mogul became known in the 1990s, questions surrounding Ramey's involvement in the incident surfaced. At issue was whether or not Ramey knew about Mogul. More specifically, some wondered if his "weather balloon" explanation was a convenient cover story intended to conceal Mogul from public view.

Ramey had a long and distinguished career, but it is difficult to ascertain how much, if anything, he knew about Mogul at the time. Air Force researchers with access to complete records concluded that he might have known about Mogul, but that is not certain.[2] However, these researchers do conclude that the wreckage—as photographed with

Ramey and described in documents of the time—consisted of material that could easily have been part of a weather balloon. Much of the design and construction of Mogul balloons was the same as was used in the era's weather balloons. In the end, it may not matter if the material was or was not from the Mogul project whether Ramey was trying to deflect awareness of the program. For those who accept the version of events laid out by the military, there is little more to the Roswell story than the discovery of some sort of official balloon device, secret or not.

The photos taken at the time, and subsequently widely published in newspapers, raise different kinds of problems. Some later UFO investigators question whether things were as they seemed in these photographs. That is especially the case among those who fervently believe Ramey was involved in some sort of government cover-up. From their perspective, a significant question is this: Were the photos in which Ramey and other officers appear with the meager-looking "wreckage" legitimate? On this matter, more than a few in the UFO community have suspected that the photos were fakes. Some with that perspective believe the supposed wreckage in the Ramey photo was not what had been recovered. Indeed, many UFO writers have suggested the actual material was sent to Wright Field and that the items shown in the photographs were substitutions.

If research by the Air Force and some UFO investigators can be taken at face value, this seems very unlikely. Indeed, the reflective material, stick-like items, and other objects in the photos seem consistent with the account that first appeared when William Brazel filed his report on Monday, July 7, when he traveled from Foster Ranch to Roswell.[3] In this respect, the material in the photos is congruent with what had been said publicly to that point.

Many other aspects of the photographs have been disputed in more recent years, as well. The later skepticism almost always focuses on details about the crash site that did not emerge until many years later. For example, some reports claim that the so-called wreckage included substantially more and substantially heavier material than is shown in the Fort Worth photos. Such claims are based on the belief that a crashed aircraft of some sort had been found and that it was far different from a balloon's remnants.

Yet, there is nothing from the 1947 record to suggest that the wreckage William Brazel found was any different from how he described it to reporters at the time. However, many UFO community members and others are not convinced. To them, the photos do not close the book on Roswell as much as they open it.

There is another element in one of the Fort Worth photos that has drawn even more attention. The questions stem from a piece of paper that Ramey is holding. On that paper, there are several lines of illegible text that are otherwise clearly visible. What exactly is written on the document is a mystery. It appears to be a telex of some sort, but the writing is unclear. That fact has fueled much debate and theorizing, drawing interest from researchers having many backgrounds and perspectives.

The University of Texas at Arlington (UTA) currently owns the original Fort Worth photos and keeps them in its Special Collections department. Of these, the picture showing the so-called "Ramey Memo" continues to attract much attention. The department has made multiple versions of a scanned close-up of the image widely available, providing public access to versions of it in different contrasts and resolutions.

Although there is much interest in this piece of paper, which Ramey is casually holding and seemingly taking little effort to hide, what it says remains unknown. Some UFO researchers claim it contains suppressed information, but the image quality is so poor that this interpretation is not definitive. Many experts who have examined it have walked away, still not sure that the actual contents of the message on the paper will ever be known. Clear answers remain elusive. At the time of this writing, UTA's website included an announcement "offering a $10,000 reward for the first person or group/lab that can provide a definite read of the Ramey memo."[4]

The technology to arrive at a definitive interpretation of the memorandum may be many years away if, in fact, it ever comes. Until the day arrives when the words on the piece of paper are entirely and unambiguously clear, it will always be possible to suggest the paper documents some secret or nefarious subterfuge. Like many aspects of the flying saucer events of 1947, it may never be possible to rule out every speculation completely.

Given that the context in which the Fort Worth photographs were produced, however, there is also little reason to conclude that the piece of paper Ramey is holding documents closely guarded government secrets or that it constitutes evidence of a cover-up and conspiracy. Would that be vaguely possible? Yes. But it seems improbable. There is nothing to suggest that Ramey made any attempts to hide the contents of the paper. On the contrary, he appears to have treated it rather casually—hardly in a manner that a person might expect if the document included secret or sensitive information. Moreover, Ramey poses rather matter-of-factly in the photo, giving the appearance that to him, the photo session was just another day at the office.

It will probably always be impossible to answer every objection that a person might raise against what amounts to the standard—and rather blasé—version of the Roswell story that officials gave once the material arrived in Fort Worth for inspection. It is theoretically possible that Ramey's photo session was staged to deflect attention away from some sort of government secret. However, none of this is to say that things were not as Ramey said they were. Overall, the explanations issued in Fort Worth appear to be credible and straightforward. That does not mean, however, that the official statements are enough to satisfy everyone.

From one point of view, it could be easy to conclude that much of the fuss about Roswell in recent decades is much ado about nothing. A government-sponsored balloon fell out of the sky and landed on the outskirts of Corona, causing a brief stir before the matter was put to rest when officials identified it as nothing more than a balloon. Yet, the story, even as it emerged at the time, is partially vague and ambiguous. There was always an element of mystery in accounts about it. In many ways, it has provided an ideal scenario that is ripe for speculation of many kinds.

It would be easy to fixate on Roswell in a way that makes it difficult to makes sense of the 1947 UFO sightings as a widespread phenomenon.

The "rabbit hole" metaphor, a reference to Lewis Carroll's classic 1865 book *Alice's Adventures in Wonderland,* is sometimes aptly applied to searches for hidden truths about UFOs. Despite much time and effort that often focus on small details of UFO incidents, it remains difficult to find answers that will satisfy everyone (New York Public Library).

Roswell is the type of story that could lead a person to fall into a meta-phorical version of Alice's "rabbit hole." It can turn into what *New Yorker* writer Kathryn Schulz describes in an essay about that term as "a long attentional free fall, with no clear destination and all manner of strange things flashing past."[5] Indeed, with its gaps and potential points of contention, the Roswell story, with its many layers, could prove to be as much a roadblock as an opportunity for better understanding the summer's unusual events.

It may always be possible to dispute one or more details in this story. Some may continue to question the sincerity, memories, and intentions of the people who claim they were involved. Yet, Roswell is only one piece of a much larger puzzle. The array of later claims and theories that people have offered about it is difficult to sort out, but how the public understood the events at the time, in the original context, is much easier to discern. The Roswell incident was taken as a significant event for only a fleeting moment in its day. Within a short time, most people decided it was not much a story and mostly forgot about it. It is possible the public was wrong, or even that they had been misled. But most people bought the story the Army Air Force was selling.

What is certain is that public disclosure of the Roswell case coincided with the apogee of Flying saucer reports that summer. After Roswell came and went in the news within a few days, the frequency of sightings dramatically fell off. Whatever was going on to cause the reports, something was changing.

⇒ 14 ⇐

A Laughing Matter

In a 1948 academic study that was one of the first to look at the subject of UFOs, Earl Wennergren examined press coverage of the sightings in the previous summer.[1] In a section entitled "levity," he observed that many people treated the saucer sightings very lightly. Wennergren had a point. Indeed, almost immediately after Kenneth Arnold's story made headlines, the jokes had started. It was a trend that continued for a long time.

Based upon his close examination of many newspaper articles, Wennergren came away with a basic conclusion. Although the saucers were "something to seriously think about," he wrote, "apparently nobody thought about it too long before they worked up a good laugh. It was a story with a punch; you could fear its implications or laugh it into gleeful greatness." And in his estimation, laughter "became the greater body in the episode."[2]

The author spends several pages repeating jokes, funny stories, and amusing anecdotes on the topic culled from the pages of newspapers across the country. Many of the items would likely not strike readers from later decades as particularly funny, but the point is not the quality of the humor. Instead, what is significant is that the nation's papers ran so many articles that did not take the sightings seriously. Interestingly, the same types of news media that frequently reported saucer incidents with apparent sincerity also published articles that implied there was not much substance to all the reports.

Indeed, the media often presented flying saucers as a laughing matter quite literally. Admittedly, many articles of this type were relatively gentle. In general, such items exuded a playful spirit that does not single out or belittle anyone. But although they lack harshness, there was a discernible thread of incredulity running through them. The result was a generally skeptical atmosphere that presented potential UFO witnesses with a dilemma. That is, would it be better to speak up and report what they thought they saw? Or would it be better to keep quiet and avoid becoming a laughingstock or the butt of the next flying saucer joke?

Many newspaper columnists, presumably opinion leaders, latched upon the UFOs as a subject ripe for playful commentary. Wittingly or not, more than a few of them contributed to the creation of a cultural atmosphere that mocked, however lightly, the whole subject. Syndicated writer Henry McLemore had fun with the topic for a mid–July piece. "I had a stern warning from the [fictitious] Columnists' Union today," he wrote. "It said that unless I wrote something about flying saucers within 24 hours that my card would be picked up, I would be fined $50 and forced to spend a week with [labor leader] John L. Lewis.... So, to save my card, I am going to tell you about the flying saucers I haven't seen."[3]

Walter Winchell, another syndicated columnist, also had something to say about the flying discs. He wrote that "most everyone has some ridiculous theory" about unexplained objects. He added that the "best line on the flying saucers, we think, was 'Anyone who tells you they've seen flying saucers must have been in their cups!'"[4] Based on the now-outdated expression "in their cups" (a reference to drunkenness), this joke was hardly subtle in suggesting that there was nothing about the saucer sightings to take seriously.

On July 10, the author of an unsigned article in the *St. Petersburg Times* noted that flying disc reports in the nation's newspapers already "were getting the typical American light treatment." Editorial cartoonists at many newspapers soon adopted flying saucers for amusing treatment, too. It was apparent at the time, then, that much of the public saw little that was of earth-shattering importance or that presented an immediate danger.

Life magazine had stayed above the fray during the first weeks of the saucer craze, but it finally addressed the subject in its July 21 edition. The magazine assigned Boris Artzybasheff to illustrate a short piece that reflected the editors' stance toward the topic.

According to the text accompanying Artzybasheff's amusingly grotesque illustration, the editors had chosen the artist to provide "the correct explanation" of the saucers. The accomplished artist had won awards for book illustration and often contributed work to major magazines. Moreover, he had worked for *Life* before and possessed what the magazine described as "long experience with pixyish interplanetary phenomena." Half of the *Life* article was turned over to Artzybasheff's comical full-page drawing. The accompanying text read, in part: "Obviously the residents of Neptune, having attained civilization far in advance of that now enjoyed on earth, are shelling the earth with crockery."[5] It was a playful take on the "saucer" language of the unexplained sightings—one of many in the media at the time—that framed the UFO wave as a humorous side-story of little consequence or concern.

Sometimes a joke is only a joke, of course. Absent other intent, sometimes a person makes fun of something to get a laugh without thinking about it having any different meaning. Maybe the humorous treatment of flying saucers was nothing more than that sometimes. Yet, whenever some new development becomes the object of jokes, it is worth asking what exactly is going on. More specifically, when the 1947 wave of UFO sightings became a popular target for wisecracks and mocking disbelief, what does that say about the phenomenon overall?

Many witnesses were reluctant to report unexplained aerial objects when the phenomenon burst onto the scene that summer. This common thread ran through many of the 1947 accounts. It was more than a result of simply having seen something strange and unusual, however. Indeed, witnesses' apprehensions stemmed from a more immediate and potentially unsettling worry—the genuine possibility that they would be ridiculed simply for telling anybody what they had seen.

It was hard to go against the grain in postwar America. An age of conformity was emerging in those years and veering from the mainstream often created a sense of unease. It was a development that sociologist David Riesman and his co-authors documented in an academic book that became an unlikely popular success. *The Lonely Crowd* (1950) examined America's rising social conformity as a response to peer pressure. With Americans increasingly were becoming "other-directed," Riesman and his co-authors reasoned that people who wanted "to be loved rather than esteemed."[6] It was not a context in which ridicule would be taken lightly.

In some respects, *The Lonely Crowd* stated the obvious, but the book's observations were especially pertinent amid the consumer culture developing at mid-century. Few other works had shone a spotlight so glaringly on the so-called crowd's influence on everyday life. Here, the authors suggested that the social world played an even more decisive role in shaping individual behavior than was commonly presumed. And Riesman made his point at a critical time, just as Americans were remaking their whole notion of what constituted success and the so-called good life.

In those years, "keeping up with the Joneses" was especially important to Americans' sense of their own identity. It was essential for being seen by others as successful. For many, if the question was how to win in life, the answer was to conform. Following the perceived wisdom of the crowd in this way led not only to validation and self-worth, however. As Riesman and his co-authors write, "The presence of the guiding and approving 'others' is a vital element in his whole system of conformity and self-justification."[7]

In a social world that places a high value on respecting norms, stepping outside the mainstream is risky. Veering from the crowd's beaten path could lead to separation from the majority, in other words. Peer pressure can be especially powerful in an "other-directed" setting, where a person's sense of self is wedded to perceptions of belonging to the crowd. As long as people conform, their social standing remains secure. But when someone departs from the approved path, the situation can get dicey. Ignoring group norms can lead to all sorts of troubling signals that a person no longer is worthy of membership in the crowd—some overt, some very subtle.

One indication that a person has veered off the path can come in the form of ridicule. Mockery of this sort can be harsh, but it can also take on an appearance that seems milder and even, at times, light-hearted.

In their book, *The Psychology of Humor*, Rod A. Martin and Thomas Ford explain how ridicule "functions as a means of establishing or maintaining control over others through embarrassment and humiliation."[8] As they write:

> Ridicule presents a particularly insidious means of social control because of the humor paradox. The humiliation of ridicule serves as a social corrective, while the humor of ridicule creates ambiguity about underlying intentions. Thus, if one challenges ridicule, he or she risks further castigation for "not having a sense of humor" or "not being able to take a joke."[9]

Ridicule can affect more than the people at whom it is aimed, however. It can also influence those who are not directly involved. In a psychological study of what is sometimes called "jeer pressure," Leslie Janes and James Olson discuss the potentially powerful influence of just seeing other people being mocked. "Participants who viewed ridicule of others," they write, "were more conforming and more afraid of failing than were those who viewed self-ridicule or no ridicule."[10] Of course, ridicule may not always be intended to have a policing effect on how others think and behave. Yet, even absent specific intentions, mockery often leads to discomfort for people on the receiving end of it.

In another sense, to make a joke of something is to tame the subject, at least on some level. People sometimes make fun of things as a psychological strategy for dealing with their apprehensions—or to borrow Anna Freud's way of stating it in a very different context, as a "defense by means of ridicule."[11] The goal in those situations, presumably, would be to soothe one's anxieties by treating the feared subject dismissively. In such cases, the motivation to mock something is as much to the benefit of the person doing the mocking as to extract conformity to group norms from others.

Ridicule's effects can be potent regardless of intentions. If a person expected to be ridiculed for reporting a flying saucer, it is reasonable to think that person may have thought twice about coming forward. After all, why would people set themselves up to be the butt of jokes by reporting they had seen weird things in the skies? Some people might, but many probably would not. A person might have wondered if it was worth the risk of potentially adverse social consequences. It seems better to play it safe and let someone else come forward. That, at least, could have seemed like a realistic way to deal with a UFO experience in the social world of the 1940s.

If this were true, then it may be reasonable to question the nature, quality, and completeness of the 1947 saucer reports overall. If anything, many people may have felt a strong disincentive for filing a witness statement. With people reasonably thinking that others would look at them warily if they said anything, the whole situation may have led to something resembling a "bystander effect." Thinking no one would believe them, or worse, that they would be ridiculed, some witnesses may have decided it would be better not to say anything and just to let it go. Let someone else report it and deal with it, they may have thought.

Some observers hypothesized that many of the UFO reports partially resulted from mass hysteria or some other form of social contagion. Such claims frequently appeared in the press. Yet, given how quickly many people got the idea that UFOs were a joke that could lead to ridicule, there seems to have been a countervailing social influence at work, too. It may be true that some, possibly even many people believed they saw UFOs due to the effect of previous reports. However, there was also a strong reason for people to keep quiet, even if they were convinced they had seen something strange.

It is impossible to know how much or exactly how these factors may have affected potential witnesses. There is no way to be sure about the extent to which filed reports represent the totality of what people saw. It surely seems likely that some unknown number of sightings was never reported officially to anyone. Whether any of those would significantly alter understanding of the phenomenon remains unknown.

What is more knowable is that UFO sightings did become the objects of jokes and ridicule. The simple fact that some of these accounts were treated this way says nothing about the reports themselves, of course. The accuracy of eyewitness accounts does not necessarily have any relationship to how people talked about them.

Yet, it seems evident that ridicule—or more precisely, the fear of it—was a complicating factor throughout the first weeks when flying saucers burst onto the American scene. The first joking comments came very soon after Kenneth Arnold's report appeared in newspapers. This attitude remained evident in the weeks that followed as a spate of sightings thrust flying saucers into the spotlight. As a result, there was an air of mystery surrounding the entire affair. Some people took it very seriously, but many did not.

Whatever a person today might believe about Roswell or the blizzard of UFO sightings around that time, it is evident that the American public was not in a panic about them. Although some people genuinely showed concern about the phenomenon, it was mostly treated as a sideshow—a diversion from life's routine mundanities in the hot summer months. Even the reports out of Roswell, which later would be interpreted by some as evidence of a unique and significant development in humankind's understanding of the universe, did little more than grab the public's attention for a few otherwise uneventful days.

A small classified advertisement in the Washington, D.C.–based *Evening Star* newspaper unintentionally reflected just how lightly the subject was sometimes treated. It reads: "Flying saucers [are] easier to trace than a living room [big enough] to house our piano; State Dept director needs 3-bedroom, unfurn[ished] house."[12] Already, it seems, the term "flying saucer" had become commonplace and amusing.

In the span of just a few weeks, unexplained aerial phenomena had secured what would turn out to be a durable place in mainstream American culture. In future years, it would be a widely and contentiously debated subject. There often would be little agreement from those holding differing opinions about what had happened or what it meant.

≈ 15 ≈

Taking Another Look

For a tumultuous two weeks that summer, UFO stories were all the rage. After building to a crescendo, the number of new reports peaked in early July at about the same time that officials at Roswell Army Air Force claimed that a flying saucer had been "captured." Eighth Army Air Force headquarters in Fort Worth soon discredited initial claims about the wreckage, however. The tide then turned. In the following weeks, there were dramatically fewer new sightings. No one had fully explained every recorded case. Indeed, a stubborn percentage of the sightings have never been fully solved. However, the public was losing interest. The news media, too, appeared to tire of the topic, even though it had made something of a field day with flying disc stories in previous weeks. Perhaps the novelty had worn off, or maybe editors felt the story had run its course.

The subject did not disappear from the news entirely, but the overall tone seemed different. With fewer new sightings to report, journalists often took a different approach to the topic when they wrote about it. With a lull in new accounts to fill newspaper column inches, writers took an opportunity to reflect on the flurry of activity that now seemed to be subsiding.

"Where are the saucers?" That was the headline of an item that ran in the July 24 edition of *Key West Citizen.* The brief article noted had already faded in prominence even though there were still many unanswered questions. "The mysterious flying saucers have dropped somewhat from the news," the unnamed writer said, "but the fact that hundreds of individuals believe that they saw something in the sky gives us another puzzle."[1] According to the article, "expert scientists" had concluded that "the amazing number of reports about 'flying saucers' have been based entirely upon visual delusions of some sort." Explaining the whole thing was "a matter for psychologists," according to the article.[2]

It seems reasonable to ask whether some psychological dimension may be involved in mass reports about phenomena lacking straightforward explanations. From this perspective, the frequently voiced suspicion that the saucer sightings may have had some social, perhaps copycat aspect makes sense. However, even if some sort of social influence was involved, that does not necessarily mean that there would have been nothing concrete behind at least some of those sightings.

As the number of new accounts diminished In July, the press started taking stock about what had just happened to put it in perspective. To be sure, many people—including military officials—realized that at least a small percentage of the reports could not easily be chalked up to delusions or illusions. If not outright mysteries, these cases at least represented unanswered questions. Maybe many were simply mistaken identifications or the result of some mass psychological effect, but some of the stories seemed to be about something else.

Brigadier Gen. Ramey had convinced much of the public that the supposed saucer wreckage in New Mexico was nothing more than a weather balloon. However, the military kept an eye on the flying saucer phenomenon and continued to gather reports of new sightings. Meanwhile, Washington officials dressed down subordinates at the Roswell Army Air Force base for their haste in issuing the "captured" flying saucer statement. A syndicated press account indicates that Roswell officers were "delivered a 'blistering' rebuke" shortly after the news broke.[3]

However, behind the scenes, intelligence personnel at the Pentagon looked into some cases, including several reported sightings that had occurred before Kenneth's Arnold by-then famous encounter and had not previously attracted much attention. The military's interest was piqued enough to take at least some of the reports seriously. That said, there is little to suggest that officials were doing much more than maintaining a watchful eye on the situation.

Simultaneously, the press continued speculating about the possible causes of the wave that appeared to be subsiding. As was true earlier, many of the reports were obvious errors or hoaxes. But the relatively small percentage of cases that still defied simple explanations were sufficient to prompt a continuing search for answers.

Some journalists began to think about what they perceived as similarities between the recent reports and a series of unexplained incidents in the latter days of World War II. It was not the first time this had been noted, but by July, the idea was discussed anew as writers tried to put the wave in perspective. Writing for the *Daily Boston Globe*, Carlyle Holt noted, "Flying saucers are a new phenomenon to the American people. To wartime flyers in Europe, they may be old stuff."[4]

Indeed, American aircrews experienced a series of unfamiliar and unusual situations in the latter months of the war. Pilots reported "mysterious engine irregularities" in which "engines would suddenly misfire, began to sputter, and fail." They wondered if the Germans had "found some way of establishing a magnetic field that could throw the timing of any electrically fired engine out of kilter." Holt further noted that crews said they saw "odd, silvery balls drifting in the skies." Army Air Force officials subsequently explained the "silvery balls" as "small strips of paper coated with metal foil" that "were dumped from aircraft to confuse radar tracking systems." Still, the reports were numerous enough to have made an impression at the time.

Although he did not mention the term, Holt's story also evoked the series of bizarre encounters with "foo fighters" in the skies over Europe near the war's end. A writer for the *Evening Star* made that the focus of one story, saying that maybe the witnesses reporting "'flying saucers'... just don't know a 'foo fighter' when they see one."[5] Describing the foo fighters as "weird objects" that sometimes gave off a "reddish light" and at other times resembled "silver globes," the objects sometimes "danced just off the wing tips, or played tag with the [U.S.] fighters in power dives," while at other times "appeared in precise formation." One American pilot said a foo fighter "Chased" him "down the Rhine Valley." At the time, officials seem to have dismissed such incidents are misinterpretations of radar interference materials and other visual errors.

Regarded as a mostly minor oddity as the war was still ongoing, the foo fighters were never the main events reported in daily news at the time. However, this is not to say that stories about them were hidden from the American public. Indeed, numerous news sources published stories about them in 1945.

While the press, the public, and even many officials struggled to figure out exactly what was going on in mid–1947, one thing had become apparent. The Army Air Force—and perhaps the U.S. military establishment, more generally—had become "the No. 1 suspect in the 'flying saucer' mystery,"[6] as one newspaper article said.

In July 1947, both the AAF and the Navy said most reports could be explained easily, though they admitted that some still needed to be sorted out. Defense officials issued multiple denials that the military owned anything that resembled the still-unexplained aerial objects. Yet, the idea that at least some of these were secret (or relatively unknown) defense projects continued to surface. Sometimes, the military agreed, especially in cases that involved information that was public knowledge. In response to a sighting over Maryland in early July, for example, a military source hypothesized that a UFO sighting could have been nothing more than "four jet fighters which cruised the area in formation."[7]

However, for the most part, defense officials claimed that the flying discs had nothing to do with them.

Still, the AAF made it a point to tell the public that it took the matter seriously and had assigned intelligence officers to review case files.[8] This was undoubtedly true, as records suggest that internally, the Pentagon still had some unanswered questions, even if it was satisfied that the overwhelming majority of sightings were nothing to cause worry.

Of course, the Pentagon had its own priorities that mainly focused on the emerging Cold War. The military was not primarily in the business of helping the public understand the recent wave of UFO sightings. That said, aeronautical research and development commanded much of the Pentagon's attention at the time. There were many projects at far-flung locations across the United States that involved futuristic technologies. Authorities publicized some of these as part of a public information campaign to keep the U.S. public from worrying too much about the rising Soviet threat. But much of the development was done quietly, as far from the public's gaze as could be managed.

Of course, testing and practicing with new aircraft means flying them. And once aircraft are aloft, it is sometimes difficult to keep them entirely out of sight. Is it possible that some unexplained accounts were actually military aircraft, even though there had been official denials? That is not an unreasonable question, especially as the government presumably would not be keen to acknowledge aerospace hardware developments that it thought would give America an advantage in a military confrontation.

Whether such speculation helps clarify what was happening is an open question. However, it is undoubtedly true that some of the public was aware that potentially jaw-dropping new technologies were in the works.

It is worth noting that the skies really were filled with new and experimental aircraft in the immediate postwar years. The media reported this often. The military was transitioning to jet-powered planes at this time, and many of these new aircraft designs looked very unfamiliar to the general public.

One new design involved the so-called "flying wing" concept. These aircraft possessed a stunning wedge-like design, essentially giving them a V-shaped, boomerang-like appearance. The flying wing was not a new idea, but it had seldom been put into practice. A jet-powered version, the Horten brothers' experimental Ho 229 fighter, was developed in Germany in the latter days of World War II. It was developed too late to put into combat, but the plan was quite far along when Allied troops captured the facility making them and removed the existing models and data for analysis.

Stateside, the American military had been working along similar lines. The Northrup Company, for example, was involved in both propeller-driven and jet versions of such aircraft during the war. After the conflict ended, Northrup continued to work on various flying-wing planes, both big and small. Although some parts of the development program remained secret, some information about new aircraft designs was surprisingly open for public consumption.

Northrup's MX-324 was brought out from under a veil of secrecy and publicly announced on July 5, 1947. Before that date, "only a few dozen persons knew of the plane's existence,"[9] according to a press account. Nicknamed the "rocket wing," the MX-324 had been tested an airfield at Barstow, California—about 100 miles northeast of Los Angeles—before the public announcement.

The MX-324 was only one of several new technologies in

Aircraft designers had long experimented with so-called "fixed-wing" planes by the time this plane, the Northrup YB-49, took to the air for test flights in the fall of 1947. The novel design of such aircraft presented a startling and unfamiliar sight to people who happened to catch of glimpse of it (National Archives/Department of Defense).

various stages of development in 1947. American newspapers carried stories about a British flying-wing British fighter, the jet-propelled Armstrong-Whitworth AW-52, in January.[10] In February, the U.S. Navy told the public about its more traditionally shaped new D-558 Skystreak turbo-jet bomber. It was designed to[11]"carry five tons of bombs 10,000 miles" and was scheduled to make its first flight in the coming weeks.

Meanwhile, the military's quest to attain supersonic flight capabilities was documented in the news media throughout the year. Reports about the rocket-powered XS-1 started in 1946.[12] As it broke speed records one after another, that technology regularly appeared in the press.

It does not seem likely that many of the still-unexplained UFO cases from June and early July were actually sightings of new-style military aircraft that the Army and Navy were testing around that time. Yet, a segment of the public was well aware that these new devices were in development.

It seems reasonable to wonder if background awareness of the latest technologies influenced some people's interpretations of the sometimes-ambiguous visual experiences they had. It was not, in other words, preposterous for the public to speculate about possible military involvement in the flying saucer episode even though officials denied it. Americans knew a little about the new technologies. News accounts had revealed some information, and that may have been enough to prompt speculation and conjecture. Americans also knew that their government had produced the epoch-defining atomic bomb in nearly complete secrecy only a few years earlier. Why, people might have asked, would it be so impossible that the saucers were something new that the government was keeping under wraps? Even in a society that was not as cynical as it would be later, it was not an unreasonable question.

⟹ 16 ⟸

National Security
and the Culture of Secrecy

When the UFO wave began, Congress was still debating changes that would profoundly affect the organization of American military and intelligence operations. After months of talk, back-and-forth negotiations, and deliberations, the National Security Act of 1947 was signed into law on July 26, only two weeks after events in Roswell made national headlines.

The new legislation brought significant change to highly fragmented defense operations. For one thing, it mandated the creation of the Air Force. (The new branch officially launched in September.) It also combined previously separate functions and placed the Army, Navy, and a new, independent Air Force under a single umbrella called the National Military Establishment. (It was renamed the Department of Defense in 1949.) And it created both the National Security Council and the Central Intelligence Agency, the latter of which was mostly built upon the wartime Office of Strategic Services (O.S.S.) and staffed by many of the same people.

The road to the National Security Act had been winding and contentious. Many Navy and Army leaders were wary of changes that they believed would alter the delicate balance of power between rival military branches. The State Department and military establishment also bickered over lines of authority and influence. Meanwhile, many members of Congress were divided about the proposed measures, which promised to shake up and redistribute power if signed into law.[1]

In the end, it took months of negotiations and political wrangling to arrive at a bill that could pass muster. When signed into law, it changed the landscape, but it did not eliminate departmental rivalries. The confusing web of agencies and departments had complicated UFO investigations before. It was not necessarily a much-improved situation after the Act took effect.

A great sense of apprehension about the threat posed by the Soviet Union lurked in the background to this massive reorganization scheme. The unlikely Soviet-American wartime alliance had never been strong, and few people thought it would last when the conflict ended. Indeed, by the time Germany fell in 1945, it was apparent that the two nations would be bitter rivals in the months and years ahead.

Even before the war ended, the emerging superpowers acted upon that presumption. Near the conflict's conclusion's end, a secret United States program, Operation Paperclip, rounded up German scientists and technologists for future use in American defense and aerospace research. The Soviets, meanwhile, engaged in similar practices, eventually relocating numerous German personnel to help staff its weapons and research programs. As World War II was ending, both sides shored up the secret weapons programs with German scientists. Some of them, such as rocket scientist Wernher von Braun, had been far from bystanders in the Nazi regime. Von Braun was a member of the SS during the war and participated in many questionable actions. Like many other Nazi scientists, however, the government brought him to the U.S. after the war to continue his research for the American military.

Advanced military technology was always part of the planning from both sides in the Cold War. The United States and the USSR devoted enormous attention and resources to the new technology, with each side hoping to gain and keep and superiority over the other. Atomic weaponry, which only the United States possessed until 1949, was the centerpiece, but aerospace and other technologies were also in the picture.

German scientific expertise in rocketry, acquired in the development of the V-2 program, became important in this regard. Much of U.S. military aerospace research was highly classified. Many people knew that former Nazis were participating in America's postwar defense research programs, but not everyone agreed with the policy. The Federation of Atomic Scientists wrote an angry letter to Truman in protest, saying it was an "affront to people who fought the Nazis and to refugee scientists denied entry to the U.S."[2] However, there was little change to the policy. Military and political leaders thought that the outcome of a future war would depend in no small measure on which side possessed the technological edge.

Across America, a shroud of secrecy fell over much postwar technological research. This aspect of the race to build the most powerful military force on the planet was not new. Restricting access to plans and capabilities traditionally has been part of military thinking. Yet, in the postwar atomic age, secrecy took on even greater importance. In the

Nazi V-2 rockets terrorized London in the final months of World War II. After the conflict, the U.S. military brought the fearsome technology and some scientists who developed it to America. This V-2 gantry, shown here long after being abandoned, was used in V-2 tests conducted at the secretive White Sands Proving Grounds in New Mexico in 1947 (Library of Congress).

technological contest with the Soviets, the ability to keep the enemy from fully knowing U.S. defense capabilities represented a distinct advantage. Keeping enemies in the dark, or even outright deceiving them, was an essential part of planning. Therefore, officials were careful in doling out information, releasing it when it was either innocuous or when there was some advantage to making it public. The military kept much of its research and development as confidential as possible.

In the late 1940s, the U.S. government remained very interested in keeping American secrets safe. In March of 1947, as part of that effort, Harry Truman had issued Executive Order 9835, the so-called "Loyalty Order." Primarily intended to find and deal with communists serving in government, the order cast a wide net. Millions of federal employees fell under suspicion in the search for spies, traitors, members of subversive organizations, and communist sympathizers. Investigators uncovered a relatively small number of suspects, but the order signaled that an undercurrent of suspicion was beginning to overtake American culture.

In some ways, it was a forerunner to the more well-remembered investigations of the House Un-American Activities Committee and the Senate hearings of Joseph McCarthy.

The search for communists in government frequently made news, as would continue to be the case for many years. In June, the State Department fired ten employees on such suspicions.[3] On the same day this story appeared in the news, another report announced the criminal conviction of a man on charges of "concealing Communist Party affiliations from government loyalty examiners." The man recently worked for the State Department, but he had been a member of the Pentagon's Office of Strategic Services during the war. Upon conviction, he faced a possible "maximum sentence of $110,000 in fines and 110 years imprisonment."[4] The actual sentence of one-to-three years behind bars was mild in comparison.

The U.S. government was clearly committed to enhancing national security. Yet, it remains difficult to determine just how much, if at all, these factors may have influenced flying saucer investigations. If the Air Force's later analysis is correct, then the classified nature of Project Mogul likely contributed to confusion about the Roswell events. Official secret-keeping plausibly may have played a part in other sightings, too.

In an environment where secrecy is highly valued, many of these details can be hard to pin down. What is more definite is that the 1947 wave of saucer reports occurred in the context of a culture that placed an increasingly high value in keeping many things out of sight. And that undoubtedly complicated efforts, then and now, to fully understand the totality of what was happening.

As the U.S. government focused on keeping its own secrets, it simultaneously was trying desperately to uncover secrets of the Soviet Union. The urgency that authorities placed on reaching that goal is understandable. After all, the 1941 Japanese attack on Pearl Harbor—the incident that plunged the United States into World War II—had been so devastating precisely because American officials had not seen it coming. If intelligence had been better, that tragedy could have been averted or at least lessened.

Whatever the unexplained aerial objects were, even sober-minded defense officials realized that they were not necessarily a trivial or frivolous concern. A column from July 12, 1947, by Washington insiders Joseph and Stewart Alsop illustrates that point. "The flying saucers have served at least to pound one lesson home," they said. "That is that the United States has developed no effective warning system against surprise attack in this age of new and terrible weapons."[5] They argued that a new early warning system, which would be expensive, was overdue. In their view, "Unless the nightmare of surprise attack conjured up by the flying saucer scare is to become a reality, or unless a secure world settlement is unexpectedly achieved, the money must be spent."

With this column, the authors were among the first writers to connect publicly the UFOs and the widely perceived Soviet menace. What concerned them was not that the flying saucers posed a real, concrete threat or that they necessarily were of Soviet origin. Rather, they worried that the UFO sightings had exposed a potentially fatal flaw in American defenses. The military's inability to say with confidence exactly what people were seeing—their failure to end speculation by providing specific facts—was the primary concern. America lacked "adequate defense preparation," they argued, especially in the "era of the atom bomb and the guided missile." Their conclusion: "We are not prepared for the worst."[6]

From this perspective, the saucers did not need to be anything mysterious or something entirely out of the ordinary to be taken seriously. A little doubt provided more than enough motivation to look into them. The simple fact that the authorities could not be entirely sure what the sightings represented was enough to expose major weakness in American defenses. In that way, the phenomenon provided a valuable and even jarring lesson.

By this time, even the public knew that the USSR was probably inching closer to developing atomic weapons. Before flying saucers had made news, the press already had reported as much, openly stating in March that "the Soviet Union is on the threshold of developing an atomic bomb."[7] So, when the New York Times story on July 9 reported that the Roswell incident had occurred "near the scene of atomic tests,"[8] a possible connection of some sort did not necessarily seem far-fetched. There certainly seemed to be enough questions to warrant looking into the matter more thoroughly.

Many officials and other experts publicly insisted that the flying saucers were not classified government projects throughout this time. The *Boston Globe* reported that the country's leading physicists had said that "'flying saucers have no connection with any secret weapons now being developed by the Army or Navy.'"[9] However, the headline to that story notwithstanding, journalist Tomas R. Henry includes a telling caveat to his article. He acknowledges that the same experts who denied the saucers were part of weapons research could "be held to such strict rules of secrecy that they could not drop the slightest hint of what they may know." If that were true, the denials would not mean much.

And that was the fundamental conundrum that authorities faced when offering official declarations about the saucers. In a society ramping up security and secrecy measures in a developing Cold War, there was a compelling reason for those authorities to be less than truthful on some occasions. With security interests trumping other concerns, they could always justify—or rationalize, at least—stretching or denying the facts about something if they thought it would protect American interests. Regardless of what a person believes was true or false about government statements, this situation almost certainly fueled distrust and suspicion among some interested parties. Some people would conclude that the government, having what they saw as a reason to lie, could never be trusted. But even for others, there would always be enough doubt to make it difficult to tell precisely when governmental sources were being completely candid instead of when they were trying to hide something. And in the Cold War, it is beyond doubt that the government often had an interest in hiding some things.

Despite apparent attempts to quell continuing interest in the flying saucers, investigations continued, although in a low-key manner. Authorities across a spectrum of agencies took statements, investigated cases, and developed case files for unexplained aerial phenomena. The pace of new reports was slowing, but both the FBI and military kept working on them. Other officials at various levels of government did, as well.

Meanwhile, Americans' interests turned to other topics as the days passed in mid-summer. With radically fewer new sightings, the phenomenon seemed to have run its course. Yet, the subject did not fade entirely from public consciousness. Although many incidents had been chalked up to mistakes and visual illusions, a number of cases stubbornly lacked completely satisfactory answers. And it was those cases, of course, that remained the problem.

On August 9, the Fourth Army Air Force, based in California, released a "report on flying saucers." it had been working on it for some weeks. Its conclusion was straightforward and perhaps as to be expected:

> There is not sufficient evidence nor testimony available to conclude whether the reports of the so-called flying discs in the Tacoma (Washington) are or any other area have any basis in fact. In view of this, the Fourth Air Force will pursue this particular investigation no further.[10]

Whether this document was intended to inform or merely to appease the public's curiosities is hard to say. Yet, even if the Fourth Air Force mostly had dropped the subject, as the report indicated, many other parts of the government had not. While the intensity of attention may have lessened, it was far too soon to say the flying saucers phenomenon was over.

⇒ 17 ⇐

Dangerous Skies

Kenneth Arnold's search for a missing military transport plane led him to detour over the Cascade Mountains in June. He never did find the downed aircraft. However, in changing his flight path, the amateur pilot ended up in just the right location to spy strange things in the sky. With that one fateful decision, Arnold inadvertently launched the flurry of UFO reports that made headlines over the following weeks.

The initial excitement about flying saucers was subsiding when, on July 24, two members of a ground search party finally located the "scattered remnants" of the missing plane at the base of the snow-covered South Tahoma glacier at Mount Rainier.[1] Park ranger Bill Butler, one of the two who made the discovery, concluded that the plane "must have plunged blindly into the side of the mountain, exploded, and practically disintegrated."[2] The discovery of the wreckage confirmed that all 32 Marines aboard the plane had perished. Although authorities already had concluded that there could have been no survivors, the grim find was still a sad outcome to the search that had started months earlier.

Air safety was a priority for military and civilian flights then, but air travel was a more precarious proposition than it would be in later years. The public's worries prompted the House of Representatives Committee on Interstate and Foreign Commerce to investigate the issue in January 1947. At hearings on "Safety in Air Navigation," some witnesses testified that air travel concerns were overblown. However, it is clear from some House members' statements and questions that the public was rattled by reported mishaps. As committee chair Charles A. Wolverton said, "In recent months, the country has been shocked by the number of airplane crashes that have occurred."[3]

U.S. military aircraft were involved in numerous accidents in the era, as well. Dozens of military crashes occurred in 1947. The frequency of incidents became so acute that a year later, in mid–1948, the Air Force felt compelled to explain. Overall, they attributed the problem to "stepped up operations and an intensified training program,"[4] but they admitted it was a difficult situation.

"Accidents have been the principal challenge to U.S. airpower," one official said.[5] It was not a new issue. Even during the war, of the 18,700 American military aircraft lost between December 7, 1941, and mid–1944, the vast majority—11,000—were destroyed not in combat but rather in non-combat accidents.[6]

The American public of 1947 was concerned about the many aeronautical mishaps. The media regularly informed newspaper readers and radio news listeners of air incidents, many with tragic outcomes. When the public's attention was directed to the skies in the summer that year, UFOs were far from the only things on their minds.

In the first week of August 1947, aircraft accidents and UFOs came together in an unfortunate incident. A B-25 bomber carrying four military men—the pilot, co-pilot, and two passengers—crashed near Kelso, Washington, in the early hours of August 1. Ironically, the tragedy coincided with "Air Force Day," a celebration designated by Harry Truman "in recognition of the personnel of the victorious Army Air Forces and all those who have developed and maintained our nation's air strength."

The earliest reports skimped on details. "' Chutes Save Two in Bomber Crash,"[7] read one headline later that day. Soon, however, more information was available. It became clear that while two aboard the aircraft survived the fiery crash, two others did not. More surprisingly, authorities subsequently identified the men who died in the accident as two intelligence officers, Capt. William L. Davidson and Lt. Frank M. Brown.[8]

As a more detailed picture of the tragedy emerged, a connection between the deceased victims and the UFO sightings suddenly became evident. Most people had dismissed the Roswell story by this time, but now the B-25 crash elicited claims that were just as shocking. It turned out that not only were Davidson and Brown intelligence officers; they had been investigating UFOs. And what is more, news accounts suggested that the officers had stowed physical evidence of the unknown objects aboard the plane—evidence that was lost or destroyed in the plane's wreckage.

Provocative headlines, such as "Crashed Plane Pilots Believed Carrying' Disc Pieces,"[9] accompanied syndicated news stories that appeared a few days after the crash. Many articles gave the distinct impression the military had acquired physical UFO evidence that had gone missing. It is not hard to imagine that many readers may have wondered whether there was more to the story than just another sad example of the aviation mishaps that were all too common in the era. The frenzy of interest in flying saucers otherwise had peaked by this time. Now, however, there was a possible new mystery with the potential to resurrect the frenzied interest in UFOs once again.

Although it was not apparent to the public initially, the B-25 crash was directly connected to Kenneth Arnold. In fact, it is doubtful that Davidson and Brown would have been on the plane or that they would have placed a cargo of "disc pieces" on the flight, except for Arnold's involvement with a reported unexplained incident that he did not witness personally.

The "disc pieces" that were supposedly on the downed plane consisted of material from an incident that allegedly occurred a few days before Arnold's sighting over the Cascades. The missing items were allegedly fragments of a UFO spotted by Harold Dahl, a salvage worker, on June 21. According to his later account, Dahl was working on a boat on Puget Sound that afternoon when he saw six unidentified aerial objects racing across the sky. As he watched, one of the objects exploded, scattering shards of a metallic substance onto his boat, into the water, and onto the beach of nearby Maury Island. The bits of wreckage were hot enough to burn his son's arm, Dahl said. One piece struck and killed the family's dog.[10]

According to his later statement, Dahl was so shaken by these startling events that he quickly put his boat ashore. He and his son then ran for cover, waiting to be certain there was no further activity before resuming the day's planned activities.[11]

Soon after that, Dahl spoke about the weird experience with his boss, Fred Crisman. When they met, Dahl showed Crisman some fragments he said had collected from the wreckage. Finding this series of events unusual enough to pass along, Crisman then contacted a magazine about it.

Crisman apparently hoped that he and Dahl would receive financial compensation for information about the incident. That consideration evidently had something to do with the outlet he decided to approach with the story. It was an interesting choice. Rather than talking to a local paper or radio station, Crisman contacted Ray Palmer, a science-fiction writer. Palmer was well-known as the editor of *Amazing Stories*, a pulp magazine that was especially popular in the 1930s and 1940s.[12] He was also interested in getting a publishing company of his own off the ground, and in that vein, he was seeking out new kinds of material.

The flying saucer reports fit congruently with Palmer's interests in other-worldly and unusual tales. When contacted by Crisman, he was interested.

It took a while to pull together a plan for how to proceed. To find out if there might be something substantial in the Puget Sound incident, he made a deal with none other than Kenneth Arnold, who, since he had a pilot's license and a plane, could fly out to meet with Dahl and Crisman.

Palmer financed Arnold's short expedition. To assist with the informal investigation, Arnold brought along Capt. E.J. Smith, a United Airlines pilot with 14 years of flight experience. Interestingly, Smith, along with the first officer and a flight attendant, had reported seeing "flying discs" in early July during a scheduled trip between Boise and Portland, Oregon.[13] As seasoned airline professionals, their testimony, which was widely reported, lent an air of credibility to the saucer phenomenon when the public was still pondering what to make of it.

When arrangements were finalized, Arnold and Smith made the trip to meet with Crisman and Dahl to hear their story and see the evidence firsthand. It had been a month since Arnold's own encounter with something strange in the sky, but he still had many unanswered questions. The Idaho pilot seemed to think that an earthly explanation for the unexplained objects was entirely possible. Precisely what that could be, however, he could not say. At the time, he later wrote, he "didn't even dream of the possibility that they [the flying saucers] could come from another world."[14] And some of what people were saying seemed outlandish to him. In a book he co-authored with Palmer a few years later, he recalled that he and Smith "did a great deal of laughing and joking about the crazy things people were saying about flying saucers" in the hours leading up to their meeting with Dahl and Crisman.

The four men—Arnold, Smith, Crisman, and Dahl—finally met on July 31. After introducing themselves and exchanging pleasantries over breakfast, they retired to a nearby hotel room for a private conversation. Crisman and Dahl then related the Puget Sound story in detail. They also showed Arnold and Smith material they said was debris from the unknown object that supposedly exploded over the Sound a few weeks earlier.

Arnold and Smith were intrigued. Both men were previously interviewed (separately) by military intelligence officers after filing their respective reports. After hearing and seeing the new story and evidence, Arnold called a military official he knew, offering to introduce him to Crisman and Dahl and show him the evidence.

A while later, Capt. Brown and Lt. Davidson arrived at the hotel where Arnold, Smith, Crisman, and Dahl were waiting. According to Arnold's later account, the two officers initially showed some enthusiasm when Crisman and Dahl related their story. Some time passed, and the two officers had a chance to examine the supposed debris carefully. But then, the intelligence officers appeared to suddenly lose interest. Concluding that the items were unexceptional, the military men cut the meeting short. They seem to have suspected a hoax and saw no reason for further questioning.

Explaining to the others that the next day was Air Force Day, Brown and Davidson said they needed to return to their base and ended the conversation. The others were taken aback by the suddenness of the meeting's end, but there was not much they could do about it. The officers seemed to have made up their minds. Brown and Davidson then packed up the evidence and their notes and, despite the late hour, headed back to the local airfield. Shortly after that, with the evidence in hand, the two officers boarded a B-25 for the flight back to their home base.

Within a matter of minutes, however, disaster struck. The plane's engine caught fire, and the aircraft crashed. There were subsequent rumors about what had happened, but officials were satisfied that it was nothing more than a regrettable accident. It was one of the many air mishaps that cause so many people of that era to worry about aeronautical safety.

Back in Tacoma, Arnold and Smith heard the news. Arnold later claimed he wondered if Dahl and Crisman were trying to fool people with their story. After the crash, however, the purported evidence was gone.

The shocking news that military UFO investigators and evidence had been involved in a fatal crash created an initial stir, but the news media quickly lost interest. As with the Roswell case, official explanations seemed to indicate nothing mysterious about the incident. It was a human tragedy in the eyes of most, not unlike the other human tragedies that often appeared in the news.

Speaking to a reporter after the crash, Smith reported that the evidence Dahl and Crisman turned over to the investigators consisted of "pieces of metal or lava" that were "extremely heavy." He (and Arnold, also) believed the fragments must have been "subjected to extreme heat."[15] However, there seems to have been little to suggest that anything about the debris was wholly unfamiliar or strange enough to cause concern.[16]

After his brief trip, Arnold knew little more than he had before meeting Dahl and Crisman. He would continue to follow UFO stories, but it was time to get back to his everyday life. Back in Boise a few days later, he once again took off in his small plane. When the aircraft was only 30 feet in the air, however, the engine malfunctioned. The plane crashed to the ground, but Arnold escaped unhurt.[17] The mishap added an ironic note to his continuing search for answers.

Within a few weeks, interest in the Puget Sound story was little more than a memory. In the meantime, the Fourth Army Air Force base in California had collected other fragments from Maury Island as potential evidence. However, authorities concluded there was nothing much to the story. The material they collected from the beach on the island was determined to be "molten metal." That was not unusual, officials said, adding that "similar material appears in great quantity in that area and other Tacoma areas."[18] In any case, reports indicated that nothing out of the ordinary had been found among the wreckage of crashed B-25.

≈ 18 ≈

The Bureaucratic Merry-Go-Round

A few days after a B-25 crash ended the lives of military intelligence investigators Brown and Davidson, the public relations officer of Tacoma's McChord Army Air Force base, issued a statement. In a rare public expression of sentiments usually held closer to the vest, the release said, "The army and the FBI are going to get to the bottom of this. It's the biggest hoax ever perpetrated, and it's not funny. Two army officers lost their lives as an indirect result of this fraud."[1]

The statement left little doubt that Army officials had already concluded that the supposed incident over Puget Sound was fake. They were not happy about the apparent attempt to deceive them. The disclosure also exposed something that federal entities usually did not admit—that they were working together. But what, exactly, did that mean? A reader could be forgiven for thinking the two organizations were coordinating their efforts and conducting their investigations in concert. However, a closer look behind the scenes suggests that the entities, though relying on each other, did not necessarily have a close working relationship.

Almost immediately after news of the B-25 crash made headlines, there were rumors about the cause of the accident. Interestingly, the FBI and Army Air Force traded preliminary information about the tragedy, as each organization tried to establish if there had been anything suspicious about it.

A memorandum dated August 6 notes that an FBI agent had been in touch with Army Air Force Intelligence, "inquiring about an article that appeared in the West Coast newspapers recently stating in substance that an airplane carrying recovered flying saucers" had crashed.[2] At this time, according to the memo, the Army Air Force command knew few details. That, at least, was the official word.

The memo's writer does confirm that an Air Force CIC (counter-intelligence) agent "was killed" in the crash and that "headquarters of the Air Force have been advised that he was on a top secret mission." Moreover, someone pertinent to the case (the identity is redacted in the declassified version of the document) "was under the impression that the CIC agent was either en route to or from an interview with [redacted], who is one of the individuals who first saw one of the flying saucers."

This much of the memorandum, if examined in isolation, may look provocative to some extent, but the final words in the document suggest otherwise. The memo ends by passing along a third-party assessment of the situation, "It was his belief," the writer says, "that no flying saucers have been recovered but that it was merely an attempt to interview an individual who previously had reported seeing one of the flying saucers." Unless the memo was intended to deceive the recipient, which seems unlikely, the document appears to confirm that officials did not think the B-25 had been carrying any substantive physical evidence of a UFO. Similar internal records indicate that federal officials were confident that the B-25 mishap was nothing more than a tragic accident.

A few weeks later, various governmental organizations were still dealing with the aftermath of the crashed B-25 and the UFO phenomenon, more generally. By this time, media interest had waned from the frenzied levels of only a few weeks earlier. However, the topic had not wholly disappeared. Therefore, some parts of the government were still tracking down leads and putting together reports in response to recent events.

An FBI memo dated August 18 follows up on a telephone conversation during which the FBI Director had been "advised that Los Angeles papers" had published that "an article indicating the Soviet espionage agents in the United States are under instruction to solve the flying discs."[3] Moreover, the memo continues, "Such instructions were believed to be based on the assumption that the flying discs were a secret weapon of the Army or Navy."

According to the memo, the newspaper article attributed this information "to a Federal investigative agency,"[4] and this was evidently a source of concern. After all, if that were true, it could very well have suggested a possible security leak. Indeed, news about ultra-secret U.S. technology, if it existed or about the activities of Soviet agents, would not have been information that the government wanted to share openly. Given this situation, the FBI appears to have looked into both the article's substance and source.

"Pursuant to your instructions," the memo concludes, "liaison representatives had contacted the Headquarters of Military Intelligence, the Headquarters of the Air Forces Intelligence, the Office of Naval Intelligence and CIG [Central Intelligence Group]. All agencies denied any knowledge of the flying discs, as well as any knowledge of the basis for this article."[5]

Such documents do not offer conclusive, incontrovertible proof that the government, at some level or in some unit somewhere, did not have knowledge or material about UFOs that it was withholding. Yet, the pedestrian tone and language of the documents have a mundane quality. Rather than looking evasive, the documents seem more like records of people simply trying to figure what was going on and to establish who knew what. Indeed, the routine nature of these memoranda—and of other known communications of the time—suggests that overall, federal authorities did not know about any such hidden knowledge or evidence.

Still, that does not mean that the different organizations were entirely confident that their counterparts were candid about what they did and did not know. Even in mid–August, communications between the FBI and the military suggest that at least some agents at the former agency were not quite sure that defense officials had told them everything about what was going on.

In an August 8 FBI memorandum, the writer (identity redacted) is blunt. The writer says:

> From the information available thus far, it does not appear that these discs should be treated other than as a military weapon. Certainly, the Bureau has no way to determine what experiments the Army and Navy are conducting ... nor to have any way of determining how far the Russians have progressed in certain experiments and whether such [discs] might be the results of experiments by the Russian army. [In] short, it would certainly appear that this is a military situation and should be handled strictly by military authorities.[6]

Another FBI memo, which was sent a week and a half later, similarly notes a recent conversation between an FBI official and a military officer. According to this document, the special agent "expressed the possibility that flying discs were, in fact, a very highly classified experiment of the Army or Navy."[7]

At the time, the military already had issued numerous denials about any secret projects that could account for the sightings. (Of course, it now is known that Project Mogul, at minimum, was being kept under wraps and that it very likely was a factor in the Roswell incident.) Due to the policy of compartmentation, which severely limited the number of people who were informed about some military projects, it would not have been surprising if even the FBI was kept out of the loop about highly classified aeronautical experiments.

Undoubtedly, the FBI was aware at the time that military officials were likely keeping some things very close to the vest. Possibly for that reason, the FBI agent mentioned in the August 19 memo was apparently "very much surprised when Colonel [redacted] not only agreed that this was a possibility, but confidentially stated it was his personal opinion that such was a probability."

The memorandum inadvertently sheds light on some other interesting details, too. The writer mentions that some unidentified aerial phenomena that had been sighted over Sweden some months earlier had caused "tremendous pressure on the Air Force Intelligence to conduct research and collect information in an effort to identify these sightings." (This was almost certainly due to Sweden's proximity to Soviet air space.) That apparently contrasted with the military's comparatively mild response to the torrent of recent UFO sightings in America. On this front, the memo says, "the 'high brass' appeared to be totally unconcerned." What is more, the officer reportedly said that "this led him to believe that they knew enough about these objects to express no concern."[8]

The document gives the distinct impression that the military contact did believe that at least some portion of UFO witnesses "saw something." But the officer also concluded that "there were objects seen which somebody in the Government knows all about."[9]

This memorandum—one of many UFO-related documents in FBI files—suggests that if not outright strain, there was at least some degree of apprehension between the Bureau and the military. The memo's writer makes that clear in the context of the conversation that the document summarizes. The unnamed FBI agent "pointed out … that if it is a fact that [military] experimentations are being conducted by the United State Government, then it does not appear reasonable to request the FBI to spend money and precious time conducting inquiries with respect to this matter." Moreover, the writer says, "it would be extremely embarrassing to the Air Forces Intelligence if it later is learned that these flying discs are, in fact, an experiment of the United States Government."

None of this proves that clandestine tests or experimental aircraft had not been the basis of at least some flying disc sightings. However, the tenor of this document, which in most other respects is a routine inter-organizational communication, suggests FBI personnel were unsure about how forthcoming the military had been to that time. The memo pressured the military to be candid by emphasizing something

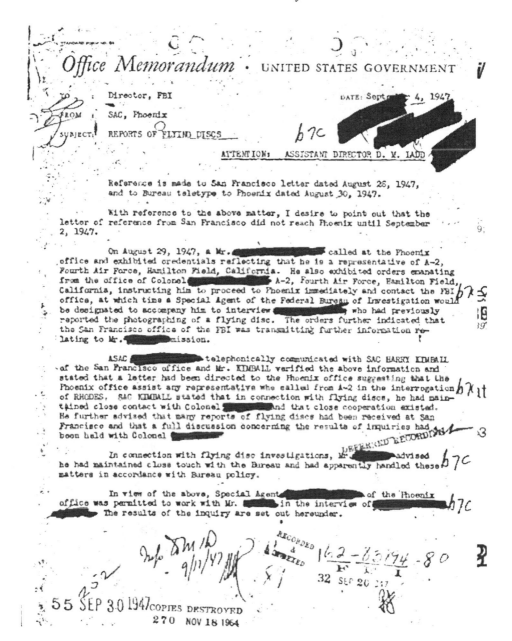

Many years after the fact, the FBI declassified and released photocopies of numerous internal documents relating to its investigations into UFO sightings. Although decades have passed since many UFO-related documents were written, much of the material released to the public over the years remains heavily redacted (FBI Freedom of Information Act Library).

obvious: future revelations could be "extremely embarrassing."[10] In a hardly subtle manner, the message implies that the FBI was not taking for granted that the military was sharing complete information. Yet, it is also the case that FBI agents would have been aware that if the military were engaged in classified projects that had triggered UFO sightings, it very likely would not admit to that, even in secure communication with the Bureau. Such is the nature of compartmentalized government secrecy protocols.

All of this raises questions about what, precisely, the government did and did not know about the B-25 incident and the whole UFO matter, more generally. Here, however, the specific language matters. It is easy to refer to the federal government, including its many divisions, subdivisions, and bureaucratic complexities, as if it were a single, coherent entity. However, that has never been the case. In reality, "the government" is not that. It is a sprawling and incredibly complex enterprise. Its various parts can be confusing and inconsistent.

The many people who populate the complicated array of sub-units in government often have access to different kinds of information and possess differing worldviews. They are not necessarily on the same page. Indeed, as Morton Halperin noted many years ago in his groundbreaking book, *Bureaucratic Politics and Foreign Policy*, even within a single area of interest, the various offices in government often behave as rivals. Accordingly, people in different units may not wish to share the information they have with people in other parts of government. In governmental bureaucracies, information represents power and prestige. People within government often treat it as a rare commodity to be shared only when there is some strategic advantage for the person or office that has it.

So, there was a working relationship between the FBI and the military, but there were also strains and potential fissures. Since the two organizations were located in different, at times rival parts of the government bureaucracy, it is easy to see that they might sometimes work at cross purposes. For this reason, it is not unreasonable to conclude that "the government" may not always have known what it did and did not know. Some parts knew some things. Other parts may or may not also have known these things. The situation undoubtedly contributed to the uncertainty and ambiguity that the UFO phenomenon inherently possessed.

As the summer progressed, governmental agencies, together and independently, pushed ahead with investigatory efforts. Many cases had been quickly dismissed, but a stubborn percentage of incidents continued to defy straightforward explanations. And although the number of new reports dwindled as the weeks wore on, it was not as though no additional sightings were reported. There was still much to sort out.

By this time, the massive number of reports from previous weeks had added up to a collection of cases distributed across a vast geographical area and involving people from nearly all walks of life. In one example, 200 witnesses reportedly saw a flying saucer at Braves Field, then home to the Boston Braves baseball club, on July 10. A witness in Cambridge, Massachusetts, backed up that report. "I don't know what it was," the witness said, "and I'm not a crackpot. But we saw something, and it looked like a saucer."[11]

The mysterious object, which was said to be about four feet in diameter, nearly hit a light pole at the nearby ballfield and then went out of view as it drifted to the ground, he added. However, "a thorough search of the neighborhood revealed nothing."[12]

≋ 19 ≋

The Twining Memorandum

When asked about flying saucers in early July, a spokesperson for the Army Air Forces candidly said, "There's something to this."[1] Yet, if that is what AAF authorities truly believed, published and unpublished documents suggest that the AAF did not know precisely what that "something" was. What they knew was that sightings continued to pile up, even though the pace was slower than before. They probably found satisfaction with the many cases that could be dismissed. But that did not change the fact that there were still a substantial number of unknowns.

Reports of new UFO sightings continued to cross the desks of officials and news organizations occasionally, but whatever was behind the earlier flurry of reports seemed to have come and gone. For the most part, the public was satisfied that the wave of UFO sightings had blown over. The news media had largely lost interest, too. As a story published July 12 in the *New York Times* concluded, "the sky seemed to have returned to normalcy."[2] As a public matter, then, the flying saucer craze of the previous weeks seemed to have run its course. The troubling cases were a relatively small percentage of overall reports, but they remained a sticking point, at least for national defense officials.

In these early days of the Atomic Age and the Cold War, the stakes were just too high for defense officials to ignore the problematic UFO cases, even if they were relatively few in number. The Soviet threat loomed large in the American consciousness, and it was not a time to rest easy. As scholar Kate Dorsch writes in a recent study of the subject, the U.S. military concluded it had "no choice but to respond to the sighting reports. Even if ninety-nine out of one hundred sightings were bogus, hoaxes, or misidentified jet planes, it only took one technologically-advanced Russian bomber to end the American way of life."[3]

Many different "scientific and pseudo-scientific explanations of the

118

mystery"[4] appeared in the press and presumably behind closed doors, too. Yet, none of these answered all the remaining questions.

In the late summer, personnel at the Air Material Command at Wright Field in Ohio, who were unsatisfied with the piecemeal accounts in the files and the press, tried to understand the unexplained sightings better. Various personnel assembled cases and conducted early analyses. In addition, they communicated with counterparts at the Pentagon in an apparent effort to establish what was and was not known about the still-unexplained incidents.[5]

Even though these events were decades ago and many documents about them have since been declassified, it is still difficult to ascertain with certainty everything that happened behind closed doors at Wright Field or the Pentagon. Yet, there is no doubt that the military—and the Army Air Forces, in particular—wanted to arrive at a more certain comfort level about the UFO events of recent weeks. If the sightings did present a threat of any kind, military leaders wanted to know what that threat was so they could develop appropriate defensive capabilities and keep the nation safe. And presumably, leaders of the Army Air Forces, which was about to be spun off as a separate military branch, did not want to be embarrassed at any future point. For multiple reasons, then, it was very much in the AAF's interest to continue investigating the flying saucers until it had reached a comfort level with the state of knowledge about them. And given its mission within the AAF, the Air Materiel Command was the logical unit to take a leading role in resolving the matter.

By the third week of September, Lt. Gen. Nathan Twining, the AMC's commanding officer, was ready to proceed. The next step came in a memorandum that seems to have been drafted by Twining's assistant, Captain Howard McCoy of the AMC Intelligence office, who had assembled a working group to investigate the matter. The memorandum, signed by Twining, is addressed to Brigadier General George Schulgen and dated September 23. The document summarizes "AMC Opinion Concerning 'Flying Discs.'"[6]

The most important conclusion is stated at the outset: "The phenomenon is something real and not visionary or fictitious."[7] This and the other judgments expressed in the document, he explained, were the result of "a conference between personnel from the Air Institute of Technology, Intelligence T-2, Office, Chief of Engineering Division, and the Aircraft, Power Plant and Propeller Laboratories of Engineering Division T-3."[8]

Having indicated something "real" about a portion of the unexplained object sightings, Twining then presented his group's other significant conclusions. For example, the group believed that some reported objects had "the shape of a disc, of such appreciable size as to appear to be as large as man-made aircraft." However, in other cases, there was still the "possibility that some of the incidents may be caused by natural phenomena, such as meteors."[9]

The group also observed that the motions and flight paths indicated in some sightings were noteworthy. "The reported operating characteristics such as extreme rates of climb, maneuverability (particularly in roll), and motion which must be considered evasive when sighted or contacted by friendly aircraft and radar, lend belief to the possibility that some of the objects are controlled either manually, automatically or remotely."[10]

The group agreed that there were some common factors in many of the unexplained reports. Notably, these included "a metallic or light reflecting surface," "absence of a trail" (usually); "Circular or elliptical in shape, flat on bottom and domed on top"; their ability of fly "in well-kept formation"; the "absence of sound"; and "level flight speeds normally above 300 knots" [about 345 miles per hour].[11]

Based on their analysis and discussions, the group speculated about the origins of the unidentified and unexplained aircraft. Significantly, they were aware that despite AMC's mission and prominence within the AAF, there could be projects elsewhere in the U.S. military too secret for them to know about. "The possibility that these objects are of domestic origin—the product of some high security project not known to AC/AS-2 or this Command," was something to consider, as Twining's memorandum indicates. The group also noted the "possibility that some foreign nation has a form of propulsion, possibly nuclear, which is outside of our domestic knowledge." Ultimately, the AMC was hampered by the "lack of physical evidence in the shape of crash recovered exhibits."[12]

Presuming that the memorandum accurately reflected Twining and his subordinates' judgments—a presumption there is no reason to doubt—the message's recommendations were sensible, even obligatory from a military perspective. Specifically, the AMC commander recommended that:

> Headquarters, Army Air Forces issue a directive assigning a priority, security classification, and Code name for a detailed study of this matter to include the preparation of complete sets of all available and pertinent data, which will then be made available to the Army, Navy, Atomic Energy Commission, JRDB, the Air Force Scientific Advisory Group, NACA, and the RAND and NEPA projects for comments and recommendations, with a preliminary report to be forwarded within 15 days of receipt of the data and a detailed report thereafter every 30 days as the investigation develops.[13]

Having provided his assessment of where the AMC stood regarding its understanding of the UFO wave of earlier weeks, Twining signed off. He was "awaiting a specific directive," he said, after which "AMC will continue the investigation within its current resources in order to more closely define the nature of the phenomenon."[14]

The so-called "Twining memorandum" is sometimes cited out of context, leading to interpretations along lines that Twining probably did not intend. For example, he and his group legitimately may have concluded there was "something real and not visionary or fictitious" about some UFO sightings. However, the memo contains no hint that this led him to believe that the UFOs were necessarily beyond the technological capabilities of the United States or some other nation, such as the Soviet Union.

Although the USSR was the United States' main adversary at the time, there were other possibilities. Those involved the possible continuing involvement of former Nazi aerospace scientists and technologists who might be working clandestinely in other countries, away from the spotlight. Spain was considered as one possible refuge where some Nazis might be working without attracting notice. Yet, as Kate Dorsch notes, as of late 1947, former Nazi scientists who were then working for the United States did know of any "important scientists" working in that country.[15] To eliminate the possibility that unknown Nazi scientists might be working on something related to the UFOs, there was some internal discussion at the Air Force about gathering more information.[16]

The fear that the Nazi aerospace and weapons scientists might be mixed up in a surprise Soviet military technology would cast some shadow over America's own Cold War efforts for many years. After all, the German war machine had made huge strides with rocketry, producing V-2s that rained terror on Britain during the war. The Americans were in an excellent position to realize that the depth and scope of the Nazi rocket program. After all, U.S. development efforts in the same direction were now benefiting from—and in Wernher von Braun's case, somewhat spearheaded by—scientists from the same pool of Nazi scientists. Considering Nazi success with rocketry and the substantial, though less publicly known at the time, progress with developing atomic weapons, it was reasonable to be extra cautious before ruling out the possibility that former Nazis, working somewhere in the postwar world, could be involved.

A close reading of the Twining memo in light of the Cold War and of Pentagon priorities of the time suggests that he almost certainly wanted to rule out the Soviet possibility, regardless of how remote that possibility may have been. Of course, this does not mean that a different set of conclusions was beyond the realm of possibility, but there is no reason to think the AMC group was thinking outside the Cold War context at this point.

Meanwhile, the FBI and Air Forces continued to debate the "possibility that the flying discs or saucers are in fact a project of the Army Air Forces."[17] Unaware that some inside the AAF were also unsure about the objects, the FBI again brought up the "possible embarrassing situation of the Intelligence Division of the Air Forces if it was subsequently ascertained that this was the truth." Discussions were enough to cause Brigadier Gen. Schulgren, the recipient of the Twining "AMC Opinion Concerning Flying Discs" memo a few weeks earlier, to write a letter to J. Edgar Hoover, the long-time FBI Director. In that document, Schulgren reportedly stated that AAF had conducted a "further search." The outcome was the same as before, however. The Army Air Forces denied it had anything to do with the sights, saying that "a complete survey of research activities discloses that the Army Air Forces have no project with characteristics similar to those which have been associated with the flying discs."[18]

In October, as the next step in an illustrious career, Nathan Twining left Wright Field and the AMC command to assume a new role. His next stop, Fort Richardson, was just outside Anchorage, Alaska. It may have looked like banishment to a remote outpost for unobservant onlookers. Considering Alaska's proximity to the far eastern edge of the Soviet Union, however, Twining was moving to a strategically important area. In this new position as commander in chief of the Air Force's Alaskan Command, he continued to play an important part in America's Cold War defense operations.

By this time, after several months of planning, the United States Air Force was up and running. Spun off from the Army Air Forces in mid–September, it was now a separate branch of the armed services within the National Military Establishment.

At the time of his transfer, Twining's superiors had not yet acted on his request for a "specific directive" to study UFOs. This had been outlined in his memorandum of September 23. It was not until late December that the proposal made its way through official channels to the point of a decision. As the eventful year of 1947 drew to a close, the Air Force created a secret new program, Project Sign. With a mission to assess any possible national security threat posed by the recent UFO phenomenon, it was ordered, as later described, were "to collect, collate, evaluate, and distribute within the Government all information related to sightings" of unexplained aerial objects.[19]

≋ 20 ≋

Life on Mars

At the time, most people did not think the 1947 wave of UFO sightings presented evidence of visitors from another planet. The number of Americans endorsing that idea would increase as time passed, but relatively few people gave it much thought initially. Military and other government officials had more earthly worries at the time, and even the general population did not gravitate to that explanation initially.

Yet, the idea did attract some attention. It seems to have been considered in passing by many people, even if they dismissed it for the time being. A few, however, thought about it more seriously, which was not wholly surprising in the context of the times. Indeed, the notion that the flying saucers could have come from another world was not solely the product of overactive imaginations. Nor was it simply the influence of science-fiction stories, which had earned a place in popular culture. The "extraterrestrial hypothesis" about flying saucers, as it is sometimes called, may have seemed unlikely to many people. Still, it was not necessarily far-fetched relative to ideas that long circulated in the culture. In some ways, that interpretation was consistent with theories that some scientists and the news media had promoted for decades.

As far back as the late 19th century, many people had come to believe that advanced life forms populated other parts of the solar system. Consequently, some scientists identified Mars as a planet that could, and possibly did, have the essential conditions necessary to sustain an alien civilization. That notion especially took hold shortly after Italian astronomer Giovanni Schiaparelli's 1877 reports of so-called "canals" on the Martian surface. These strange, much-discussed features fueled much speculation. Later, it turned out that the so-called canals were little more than optical illusions. Until then, however, the canals' presumed existence sparked imaginative, if misguided, scientific conjecture about their origins and nature.

From the very beginning, a translation issue was part of the problem. Schiaparelli used *canale* (plural *canali)* to describe the lines he saw (or thought he saw) on the Martian surface. In Italian, the word corresponds to *channel* and could refer to a naturally occurring geological feature. When reports made their way to the English-speaking world, however, the similarity of the Italian term *canale* to the English word *canal* led to a misunderstanding. Many people presumed that Schiaparelli was speaking of "canals," meaning waterways constructed by intelligent beings. That was markedly different from designating them as geological features, which the original language implied.

An American named Percival Lowell inadvertently added to the misunderstanding. Born to a prominent Boston family in 1855, Lowell was a Harvard graduate with many interests. He was particularly drawn to astronomy and, by the 1890s, developed a particular fascination for Mars and Schiaparelli's descriptions of the Red Planet's *canali.* Having the means, Lowell established a new observatory in Flagstaff, Arizona, where the night sky was dark and the view of the heavens clear. Almost immediately after that, he began studying Mars in earnest.

As he added to his knowledge—or what he thought was knowledge—Lowell constructed detailed explanations for the "canals." It did not take long for him to draw remarkable conclusions that he soon began to share. In a lecture delivered in Flagstaff in 1896, he described the canals on the faraway planet. A local newspaper summarized Lowell's remarks. The former Bostonian described the planet's surface terrain, atmosphere, and other physical features. He told the audience that "the [Martian] canals run pole to pole, with lateral at regular intervals" and that "patches of vegetation" could be found "at the canal junctions."[1]

Lowell's most astonishing assertions, however, were about something else. According to a published account of the lecture, Lowell claimed that "Mars ... is without doubt inhabited." And not only that. He also said that "the Martians are a people of high intelligence, mathematicians of the first order and of unknown form."[2]

These were undoubtedly bold claims, but Lowell seems to have had little doubt about them. Confident that his and others' initial observations of canals on the Red Planet must be correct, he had interpreted all his data based on that presumption. More than that, he filled in missing pieces of the puzzle with speculations about intelligent life forms on the alien world that appear, to modern eyes, a remarkable stretch from the source data.

The most striking aspect of Lowell's detailed conclusions was not that he had dared to imagine a scenario about mathematically and technologically advanced beings on Mars. Instead, it was the unbridled confidence he placed in his conclusion that the canals must have been intelligently designed. Yet, in retrospect, it is evident that something had gone wrong as he developed his theories.

To his credit, Lowell diligently tried to amass more detailed, state-of-the-art observations about Mars. But there were still significant gaps in the information. The trouble—which, unfortunately, he did not recognize as trouble—came at the next step.

At the point when he searched for a scenario that would fit the "facts" as he understood them, Lowell prematurely fixated on only one speculation. His observations, Lowell concluded, could only be explained if civilized life existed on Mars. And after adopting this view, he then discounted any other possibilities. Percival Lowell was undoubtedly an intelligent, successful, and well-educated person in many ways. In retrospect, however, he vastly overestimated his reasoning powers. As a result, he prematurely dismissed the possibility of other explanations.

Brimming with self-confidence, Lowell subsequently made a career promoting his life-on-Mars hypothesis. He lectured and wrote about Mars and Martian life for many years. In time, and with the cooperation of a rising newspaper industry looking for attention-getting stories, his ideas about life on Mars reached a broad audience.

Lowell authored several books on the subject. *Mars and Its Canals,* for instance, was published by the reputable Macmillan Company in 1906. Writing in what, at the time, was contemporary scientific prose, Lowell began by outlining a comprehensive and observation-based description of his findings about Mars. Much of it is very interesting. But over the book's many chapters, his presentation orchestrates the data so that it builds to one grand conclusion. "That Mars is inhabited by beings of some sort or other," he says, "we may consider as certain as it is uncertain what those beings may be."[3]

By this time, Lowell had developed a complicated set of arguments to support his assumptions. Some of them are remarkably detailed, especially considering the gaps in the data from which he drew his conclusion. Indeed, the astronomer makes some extraordinary claims. He takes the Martians' scientific and engineering brilliance almost for granted. How else, he seems to ask, could they have built the remarkable canals? The Red Planet's inhabitants are "necessarily intelligent and non-bellicose," he says, adding that there are "eminently sagacious," as well.[4]

Lowell's Martian-civilization theories were very well circulated. His ideas were given a much wider public airing than the judgments of those who did not necessarily share his conclusions.[5] And indeed, there was always some doubt about Lowell's contentions about Martian life within the scientific community.

Yet, the media typically presented Lowell's views about Mars uncritically. For example, *Scientific American* published a lengthy review of *Mars and Its Canals* in 1907, shortly after the book's publication.[6] It exhaustively summarizes Lowell's argument without taking a position on the book's claim of intelligent life on Mars. The review does employ language—such as "Prof. Lowell would have us believe" or "in Prof. Lowell's opinion"—in an apparent effort to distance itself slightly, though not forcefully, from some of Lowell's more remarkable conclusions. But the review does not suggest that Lowell was unhinged or spewing nonsense—far from it.

Lowell's ideas found dependable champions in the nation's newspapers and magazines amid the excitement of the new century. His claims about Martian civilization made regular appearances in the press throughout the early decades of the 1900s.

This serves as a reminder of an essential fact of cultural life in America. Years before the 1947 UFO sightings, belief in intelligent, technologically advanced life on Mars was mainstream. Even if the scientific community did not accept the idea entirely, the media often presented it as a plausible conclusion.

That said, other scientists eventually began to offer a very different view. For example, in 1909, astronomer Eugène Michel Antoniadi, who was working at a French observatory with a large new telescope, was able to see Mars more clearly than ever before. In previous years, he, too, had believed earlier in the Martian canals. However, the new and improved view of the Red Planet made possible by better equipment led him to a different conclusion. The apparent Martian canals were merely optical illusions. With powerful new telescopes, that became obvious.

Although the Martian "canals" were soon debunked in the scientific community, in some ways, it was too late to change course in the public sphere. The idea was already firmly implanted in the culture, and it would prove difficult to dislodge. Although many scientists began to doubt the idea of Martian civilization, the idea persisted among the overall population. This was often true even among people with at least modest scientific credentials.

So, new findings, which convincingly contradicted Lowell's claims, did not necessarily translate into quick changes in the public's beliefs. As the years wore on, portrayals of imagined life on Mars continued to appear in the press. Many of these depictions, most of which were somewhat based on Lowell's theories, possessed an adventurous, fantastic quality. For instance, one newspaper article from 1909 described

"Aerial Houseboats and Villages of Mars." The story includes wondrous speculations and is accompanied by a nearly half-page drawing of fanciful airships.[7] Another typical report from 1913 provocatively asked, "Is Mars Trying to Signal Our Earth?"[8] It describes a "subterranean tunnel constructed by the scientists of Mars which has been devised to focus upon the Earth a cold radium light of tremendous brilliancy."

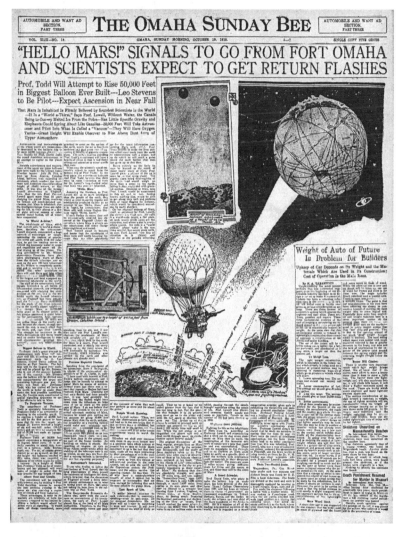

Many articles about life on Mars appeared in American newspapers in the early decades of the twentieth century. This front-page story from a 1919 edition of the *Omaha Sunday Bee* was only one of many such items to make astonishing claims about Martian civilization (Library of Congress).

Many such articles merely extended and exaggerated the ideas of Lowell and like-minded people. Others, however, bordered on the preposterous, even in the context of the times. An article from 1912, for example, reported a bizarre theory: "Mars Peopled by One Vast Thinking Vegetable."[9]

Life-on-Mars stories seem to have appealed to members of the general public, most of whom had little education in the sciences and were not in a good position to judge the likely veracity of claims about life on Mars. In many newspaper and magazine accounts, the subject was sensationalized. Editors and writers often appeared to aim more for entertainment value than reporting. Yet, the repeated publication of stories presuming intelligent life on Mars slowly built a mountain of material that supported that presumption, even if it was at times half-hearted or even ill-advised support.

When radio technology burst onto the media scene, the pioneer inventor-electrical engineer Guglielmo Marconi joined the fray. "The recent announcement of Senatore Marconi stating that he feels convinced that certain radio signals, which he has received on an enormously long wave length [sic], come from the planet Mars," wrote H. Gernsback in a 1921 edition of *Science and Invention*.[10] It was not a new conclusion for the magazine. "We have always upheld the contention that there is life on Mars," Gernsback added. "All conclusion, scientific as well as otherwise, point to this."

By the 1920s, academically trained scientists increasingly discounted that there was life—or at least, advanced life—on Mars. Improved technology yielded data that just did not support Lowell's conclusions.

Interestingly, by the early 1930s, the notion that there could be life on Mars started to look plausible once again, even among scientists. As an article in the widely circulated *Popular Mechanics* magazine reported, "Recent results have proved that Mars has an atmosphere; that its temperature ... rises at noon to fifty-five or sixty degrees Fahrenheit; that clouds float in its skies and rains probably water its lands, and that life of some kind is possible there."[11]

Life may have looked possible, but intelligent life was another matter. However, regardless of scientists' doubts, the idea was well established by the 1930s and 1940s. Whether a person believed in a Martian civilization or not, it was a view that was widely known. Scientists—or many of them—may not have embraced the notion of intelligent life on the faraway planet, but it was hardly a fringe view at the time.

An article published in *Popular Science* during World War II highlighted an important issue. "Mars, for the average person, is a planet endowed with romance and mystery," said its author, Harvard astro-physicist Donald H. Menzel.[12] He continued:

> Scientists, fiction writers, and comic-strip artists have unwittingly co-operated to popularize the belief that Mars must be inhabited. ... Everyone, it seems, is ready—almost anxious—to find facts tending to confirm the view that there is life on Mars. And this life, to be interesting, must possess human—or, preferably, superhuman—qualities.[13]

After World War II, many people seem to have adopted a cautious view about prospects for life on Mars. Given that it was mentioned in 1947 newspaper stories about flying saucers, it seems likely that Orson Welles' sensational 1938 "War of the Worlds" broadcast played a role in that development. The fallout from the Welles broadcast appears to have prompted many people to be wary of stories about visitors from another world. It was not a surprising result. After all, some listeners had mistaken Welles' radio play as a news account when it was the first broadcast. Many were likely embarrassed when it soon became apparent this was a colossal misunderstanding. Indeed, the broadcast was often discussed as if it had been a hoax that easily fooled gullible people. With that memory relatively fresh in people's minds, many may have resisted the conclusion that the UFOs were from some other planet, at least at the outset. It was, perhaps, too close for comfort to the adage: "Fool me once; shame on you. Fool me twice; shame on me."

Regardless of the "War of the Worlds" broadcast's after-effects, however, in the context of the late 1940s, wondering if the 1947 UFOs might be spacecraft from Mars was not necessarily a crackpot idea. For years, major publications and scientists had said there could be intelligent life on the distant planet. Moreover, the idea had often appeared in many of the same news media reporting about other, more ordinary news of the day.

By the 1940s, then-recent discoveries led many scientists to conclude that intelligent life on Mars was improbable. As the author of a 1944 science textbook wrote, "conditions favourable to life [on Mars] are over, or, at all events, drawing to a close."[14] It was the prevailing wisdom among scientists of the time.

For ordinary people in the new Atomic Age, however, many things that once had seemed impossible no longer looked that way. Humankind had unlocked the atom's secrets and was quickly developing rocket technology with the dream of traveling into space. As far as the general public was concerned, who could say for sure that the shiny objects in the skies could not possibly be travelers from another world?

≈ 21 ≈

Project Sign

In late 1947, Brigadier General Nathan Twining's superiors finally approved the intensive UFO study he had recommended in September. Finally, Project Sign was almost ready to commence operations. At the time, program leaders did not think visits from Mars or any other extraterrestrial world provided the likely reason for the previous summer's wave of flying disc sightings. Earthly explanations and simply mistaken identifications seemed more likely. Yet, unanswered questions remained. And until those could be laid to rest, some effort to settle the matter seemed worthwhile, even necessary, for U.S. defense purposes.

As Project Sign was about to get underway, yet another fatal plane crash tied to UFOs intervened. It was just five months after a B-25 bomber accident had killed two UFO investigators and destroyed what some described as physical evidence. The new incident was even more directly connected to unexplained aerial phenomena. It involved a military jet that met a disastrous end in pursuit of a UFO.

On January 7, 1948, Captain Thomas F. Mantell, a 25-year-old pilot in the Kentucky Air National Guard, departed from Atlanta at 1:45 p.m.[1] His one-person, single-propeller P-51[2] was one of several planes on what should have been a routine flight that afternoon. It did not turn out that way.

Headlines from following days told part of the sad story: "Airman Killed Chasing 'Flying Disc'"; "Flaming Red Cone Seen by Ohioans"[3]; "Pilot Dies Trying to Follow 'Flying Disk' in Kentucky"[4]; "Ball of Fire in Skies Excites Southern Ohioans."[5]

Mantell, an experienced World War II veteran flyer, was the flight leader that afternoon. At first, nothing was out of the ordinary. As the planes in Mantell's group flew over Kentucky, however, the situation began to change. Mantell received radio instructions from Godman Field at Fort Knox. The airfield's commander, Colonel Guy Hix, had spotted something "strange" in the sky. Area residents saw the objects (or light, or whatever it was), too. For those who saw it, there was little doubt that they had seen something very unusual. Col. Hix wanted the pilots to check it out.

According to later press accounts, the witnesses reported seeing "luminous objects floating in the sky"[6] and a "flaming cone trailing a gaseous green mist." The object (or objects—that detail is not consistent in the reports) sometimes appeared to be "suspended in the air." At other times, however, it traveled with "what appeared to be terrific bursts of speed."[7] According to military personnel, it was a visual spectacle to behold. One witness at Godman field spoke of "intense brilliance ... [that] pierced a heavy layer of clouds." It was also "very white and looked like an umbrella," added Hix.[8] Whatever people saw, it was no fleeting vision.[9] Indeed, reports indicate that the objects were visible for up to 35 minutes.[10] Within that time, the tragedy unfolded.

Following orders, Mantell redirected the group's flight path to pursue the object. One plane was low on fuel and left the group to land. The other three aircraft, led by Mantell, headed towards the object, which was not in their direct field of vision at first.

As he pursued the target, Mantell started to get ahead of the others. As his P-51 rapidly climbed in altitude, he seems to have become separated from the other two remaining in his group. According to reports from the following day, Mantell's fighter flew "too high" and too fast. As a result, he apparently "lost consciousness."[11] According to details released shortly after the incident, Mantell was "flying without oxygen equipment."[12]

According to a witness on the ground, Mantell's plane flew erratically. It "circled three times like the pilot didn't know where he was going, and then [the plane] started to dive from about 20,000 feet. About halfway down, there was a terrific explosion," the witness said.[13] Pieces of the plane's wreckage fell to the ground. Unfortunately, Mantell did not survive.

The fatal mishap was widely reported in the press, which treated it as the return of a familiar subject. "Don't look now or you might see another one of those flying saucers," said one newspaper article.[14] The most-reported—and by then, very familiar—explanation for the incident was that the UFO was nothing more than a weather balloon. Astronomers at Vanderbilt University (who presumably were not first-hand witnesses to the incident) ventured that guess. That seemed to satisfy most people. Local weather officials said they were unaware of any such balloons being used in the area that day,[15] but it was still possible. Whether it was a weather balloon, or a widely observed optical illusion, or something else, never was determined definitively. In any case, the episode added a new set of potential questions into the mix as Project Sign initiative to formally launch.

Project Sign officially began its work on January 22, 1948. The group collected cases primarily from the military branches but also included some from other sources. After assembling the material, there were hundreds of files to sort through and examine. For a small group, the volume of cases presented a challenge. And as scholar Kate Dorsch notes, it did not take long to determine that Project Sign would need help to analyze the many reported incidents thoroughly. When necessary, therefore, the group brought in outside personnel to assist. These included experts from the weather services, other specialized military units, and external organizations cleared to handle sensitive material.[16]

Over the following months, Project Sign investigated more than 240 cases from the United States and 30 from other nations. A report from early 1949 notes that the group dismissed about 20 percent as nothing more than "conventional aerial objects."[17] Another 20 percent, they said, turned out to be "weather or other atmospheric balloons."[18]

At the time, the group was still awaiting reports that could help clear up some of the still-unexplained cases. Already, they had received preliminary feedback from "an astrophysicist at Ohio State University and by psychologists of the Aero-Medical Laboratory" of the AMC. After 12 months, they could account—or expected they could soon account—for many of the incidents. A sizable number of the cases still had unknown origins, but project leaders believed that eventually, they might be able to explain an unspecified but "appreciable number of the sightings."[19]

Yet, such predictions ran contrary to the direction in which Project Sign was heading.

As the progress report affirms, the group understood its mission to be directed primarily toward collecting data. Analysis, though ongoing, was a secondary concern and focused chiefly on cases perceived to have potential international security implications. As a result, unanswered questions largely remained unanswered. The group lacked the resources or mandate to do much else. In any case, many cases lacked sufficient details to allow for meaningful analysis. Moreover, some group members believed that a number of the UFO incidents could be related to U.S. military activities beyond the knowledge and, by implication, beyond the security clearances of Project Sign members.

In general, the tone of this early-1949 report does not come across as alarmist in any respect. On the contrary, it gives the impression that there was very little cause for concern. This is apparent in the report's recommendation, which states: "Future activity on this Project should be carried out at the minimum level necessary to record, summarize, and evaluate the data received on future reports and to complete the specialized investigations now in progress."[20] It appeared, therefore, that Project Sign's official position was that the UFO matter safely could be put on the back burner.

Intriguingly, however, the report also included a significant amount of discussion about the potential extraterrestrial origins of at least some UFO sightings. The report, as submitted, did not add much weight to such speculations. "All information so far presented on the possible existence of space ships [sic] from another planet have been largely conjecture."[21] However, it is clear that the group dutifully considered this possibility enough to warrant significant attention in the progress report. Thus, while the document largely discounts an extraterrestrial explanation as "highly improbable,"[22] it nonetheless considered it. That the report devoted as much attention to it as it did, especially since it publicly dismissed all such talk, was a noteworthy development.

A long memorandum included in the report discusses the extraterrestrial hypothesis. It was written by nuclear physicist George E. Valley, a professor at the Massachusetts Institute of Technology and member of the U.S. Air Force Scientific Advisory Board.

Valley, who worked with the military during the war and was well respected, had prepared a document called "Some Considerations Affecting the Interpretation of Reports of Unidentified Flying Saucers." It runs eight single-spaced pages in the appendix of the Project Sign report. For the most part, it reads as more of the same. Valley finds little to cause concern. Indeed, as Kate Dorsch notes, his memo "reads like a debunking effort"[23] and somewhat glosses over the small but not insignificant number of cases that Project Sign still could not explain.

Yet even Valley concluded the matter warranted additional study. Among his recommendations, he suggested that more focused research could be conducted by "a meteorologist" and "an aerodynamicist." And although it was beyond his expertise, Valley also suggested looking into psychological aspects of the witness statements cases more thoroughly. These, he wrote, should be carried out by "a competent staff of statisticians and mass-psychologists."[24]

Over the months of its work throughout 1948, Project Sign leaders also consulted with the RAND Corporation. The prestigious think tank, which was then relatively new, had provided the military with specialized and often highly sensitive research and analysis services before. As a result of its work for Project Sign, RAND submitted a technical letter that covered several possibilities and assessments.

The RAND letter author, J.E. Lipp, was then assigned to the

organization's Missile Division. He had written some of the most compelling parts of a previous RAND report, *"Preliminary Design of an Experimental World-Circling Spaceship,"* for the military in 1946. Given that recent background, he seemed like a solid choice to examine some aspects of Project Sign's work.

Lipp looked especially closely at the technical requirements for interplanetary travel and the underlying science that would presumably be involved. He makes some interesting observations about the flying saucers. The "distribution of flying objects is peculiar, to say the least," he writes, adding that the "lack of purpose apparent in the various episodes is also puzzling." He also notes that if the UFOs were extraterrestrial visitors "feeling out" earth's ability to defend itself, then it was odd that they "keep repeating the same experiment."[25]

After presenting a lengthy review and analysis, Lipp concludes with these two sentences: "Although visits from outer space are believed to be possible, they are believed to be very improbable. In particular, the actions attributed to the 'flying objects' reported during 1947 and 1948 seem inconsistent with the requirements for space travel."[26]

Lipp's assessment added some weight to Project Sign's general conclusion that an extraterrestrial explanation for the UFOs was unlikely. However, it still did not clear up the many questions about UFO cases that had yet to be closed. And by its own account, a significant number of cases were still open, even though some project personnel expected them to be cleared up eventually.

During its investigations, Project Sign also secured the services of an Ohio State University astronomer. This new consultant was J. Allen Hynek. When he was first contacted by Project Sign in 1948, he was working as an associate professor at Ohio State University (OSU), aiming to build the school's astronomy program and his own academic reputation. The professor was not well known beyond specialized academic circles at the time, but he would later become prominent within the UFO community and even the culture at large.

Only 60 miles away from AMC's headquarters at the then-recently renamed Wright-Patterson Field, OSU was a logical place for Project Sign to look for consulting support. Hynek possessed the right qualifications: he was a Ph.D.-level astronomer and was willing to help. Hynek's job for Project Sign was to examine the case files from a trained astronomer's vantage point. His task was to determine if any previously unnoticed astronomical phenomena might help explain some of them.

His review, which took much time to finish, ended up mostly agreeing with what had already been suggested. Two-thirds of the cases, he decided, seemed to be nothing more than mistaken or incorrect identifications. People had seen human-made objects or known astronomical features and misinterpreted them. Some sightings still lacked a clear explanation for reasons such as insufficient detail and lack of precision in the data. After all that, however, a number of cases still were classified as unknowns.[27] These would continue to be the crux of the problem and the source of much future controversy.

At the time, Hynek was satisfied with the general direction of the group's conclusions, and he signed off on Project Sign's overall assessment. Although later, he would express doubts and change course, the professor did not make waves during his initial involvement with Project Sign. After submitting his report, the professor turned his attention back to OSU. He continued his work there until later when he was asked to come work for Project Sign's successor project some months later.

New UFO sightings occasionally popped up as Project Sign was doing its work. At least one of these turned out to be significant. In the early morning hours of July 24, 1948—little more than a year after the great wave of sightings in the previous year—one sighting would prove to be polarizing.

The incident unfolded quickly. In the clear night sky over Alabama, two Eastern Air Lines pilots spotted something highly unusual while flying a DC-3 on a routine trip between Houston and Atlanta. Initial press reports described the unknown object as a "wingless mystery plane, spurting fire."[28] The two men in the cockpit and the chief witnesses were Captain Clarence S. Chiles and co-pilot John B. Whitted. Each was a seasoned aviator. They both had wartime flying experience before joining Eastern Air Lines and were far from novices who were likely to be easily rattled.

The encounter occurred in the middle of the night, and most of the passengers were sleeping. However, one who was awake verified the incident. "A flash of cherry red fire"[29] had suddenly appeared, he said. A similar report was filed by a witness on the ground, too.

Based on these multiple accounts, it appears that something unusual happened. Precisely what was difficult to say. The incident had puzzling features on its face, but it was not necessarily a shocking or especially novel case. Yet, the sighting would prove to be polarizing when it came time to explain it.

≈ 22 ≈

Quest and Conspiracy

From a later vantage point, it sometimes appears that Americans fixated on the flying saucers for months after the 1947 wave of sightings. For the most part, however, that conclusion is wrong. UFOs sometimes did capture headlines, but the topic was only one of many vying for public attention. For the most part, after a few weeks of initial excitement, the public moved on to other topics, and UFOs would only occasionally recapture their attention. Indeed, flying saucers or not, life continued in all its aspects. Americans still followed their favorite radio shows and sports teams, still went about their ordinary lives, and still went to the movies.

One film that attracted attention was director John Huston's classic *The Treasure of Sierra Madre.* It opened in January 1948, just before Project Sign began operations. This was a different kind of film that simultaneously broke with some traditions even as it reinforced others. In some ways, this movie hints at cultural dissonances that were just beginning to emerge in the postwar society.

Consider, for example, a scene near the film's end. One of the main characters, Fred Dobbs, an unlikeable man played by Humphrey Bogart, is murdered by the bandits he previously had double-crossed. Dobbs is on horseback and carrying sacks of gold dust at the time, but the bandits never realize that fact. Indeed, when they cut open the bags, they mistakenly think the gold dust is nothing but worthless dirt. They never recognize their mistake as it blows away in the wind.

The film's plot about an obsessive hunt for gold provides Huston with ample opportunities to ponder human foibles. Almost all the main characters are plagued by wrong turns, misinterpreted opportunities, and disappointing outcomes. In many stories of this type, someone might arrive to save the day. But as professors Robert W. Rieber and Robert J. Kelly observe, in *The Treasure of the Sierra Madre*, such " a savior never appears."[1] Instead, audiences are left to ponder a conclusion that may seem disappointing and unsatisfying.

In that respect, *The Treasure of Sierra Madre* may have hit too close to home for some. As a parable about an epic quest gone awry, it may have touched on things that many viewers preferred not to ponder. Americans always seemed to be searching for something in the postwar years. And they often seemed eager to find someone who could clarify and solve all their problems, too. But in this movie, director Huston delivers a story that meets none of those expectations. For some, *The Treasure of Sierra Madre*'s stark suggestion that some pursuits never work out may have been unnerving.

As popular culture provided Americans with diversions and things to ponder, a parade of national and international stories filled the news. There was no shortage of concerning new developments throughout 1948 and 1949. For instance, the Soviet blockade of West Berlin, which lasted from June 1948 until the spring of the following year, was a significant worry. However, it was only one of many topics that demanded attention. With so much happening all around them, the topic of UFOs mostly blended into the background as far as most people were concerned.

Mid-century America—the world in which the wave of flying disc sightings unfolded in 1947—had many grey areas. It was often hard to know things with complete certainty. Life seemed more complicated than ever. For many people, it was an unsettling situation. And like the bandits in Huston's film, sometimes people looked directly at something without realizing what it was.

Americans looked out on a world fraught with many uncertainties and ambiguities in the late 1940s. For people who had grown accustomed to seeing the world in sharp black-and-white contrasts, this was alarming. That traditional way of approaching life seemed to be under strain—perhaps even breaking down. Anxious about this brave new world, the public did not always know who or what to believe.

In Congress, the House Un-American Activities Committee (HUAC) sometimes played out the ongoing struggle between ambiguity and certainty. Its high-profile hearings often functioned as a political stage upon which committee members argued about how to distinguish between things that were unquestionably true or false, on the one hand, as and those that could be true but were not necessarily so, on the other. For the general public, the truth that emerged from Congressional hearings was often in the eyes of the beholder.

In 1947, HUAC had investigated Hollywood. Congress aimed to find hidden communists who might be working in the entertainment industry. Many celebrities, including Walt Disney and Ronald Reagan, testified. Disney and a few others sided with the accusers, saying they were certain communists lurked in the film business. The little concrete evidence was sometimes lacking, but the hearings exposed the accused to public and legal scrutiny. In the end, lives and careers were ruined.

In 1948, during the months when Project Sign was investigating UFO sightings, HUAC began an inquiry that achieved even more notoriety. In its continuing hunt for communists, HUAC set its sights on Alger Hiss, a former State Department official. What people thought when the investigation was over depended on how they made sense of the case's many ambiguities and assumptions.

A man named Whittaker Chambers dragged Hiss's name into the limelight in 1948. It was Chambers who testified that Hiss had belonged to an underground communist group in the 1930s. Hiss denied the allegations, but the case became a news sensation. Staunch anti-communist House member—and future U.S. president—Richard Nixon took an especially keen interest in it and helped keep Hiss in the headlines for months.

Two sensational trials ensued. The first ended with a hung jury, but Hiss was found guilty in the second, which ended in January 1949. The verdict applied only to perjury charges because the statute of limitations on more severe espionage charges had run out. But it was still a devastating outcome for Hiss, who was sentenced to five years in prison.

The Hiss verdict was clear but controversial. Some people, including Richard Nixon, were convinced of Hiss' guilt and his collaboration with communism. Others, however, were troubled by evidence they thought was flimsy and possibly even fabricated.

In some ways, the Hiss prosecution was one of the opening salvos in America's mid-century search—some called it a "witch hunt"—for communists. It was no quest for gold, but it was an undertaking that was pursued with similar vigor and obsessiveness. The House Un-American Activities Committee—and later, Senator Joseph McCarthy's Senate hearings—left few stones unturned in its zealous pursuit.

Sometimes beginning with little more than rumor and innuendo, Congressional investigations tried to establish the truth. During many months of searching for hidden communists, Americans entertained fears that conspiracies could be undermining the nation. In these formative years of the Cold War, suspicions that conspiracies were hiding truths from the American public slowly crept into many corners of American life. Indeed, more than a decade before Richard Hofstadter would write about the topic in his famous essay, "The Paranoid Style in American Politics,"[2] the belief that dark, hidden forces were scheming to bring down the nation became an increasingly mainstream notion.

People can get swept up in conspiracy thinking about almost any topic, especially if the subject defies easy explanation and is riddled with ambiguities and uncertainty. That is not to say that conspiracies did not exist. Sometimes they really do. The hidden nature of conspiracies, real and imagined, adds to the confusion, however. It is often tough to tell whether suspicions are well-founded or not. For these and other reasons, conspiracy theorizing can get out of hand.

Rising conspiracy fears, combined with the U.S. government's intense, Cold War–fueled interest in secrecy, created conditions that ensnared efforts to understand the UFO phenomenon. Conspiracy was not necessarily an unreasonable possibility to consider in that context. After all, the government hid many things under the umbrella of official secrets, even if most had nothing to do with flying discs. Soviet agents and sympathizers, organized crime syndicates, and potentially other clandestine groups did engage in nefarious scheming in some instances. Fears of conspiracy may have been overblown in some cases, but such suspicions were justified in others.

Considering those circumstances, it is not surprising that some people began to harbor doubts about whether authorities were telling them the truth about flying saucers. Americans knew there was much their government did not disclose about many topics. National security worries made sure of that. If this was so, how could anyone be sure official UFO denials could be taken at face value? Maybe there was something about the mysterious discs that authorities wanted to be kept from view. Whether an actual UFO conspiracy existed or not, it could have seemed a reasonable question at the time, given the circumstances. It all came down to a matter of trust.

Interestingly, differing perspectives—possibly even outright dissension—among Project Sign personnel inadvertently may have played a role in fostering UFO conspiracy theories. As the investigations wore on, the available evidence suggests two different schools of thought emerged about the UFO question. The idea presented to the public—and senior officials supported—was more or less as expected: even the unsolved cases were almost certainly illusions, natural phenomena, or misidentified human-created technology. If this is all there had been to the story, there would be little basis for controversy.

There was more, however. Some Project Sign associates appear to have suspected that different interpretations could not be ruled out completely, at least not without further research. Maybe they thought the oddities in a few cases did not fit the official explanations. Or perhaps they just wanted an airtight case and did not believe one had been developed yet. Or possibly some Project Sign members had decided that an extraterrestrial-origin thesis was worth further consideration, after all.

Whatever their exact thinking, secondhand evidence (and some documentary material produced with Project Sign itself) suggests there may have been disagreement about the off-world explanation within the project. For one thing, the group's confidential February 1949 status report, which was created for military use only, devotes a substantial amount of space to refuting the idea.[3] For whom were these arguments prepared? Was the purpose to provide a set of points that could be passed along to members of the general public who were skeptical of the official position? Or did the report go to these lengths to persuade members of Project Sign itself? These are intriguing questions, but it may never be possible to know precisely why so much effort was devoted to arguing against the idea.

The 1949 report's refutation of the extraterrestrial explanation may have been nothing more than an effort to cross *t*'s and dot the *i*'s in the official version of events. However, it is also possible that the many pages arguing against the theory, which involved bringing in outside experts such as the RAND researcher, were aimed at quelling internal dissent about the report's mundane conclusion.

Many accounts, appearing in a wide range of sources, favor the latter interpretation. For instance, in an academic book from the 1970s, University of Nebraska historian David Michael Jacobs[4] suggests that there was indeed disagreement among Project Sign members and that some Sign participants had decided "the evidence indicated the UFOs were of extraterrestrial origin." Yet, as Professor Jacobs readily adds, that assessment is primarily based on an after-the-fact written by Edward J. Ruppelt, an Air Force officer who, at the time, was assigned to sort of UFO investigations.

After leaving the military, Ruppelt wrote an influential book, *The Report on Unidentified Flying Objects*, which was first published in 1956. In this work, he says he saw a now-lost document that was allegedly created in 1948. According to Ruppelt's account: "In intelligence, if you have something to say about some vital problem, you write a report known as an 'Estimate of the Situation.' A few days after the [United Airlines] DC-3 was buzzed, the people at ATIC [AMC's Air Technical Intelligence unit] decided the time had arrived" to write such a document. It seems, therefore, that the startling account of United pilots Chiles and Whitted was enough to push some Project Sign personnel into taking a stand.

Supposedly, copies of this document were gathered up and destroyed in the 1950s, which means that anyone outside the original group of people who saw it must rely on Ruppelt's general description of its contents. That, of course, presumes Ruppelt's reports about it are true and accurate, which is challenging to prove with complete confidence. Nevertheless, many UFO devotees and academic researchers take Ruppelt more or less at his word. They presume the "Estimate" existed and that it expressed the thoughts that Ruppelt said it did. That appears to be a reasonable conclusion. Still, despite numerous efforts, an extant copy of the document has yet to be found. Like many other aspects of the UFO story at mid-century, a person's beliefs about the existence of the "Estimate" and its contents will be influenced by who and what that person chooses to believe and what standards of evidence that person deems necessary before drawing conclusions.

In the case of Ruppelt, many may choose to give his solid service record and his experience working on two Project Sign successor programs—Project Grudge and later, Project Blue Book—as evidence in favor of accepting his statements. That said, Ruppelt remains a somewhat controversial figure among UFO researchers. He initially seemed to be considering several possible explanations for the unsolved UFO cases. However, by the time of his book's second edition, which was published shortly before Ruppelt's death in 1960, he seemed to have changed course. In the newly expanded edition, he wrote of UFOs as a "Space Age myth"—language similar to Carl Jung's description a year earlier.[5] Ruppelt's final words on the subject were an apparent dismissal of the extraterrestrial explanation, damaging his reputation among many advocates of that hypothesis.

Whatever his observational skills and motivations, Ruppelt makes a surprising assertion in his book. According to his account of the "Estimate," some Project Sign members had concluded that the UFOs "were interplanetary!"[6]

If the "Estimate" existed and Ruppelt's description of it is accurate, this was an extraordinary claim. If true, that suggests persons inside a focused military investigation, with access to many materials that were closed to the general public, had accepted the possibility of an explanation that was not only remarkable but also at odds with the Air Force's public position.

At this point, it is reasonable to ask: if Ruppelt's account of the "Estimate" is accurate, why did the public not hear about it at the time? On this question, Ruppelt explains that while a few Project Sign members did hold that view, the project's leaders and their superiors decidedly did not. According to Ruppelt, the "Estimate" was sent up the chain of command, more or less without comment, until it reached "the higher echelons of the Air Force."[7] At this point, the "Estimate" finally reached General Hoyt S. Vanderberg.

Then serving as the Air Force Chief of Staff, Vanderberg saw little merit to the extraterrestrial hypothesis. According to Ruppelt, the general "batted back down" the "Estimate" because "the report lacked proof." What allegedly followed was the stuff of conspiracy-theory legend: "the estimate died a quick death," Ruppelt writes. "Some months later it was completely declassified and relegated to the incinerator."[8]

A few copies of the "Estimate" supposedly escaped fiery destruction, one of which was the one Ruppelt allegedly saw. The scant surviving documents of the document (if this report is accurate) "were kept as mementos of the golden days of the UFOs,"[9] he said.

Since the 1950s, the "Estimate" has become a subject of widespread interest to many people interested in UFOs. Given its startling contents, it is not surprising that the search for an existing copy of the document has become something of a quest for UFO researchers and enthusiasts. To date, however, the hunt has been unsuccessful. A preserved copy may never surface.

If Ruppelt's account is accurate, it is not difficult to see the Air Force's efforts to keep its internal debate about extraterrestrial theories away from public view may have created a new problem. Indeed, it may inadvertently have helped fuel the type of conspiracy thinking and suspicion that would follow government declarations about the phenomenon for years to come.

≋ 23 ≋

Project Grudge

In early 1949, the Air Force gave Project Sign a new name. Project Grudge, as it was now called, continued to collect data about unexplained aerial phenomena. But, as had been true from the beginning, the officers overseeing the effort believed the unexplained aerial phenomena did not present a significant concern. Nor, in their opinion, were the UFOs from outer space. Taking these assumptions as more or less as marching orders, managers of the newly renamed program continued to oversee the Air Force's study of the problem.

But built into the focused set of assumptions underlying Grudge was a new way of understanding the "problem." Throughout the months of research conducted under the Project Sign banner, program personnel considered many potential scenarios that might explain the stubborn cases that still lacked a convincing explanation. The internal report from February of 1949 contained many pages devoted to exploring multiple possibilities, suggesting a relatively open-minded investigation. Even if the most influential Sign personnel thought there was not much to worry about, the door was still open for conclusions that could go in unexpected directions.

With the shift to Project Grudge, however, that no longer seemed to be the case. Instead, Grudge operated as though a verdict—the conclusion that the UFOs were not from another world and were probably not a Soviet threat, either—was already in hand. Of course, officials knew there were unsolved cases, but they seem to have decided not to lose sleep over it. With that in mind, Grudge leaders did not see the issue facing the project as solving a mystery. Rather, as things stood, their mission was primarily about convincing the public there was no need to worry.

Indeed, Grudge personnel began to devote less time and effort investigating the specifics of UFO sightings than looking into the people who reported them.[1] Perhaps that was all they could do. It would have been costly to undertake more thorough investigations even if program leaders wanted to do that. It appears, however, that they did not. Instead, the top officials had already decided there was not much worth such efforts. And if anyone on the Grudge staff was a strong advocate of the extraterrestrial hypothesis, such person or persons seem to have kept quiet about it. Thus, while there is evidence to suggest the interplanetary theory was taken seriously by some during the months of Project Sign, that seems to have changed as Project Grudge went forward.

There is no reason to doubt the sincerity of Project Grudge personnel and other Air Force leaders. They probably did believe that UFOs were not threatening and did not come from some other planet. But they also knew there were sightings that even the experts could not explain and that new incidents—some of which also baffled their own experts—continued to occur, too. For reasons that are probably varied and may never be fully known, however, the unresolved cases were not enough to cause Air Force superiors great concern. Still, Grudge personnel went about their work—or at least went through the motions of doing so. They collected cases and filed the paperwork even as program leaders pushed ahead with what amounted to a public relations campaign to discourage public interest in the topic.

On April 27, 1949, the National Military Establishment (renamed the Department of Defense later that year) issued a statement through its Office of Public Information. It was a very long memorandum that summarized the findings of "Project Saucer." (The Air Force was still not revealing some details about the program, including that its actual name was Project Grudge.) The document reviewed the history of the "flying saucer" sightings from Kenneth Arnold forward. It included details and explanations that generally described UFOs as an intriguing but ultimately fairly innocuous phenomenon. The memo mostly refrained from openly mocking the reports, and it admitted that some cases remained unresolved. Overall, however, it mainly discourages speculation. Consider, for example, these passages:

> All of the information so far presented in project "Saucer" on the possible existence of space ship from another planet or of aircraft propelled by an advanced type of atomic power plant have been largely conjecture.
> To sum up, no definite conclusive evidence is yet available that would prove or disprove the possibility that a portion of the unidentified objects are real aircraft of unknown or unconventional configuration.[2]

A few days after the press release, *Saturday Evening Post*, the popular magazine, published a two-part story primarily based on information from the Air Force. Authored by veteran reporter Sidney Shalett, the article appeared under the authoritative-sounding headline "What You Can Believe About Flying Saucers."[3] He claimed he had extensively researched the topic "with what seemed to be the wholehearted co-operation of the Air Force."[4] Armed with his new understanding, Shalett said, he aimed to set the record straight.

Shalett repeats what people already knew—that many saucer reports were hoaxes, mistakes, and misidentifications of various kinds. But he also admits that some incidents—including many from "respectable" sources—remained unsolved. He further acknowledged that the witnesses included people who were not simply casual observers. Instead, scientists, commercial pilots, military personnel, public safety officers, and other professionals were among those who had verified some of the sightings. The reports of these people, he implied, could not simply be dismissed without some consideration.

The *Saturday Evening Post* story summarizes the 1947 UFO wave and some similar incidents in the following year. Among the latter cases is the fatal Mantell incident. Here, Shalett suggests that authorities had since decided there was a strong possibility the pilot was chasing the planet Venus. The Venus theory, Shalett writes, was confirmed as plausible by Air Force consulting astronomer J. Allen Hynek. (Interestingly, Hynek also is quoted as saying he found it "a little surprising that it was so easily picked out during daylight by the naked eye."[5])

Another possible explanation—and by then, a familiar one—involved scientific and military balloon projects. Misidentifications related to these objects, Shalett suggested, could explain many cases. According to the article, towering "translucent plastic balloons used by the navy for cosmic-ray research" were plausible culprits in many sightings. These types of balloons rose high into the atmosphere and drifted across a wide range of the U.S. skies where they easily could be misidentified from the ground. Shalett notes the Navy's Skyhook project, involving "huge, translucent" balloons, each with a "long tail ... [that can rise] 100,000 feet or more into the air."[6]

Other military projects could provide answers for numerous sightings, too, according to Shalett's account. For example, he writes, "Some of the sightings have been in the White Sands, New Mexico, area, where the frightening marriage of the German V-2 [missile] WAC Corporal [an early U.S.-designed rocket] is being forged, and the conclusions are obvious." He also cites Air Force and Navy projects, some of which were classified, that were "filling the air with strangely shaped experimental planes—needle nosed things which break the sonic barriers; a 'flying flapjack' plane that really looked like a saucer, but now has been dropped by the Navy; eight-engine 'flying wing' bombers"[7] and more.

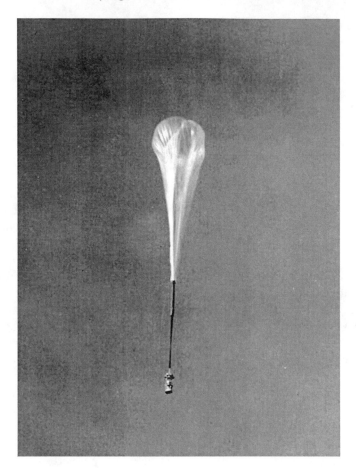

Specialized meteorological and military balloons were frequent suspects in reported UFO sightings during the late 1940s and early 1950s. Many of these, such as this Project Skyhook balloon photographed in 1957, were massively tall and had surfaces that shimmered in the light, sometimes confusing witnesses who saw them at a distance (Office of Naval Research, U.S. Navy).

Overall, while Shalett acknowledges that some flying disc sightings still were not fully understood, he gives readers the impression that there is no cause for alarm. He writes:

> When I went to Wright Field armed only with reports of what witnesses said they had seen, the Great Flying Saucer Scare seemed reasonably mysterious to me. When I had finished my investigation in Dayton, Washington, and elsewhere, the thing seemed less mysterious than odd. There are any number of logical and perfectly normal solutions by which most of the saucer sightings can be explained.[8]

The conclusion of Shalett's two-part article was published the following week, on May 7, 1949. Here, the writer devotes much space to senior military officials' views—or supposed views on the UFO topic. (Their private opinions may or may not have been the same as those recorded in the article, but at least for public consumption, they all had the same perspective.) They saw next to nothing to warrant worry or concern. Shalett describes the situation bluntly: "The men who constitute the high command of the United States Air Force do not believe in flying saucers, disks, space ships from Mars—or Russia."[9]

To bolster his perspective, Shalett offers further possible explanations for the unexplained phenomenon. He repeated the usual list of suspects—"vertigo, hypnosis, and other sensory illusions ... at high altitudes"—as reasons for some open cases. The possibility that "mass hysteria" was involved—a conjecture that had been considered since the wave of sightings in 1947—was also mentioned. Perhaps, he suggests, many sightings were due to "the jittery age we live in, particularly since our scientists and military spokesmen have started talking about sending rockets to the moon."[10] "It is small wonder that harassed humans, already suffering from atomic psychosis," he adds, "have started seeing saucers and Martians."[11]

The Air Force probably regarded the Shalett piece as a public relations coup. *Saturday Evening Post* was a widely beloved and trusted publication. The appearance of reassuring messaging in the popular weekly all but guaranteed that millions of Americans would likely see it.

On the surface, the Air Force's message, as filtered through Shalett's article, seemed to be straightforward and unmistakable. It was as if the newest, most aerospace-oriented branch of the U.S. military was saying not to be taken aback by reports of flying saucers because they looked into it and turned up nothing. To a large extent, that probably was the way officials saw the situation. Yet, being almost certain that the UFOs did not represent some new threat or unknown was not the same as being entirely sure of that belief. Although small in number, a few puzzling new cases continued to emerge. The falling may have been that these did not amount to much, but officials did not believe they could afford to ignore the baffling cases entirely in the dangerous Cold War years.

According to many sources, many ordinary people wondered if they should believe everything officials told them about the flying discs. As aerospace historian Curtis Peebles has written, many journalists were well aware that "the Air Force was very interested in flying saucer reports." For some of them, he says, "the Shalett article seemed contradictory."[12] It seemed to some reporters as though the Air Force was

trying to convince the public the UFOs were nothing to warrant interest, on the one hand, while it continued to appear very interested in
them, on the other. According to Peebles, this fed "vague, undefined suspicions" that had existed since the summer of 1947. As he said, "The suspicion grew that there might be more, that the article was an attempt by
the Air Force to hide what it 'really' knew."[13]

Perceptions were a significant factor. The Air Force did not need to
know a lot more than it publicly admitted for people to get the idea that
it did. (It certainly knew of classified military projects that might explain
some sightings, for example, but it wished to keep those secrets at the
time.) Nevertheless, in the face of ambiguities and unknowns, appearances mattered. So, when the Air Force, perhaps somewhat clumsily,
tried to assuage the public's fears of an unknown threat, it inadvertently
may have accomplished the opposite in the eyes of some.

In December 1949, Project Grudge issued what would be its final
report, "Summary of the Evaluation of Remaining Reports." Once again,
it discounted any extraordinary explanations for the saucer sightings.
Instead, the document repeated the by-then standard possible answers
for the cases cited. In addition to reports that were simple mistakes
or hoaxes, the "Summary" noted "war nerves" and "pyschopathologi-
cal persons" among the explanations. Whether intended or not, the
"Summary" document seems to have further marginalized UFOs and
the witnesses who said they saw them. In some ways, it comes off as a
heavy-handed attempt to stigmatize the whole phenomenon—an effort
to change the subject and keep it changed.

However, if those were the intentions, Project Grudge's "Summary" fell far short of the mark. Curtis Peebles is correct in observing,
"rather than clearing up the situation, it raised even more questions in
the minds of some."[14]

It is difficult to know if Air Force officials realized their efforts
to tamp down public interest in UFOs could backfire. Regardless of
that, they *did* recognize that the mere existence of an Air Force project devoted to UFOs was probably fueling rather than dampening public interest in the topic.[15] Since the whole point of the program initially
had been to reassure the public and lessen attention to the unexplained
reports, they determined that Grudge was having substantially less than
the desired effect. Deciding that Project Grudge had outlived its usefulness by this time, the Air Force announced its cancellation on December
27. However, by then, it was too late for the Air Force to salvage its original purpose of moving public attention away from UFOs.

If Air Force officials believed that they had devised an effective
strategy to persuade the public there was no need for concern about

UFOs, they would soon realize they were mistaken. Project Grudge elicited little of the outcome that Air Force officials wanted.

In retrospect, Project Grudge may have been a lost opportunity. In somewhat single-mindedly pursuing a mission to persuade the American public that UFOs were no danger, the program directed resources to that end at the apparent expense of delving more fully into the cases it wrote off as unsolved. By concluding their accounting of the unresolved incidents was good enough, authorities misread how that might appear from the outside.

The military may have been confident in a risk assessment that placed flying saucers at a low priority. Their job, after all, was to make such determinations. However, the general public was very unaccustomed to that kind of situation analysis, however. To them, the issue could—and for some, did—look very different. Thus, even though officials may have been correct in reassuring the public that nothing extraordinary had happened, that conclusion struck some as premature and disingenuous under the circumstances.

Over the months when Grudge was operating, the world situation dramatically changed. Then, in late summer, a long fear development became a reality: The Soviet Union had developed its own atomic bomb. It was several years earlier than most Americans expected, and it significantly altered the geopolitical landscape. "The period of atomic monopoly is over," said an editorial in *Life* magazine. "Now the U.S. and the Soviet Union face each other, Bomb to Bomb."[16]

⇒ 24 ⇐

The Flying Saucers Are Real

Despite Project Grudge's efforts to cool public interest in unexplained aerial phenomena, some people remained unconvinced by statements that nothing important was happening. One of those people was Donald Keyhoe, a 1919 graduate of the U.S. Naval Academy. He was a seasoned aviator and a Marine Corps officer until injuries from a plane crash ended his military service in 1923. After recovering, he was employed by the Civil Aeronautics Branch of the Commerce Department for a time and then worked briefly with the famous pilot Charles A. Lindbergh. In 1928, Keyhoe wrote a book about the latter experience called *Flying with Lindbergh*. In the years that followed, he pursued a writing career, publishing articles in well-known magazines such as *The Saturday Evening Post, The Nation,* and *Reader's Digest.*

Keyhoe received a telegram in May 1949 that would alter the trajectory of his career. Ken Purdy, the editor of *True* magazine, wanted to know if Keyhoe would be interested in conducting an independent inquiry into the flying saucer story. The editor said he had been told the UFOs might be a "gigantic hoax to cover up [an] official secret." The "flying saucer mystery" might make a "terrific story," Purdy wrote. Purdy hoped Keyhoe would write such an article for the magazine.[1]

Intrigued by the idea, Keyhoe met with Purdy soon after. In their discussion, it turned out that the two men had already drawn somewhat similar conclusions on the subject based on published accounts. Both agreed that the saucers were real and not illusions. They also decided that they were not satisfied with the official explanations to date. *Saturday Evening Post*'s two-part article about flying saucers had recently been released, mainly based on information from the Air Force. Neither Purdy nor Keyhoe believed its basic conclusions, however. There were too many gaps and too many questions for their liking, and they talked about alternate explanations.

It was evidently Purdy who brought up the main elements of a theory that Keyhoe soon adopted, as well. The two men already agreed that the Air Force was hiding something. That much was common ground. However, Purdy's ideas went somewhat further. He speculated that the UFOs were spaceships from another planet and, what is more, that the Air Force not only already knew this; it actively was covering it up.[2]

In essence, therefore, the two men had developed all the components of what would later become an elaborate conspiracy theory about UFOs—one to which others would later make additions, adaptations, and variations. However, the common core ideas were there at the start: extraterrestrial aliens had arrived; the government knew it; the government was hiding it. These elements were soon to become an article of faith for Keyhoe and countless others as the years passed.

The main parts of this theory were there initially, but Keyhoe's public articulation of it was still some months away. He would need time to research and outline this vision before it would be ready for publication in the January 1950 edition of *True.*

When he set out to gather more information, Keyhoe already had a clear idea of where his investigation would lead him.[3] That approach— determining the outcome and then finding the evidence to support it— may have made sense to him. However, it raised the potential specter of confirmation bias, which was poised to contaminate his reasoning process. Indeed, his predetermined convictions likely did compromise his efforts to understand the phenomenon.

The writer was correct about some of his initial observations, though. The Air Force's explanations did have gaps. Public acknowledgment of unsolved cases were admissions of that fact. He was also right that Air Force's press statements seemed designed to divert attention away from the UFO subject, too. That was a solid observation. At that point, however, Keyhoe made an enormous leap in logic. He decided that the questionable aspects of the Air Force's account could lead to one and only one set of conclusions: recent events involved extraterrestrial spaceships and a massive government cover-up. Having made that determination, he apparently believed no other explanation could better explain the strange phenomenon.

Armed with his convictions and enthusiasm for the project, Keyhoe spent the next several months tracking down people to interview and scouring published evidence. It did not always go smoothly. Despite his military background, Air Force personnel apparently did not want to talk to him.[4] Given that the Air Force possessed the most complete case files and data, that was a drawback.

In Curtis Peeble's view, what came next brought the "basic flaws" in

Keyhoe's research methods to the surface.[5] First, there was almost nothing in terms of physical evidence. (Recall that at the time, the Roswell case had long been forgotten.) Added to that, the people with whom Keyhoe communicated often had little firsthand knowledge. Since Keyhoe mostly dismissed Air Force statements as untrustworthy, he had few sources other than these same people whose views were influenced by media accounts and other people. According to Peebles, Keyhoe's "sources were relying on newspaper accounts, rumors, and airport gossip to shape their opinions."[6] It was a significant complication, though apparently not one that Keyhoe thought much about.

But such limitations did not deter him. If anything, Keyhoe's convictions seem to grow stronger as he continued his research. Reading and hearing things that supported his beliefs about an extraterrestrial conspiracy, he appears to have given little consideration to any other view.

By year's end, Keyhoe was ready to present his theories about the flying saucers to the public. His article, "The Flying Saucers Are Real," appeared in *True* magazine's January 1949 edition. It covered a wide range of theories and speculations.

In explaining his thought process, Keyhoe reported that the government's "on-and-off, hot-and-cold contradictory statements" about the UFOs did not impress him. He told readers that his research led him to conclusions far different from the official position of the Air Force. Rather than the phenomenon essentially being much ado about nothing, as the Air Force seemed to claim, Keyhoe said the government was sitting on a big secret that was likely to become public soon.

By this time, the writer had fleshed out his ideas with many details. Keyhoe now claimed, for example, that the saucers had a much longer history with humans than the public realized. "For the past 175 years," he wrote, "the planet Earth has been under systematic close-range examination by living, intelligent observers from another planet."[7] The latest wave of sightings, in 1947, was a herald of things to come, he said. Soon, he believed, the truth would be unveiled. "The official explanation may be imminent," he told a reporter. "When it is finally revealed, I believe the elaborate preparation—even the wide deceit involved—will be fully justified in the minds of the American people."[8]

Keyhoe's big secret was the claim that the government knew the UFOs were vessels carrying visitors from another planet. As he saw it, this was life-altering news that could easily spark widespread fear. Since revelations of such magnitude would be too shocking to disclose abruptly, he suggested, the government was taking the time to reveal everything it knew. Keyhoe theorized that officials were laying the groundwork so that humanity could cope with the revelation without succumbing to worldwide panic.

Although his article does allow for the possibility the saucers eventually could "prove of earthly origin," Keyhoe implies he thought that was unlikely. Instead, he writes, "It is the opinion of *True* that the flying saucers are real and that they come from no enemy on Earth." Still, he did not regard the UFOs as a danger. "Even the stoutest believers in the disks do not think any mass invasion from space is possible at this time," he writes.[9]

In the final sentence of his article, Keyhoe quotes what he calls a "warning" from the Air Force: "The saucers are not a joke."[10] On the surface, the quotation appears to be a simple caution. However, from one perspective, it is a clear statement about the reality of a situation that Keyhoe believed should be taken seriously.

In hindsight, these words also might apply to something else. They can easily be interpreted to be not only about the saucers but also about the people who believed the objects were of otherworldly origin. These people wanted to be taken seriously and not viewed as laughing stocks, which was often the case. Indeed, from Kenneth Arnold forward, many UFO witnesses and many UFO believers desperately wanted to be treated as intelligent, dignified people—not as delusional fools. Often, however, the reality was otherwise.

Of course, Keyhoe may have intended the final words of his piece simply to refer only to the saucers and not to the people who believed extraordinary things about them. The language he uses is revealing, however. It suggests that already, people were dividing into two camps on the issue, each possessing a dim view of those in the other camp. On the one hand, he talks about "skeptics" and "sincere disbelievers" who think "all the saucers were mistakes, illusions, hoaxes, hysteria, and mass hallucination." On the other hand, he speaks of the "believers."[11] Much of the article seems designed to present members of the latter group as "logical and reasonable,"[12] the words that he uses to refer to himself and, by implication, the *True* staff, all of whom are presented as believers.

Interestingly, this dichotomous framework appears to have left room for a little middle ground. It was as if the UFO issue were a stark contrast of black and white, with no shades of grey. Either the government was entirely correct, or the "believers" were. It was all one or all the other. Arguably, this was not the optimal way to approach a situation with inherent unknowns and ambiguities.

Various misunderstandings may have helped fuel the extraterrestrial conspiracy viewpoint. Some people at the time, Keyhoe among them, were convinced the Project Grudge (or Project Saucer, as it was still called publicly) was working at a breakneck pace behind the scenes. Presumably, as Keyhoe implies, they were researching the alien spacecraft extensively and learning as much about the sightings as possible.

That, however, seems far removed from the actual situation. Whether it was advisable or not, military investigators believed that the flying saucer issue was not a significant concern. Accordingly, it appears that very little genuinely investigative work continued. It could hardly have been otherwise since personnel had been reassigned and the budget slashed. What little work that continued amounted to not much more than a few people going through the motions. It is what bureaucracies often do in those sorts of situations.

In retrospect, the emergence of a relatively cogent extraterrestrial conspiracy theory about the saucers at the same time the military pulled back from its investigations was momentous, at least in terms of cultural impact. Authorities obviously hoped that the public would move on and leave the UFO phenomenon as something that was mostly over and done. Yet, although military officers may have been satisfied that enough—not all, but enough—questions had been answered to draw that conclusion, this reasoning was not something that the entire public similarly accepted. It turned out that the open questions—those that remained unanswered but did not overly concern the military—were more than enough to fascinate many. So, while officials may have been ready to let the matter drift into the background, it seemed that this was just the beginning of interest in the topic for the American public.

Authorities appear not to have realized the long-term implications of this at the time. That misreading of the public's attitude led to another lost opportunity. Indeed, in the future, the doubts that were left unaddressed and the questions that were left unanswered would fuel skepticism about official statements about UFOs for many years.

As it was, Keyhoe's article was widely read upon publication. Meanwhile, Fawcett, the outfit that published *True*, realized it had something that could attract much attention. Keen interest in the magazine piece suggested that a book on the topic could also be successful. So, in short order, Keyhoe quickly went to work expanding the article into a book.

It only took a few months before the book was ready for publication. As its release date neared, editor Jim Bishop claimed that the military was trying to stop its publication. Fawcett was under "a lot of pressure" to abandon it, he said, but the company pressed on anyway. "If they [defense officials] can prove publication will do the country harm, involve national security, we'll withdraw it," he told a reporter.[13]

Whether this was hype or reality is difficult to judge. In any case,

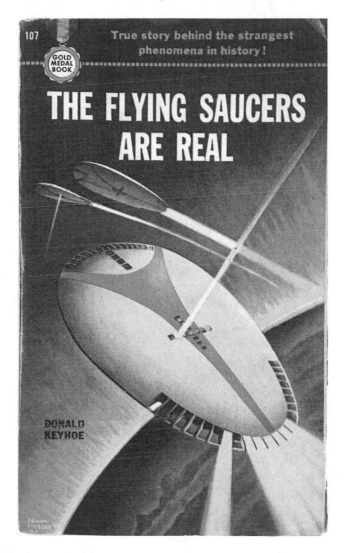

Donald Keyhoe's *The Flying Saucers Are Real* was one of the first widely circulated books to present the theory that flying saucers came from another planet and that the U.S. government knew more than it was saying. These ideas later became a mainstay of the so-called UFO mythology (author's collection).

military officials promptly denied Bishop's claims. A spokesperson said that the Pentagon had "no interest" in the book and that defense officials "had never even heard" of it.[14] Whether that was entirely true is debatable since Keyhoe's article had created a stir, and Fawcett was promoting the book version of the piece at the time. However, given that the

Air Force had apparently decided the saucers were more of a distraction than any kind of threat, these statements were consistent with officials' public views. It seems reasonable to surmise that authorities may have decided that outright banning the book would draw more attention to it at a time when they were hoping to convince the public to stop thinking about the topic altogether.

The book was soon released. Like the earlier article, it was entitled *The Flying Saucers Are Real.* It proved to be popular and demonstrated that Fawcett was right in thinking there would be a good market for such a book.

Meanwhile, the Pentagon seemed to be losing its undeclared war that focused on dampening public interested in the flying discs, at least in some ways. In October, many American schoolchildren paged through the latest edition of *My Weekly Reader,* a publication widely distributed to schools across the country. In its pages, young readers came across an interesting item. An article by Tom Trott (evidently a pseudonym) quite matter-of-factly told children, "Some saucers are real. They belong to our Air Force."[15]

Eleanor M. Johnson, *My Weekly Reader's* editor at the time, told the Associated Press that the decision to address the topic was simple. She wrote that in order "to calm any hysterical fears some children might have built up from hearing too much talk about mysterious flying objects from other planets or deadly flying weapons of our enemies. ... We wanted to reassure them by telling them the saucers are our own and will serve a good purpose."[16]

Whether the article had the intended effect or not, the item seems unlikely to have aided the Pentagon's goal of changing the subject. Nevertheless, whether government officials liked it or not, by the mid-point of the 20th century, the UFO topic was firmly implanted in America's cultural landscape.

≡ 25 ≡

Project Twinkle

Project Sign and its successor, Project Grudge, worked to figure out the flying saucers that thousands of people saw in the mid-century skies. Although at a much slower pace than in mid–1947, the list of sightings continued to grow. One of the most prominent new cases occurred near Fargo, North Dakota, in early October 1948. In that incident, Lieutenant George Gorman, a National Guard fighter pilot, engaged in what was reported as a half-hour "dogfight" with a "mysterious ... disk-like object which outran and outmaneuvered him" in the night sky.[1] Witnesses on the ground, which included two men in the control tower, watched the incident unfold, apparently just as dumbfounded as Gorman was about what was happening. A few months later, Air Force investigators determined that the object Gorman had been chasing was an Air Weather Service balloon.[2] However, that claim struck some as unlikely, and many UFO researchers still do not accept it as the true explanation.

As the Air Force continued to collect information on the flying saucers, a slightly different aerial phenomenon also drew attention. In far-flung places across the country, many witnesses reported seeing strange and fast-moving green fireballs. Whether they were some sort of meteor activity or other natural occurrence was hard to say for sure. But the number of sightings drew attention. More unsettling than that was that some of the unusual and unknown fireballs appeared near sensitive military installations.

An incident on December 5, 1948, is usually cited as the event that triggered an organized response to the green lights. On that date, pilots in two separate aircraft—one military and one civilian—witnessed something that seemed unexplainable in the distance. Personnel aboard a C-47 Air Force transport made the first report. At 9:05 p.m. and again at 9:27 p.m., they saw a large, brilliant green light in the distance. The large size and intense luminosity were very unfamiliar. It was so much

157

out of the ordinary that it prompted the pilot to report it to Kirtland Air Force Base in Albuquerque.[3]

Independently, the pilot of a commercial Pioneer Airlines plane in the vicinity also reported seeing something strange, possibly a "shooting star," just after 9:30 p.m. According to this witness, the object did not behave like a meteor or other natural phenomenon. Like what the Air Force C-47 pilot had said, the Pioneer pilot noted that the thing remained on a horizontal path and did not appear to be descending as would have been expected if it were a meteor or similar object. Even more alarming, the Pioneer witness said the object had headed toward the plane. In fact, for a moment, he feared it would strike his aircraft head-on.[4]

Reports of meteors streaking across the skies were not unusual in that era, especially in Western states. "A brilliant fireball or meteor streaked over the southwest states Thursday night and exploded in a burst of flame," read a newspaper report in mid–October of the same year. "It was a ball of yellow fire with an outside edge changing from red to green," said one witness.[5] That incident was widely reported and visible from parts of California, Arizona, Nevada, and Colorado.

Earlier in the year, many people thought they saw a plane crash in the northern part of California. That was evidently a mistaken impression, however. The American Meteor Society determined that the "brilliant green fire ball" was not an aircraft in trouble but rather that it was almost certainly a meteor. Moreover, the "Green Dragon meteor," as one press account called it, was only one in "a series [of such sightings] over Oregon, Washington, and California" in recent months. American Meteor Society scientists noted that in each of those cases, which substantially predated the C-47 and Pioneer Air Lines reports in December, the objects were noteworthy for their "predominant [green] color and the long gaseous 'tail' seen behind it."[6]

Such incidents, which appear to have not been widely reported in earlier years, would become widespread after the December 5 sighting. A report from a few months later, in April of 1949, was typical. A "'large, green fireball,' illuminated northern Arizona was sighted early today," according to a syndicated press report. An official at the American Meteor Society who witnessed the object described it as "the largest and brightest I have ever seen."[7]

Similar incidents would occur fairly often for several years. Although these sightings were geographically spread out, the bulk of the reports—and the primary cause of worry—were in the Southwest. Not insignificantly, the region was home to sensitive facilities such as the Los Alamos National Laboratory and the White Sands Proving Grounds, critical to the nation's atomic weapons program. Other vital military bases were nearby, too, including the Nevada Test and Training Range, a section of which is better known by its later unofficial name, Area 51.

It was that proximity that prompted military concerns in late 1948 and early 1949. Defense officials recognized that the fireballs might have been natural phenomena of some sort. However, they did not want to take any chances that they represented some other, unknown danger. So, as more fireballs appeared over Southwestern states, authorities decided that some investigation would be needed.

The green fireballs appeared to be a somewhat different phenomenon from the flying saucers. The mysterious lights seemed to warrant a separate inquiry. Therefore, with the fireballs presenting new kinds of questions that needed answers, officials organized a meeting of relevant personnel to establish what they already knew and how to tackle the remaining questions. A series of meetings, beginning in February 1949, was promptly authorized with the expectation that a plan of action would be forthcoming.

Officials organized several meetings with the hope of reaching a better understanding of the green fireballs. One was held at Sandia National Laboratory next to Kirtland Air Force Base.[8] The other venue, which is more widely cited, was the research lab in Los Alamos.

Twenty-five miles northwest of Santa Fe, the Los Alamos facility had been home to the ultra-secret Project Manhattan, where work for the first atomic bomb had been completed just a few years earlier. Los Alamos remained an especially critical nuclear research facility in the postwar years. It was a fitting venue where experts and military leaders could come together to ponder a course of action.

The Sandia and Los Alamos conferences brought together an impressive array of attendees. In addition to Air Force officers and intelligence experts, the group included representatives from the Armed Forces Special Weapons Project and various federal agencies. Scientists from several organizations, including the Atomic Energy Commission and the University of California (which was then running the Sandia lab), also attended.[9]

Among the scientists in attendance was Dr. Lincoln La Paz, director of the Institute of Atmospherics at the University of New Mexico. Other prominent scientists in the group included Dr. Edward Teller, who was already working on developing the hydrogen bomb at the time, and Dr. Joseph Kaplan, a physicist who specialized in atmospheric phenomena.[10]

Various accounts of the meeting suggest that it was mostly La Paz who had doubts about classifying the green fireballs as natural occurrences. He was well aware that meteor fragments in some circumstances could cause fireballs vaguely similar to those that had been recently reported. However, he thought the specific cases under consideration included descriptions that simply did not fit with the expected behaviors of bright lights caused by meteors. Specifically, the path of the objects in the sky was level and not descending. This trajectory, he believed, was "too flat" to have been the result of a meteor.[11] The reported intensity of the green color also bothered La Paz. The description seemed off to him. Perhaps, he speculated, these were some sort of unknown aircraft.

The other scientists—namely, Teller and Kaplan—were not bothered by apparent discrepancies in the meteor explanation. La Paz was a respected scientist, but the others thought his perspective was based on assumptions more than hard evidence. Again, this was a case where the lack of physical evidence meant that people charged with analyzing the circumstances had to interpret witness accounts. There was much room for error or a simple difference of opinion when making judgments.

The investigation into the bright green fireballs was formalized and given the somewhat unusual codename of Project Twinkle. When the Sandia and Los Alamos meetings concluded, only La Paz seems strongly believed the objects might not be natural phenomena. The others still thought there simply was insufficient data to conclude that the fireballs were anything of concern. However, although they suspected the fireballs were astronomical or atmospheric in origin, they could not precisely say what they were. With that in mind, they decided to set up an observation post hoping that it would produce concrete evidence.

After considering the high concentration of reports in the Albuquerque region, a location in the Sandia Mountains seemed to be the best site. So, in the spring of 1949, Project Twinkle set up an outpost there and brought in spectrographic equipment that could collect data around the clock[12] as a "crew kept vigil."[13]

If Project Twinkle managers had high hopes, they were initially disappointed. As a later article in *Life* magazine recounted, "Ironically, while fireballs continued flashing everywhere else in the Southwest, they saw nothing until Project Twinkle was transferred to Holloman Air Force base at Alamogordo, New Mexico."[14] In the new location, there were "a few sightings," but little came of it. It proved impossible "to make satisfying calculations because of the fireballs' great speed."[15] In other words, months of collection activity resulted in little new data. In the end, there was nothing from which to draw conclusions that were any more certain than when they started.

Yet, people scattered across the country still reported the

mysterious fireballs occasionally. Since the Air Force was not entirely sure what to make of the reports, they authorized other efforts to track down additional information about them. Quietly, officials arranged to install technologically advanced equipment from the Signal Corps at selected Air Force bases. Meanwhile, the Air Force enlisted the help of the nation's air traffic controllers. Under a veil of secrecy, the Air Force issued specialized cameras to some of these personnel. The authorities hoped that if any of the fireballs appeared near one of their airfields, the chosen air traffic controllers would be able to gather relatively high-quality photographic evidence.[16]

Military leaders wanted to know more about the fireballs, but they did not want to draw public attention to the government's interest in the matter. So, as was the case with the Air Force's other UFO investigations, the data-gathering activities under Project Twinkle's auspices were highly classified. Based on her research, writer Annie Jacobsen concludes that military leaders were determined "that under no circumstances was the public to know that the Air Force was investigating UFOs."[17] Evidently, according to Jacobsen, even if members of Congress inquired, Air Force officials dodged the subject.[18]

In the end, nothing seems to have come from the efforts of Project Twinkle. Some members of the program found it odd that "the sightings had stopped as soon as the Air Force started observing," according to historian David Michael Jacobs.[19] There seems little doubt that some, perhaps many of the sightings, were cases in which people did see something unusual. But as with the flying saucer sightings, many incidents seemed to involve either misidentification of known astronomical or atmospheric phenomena, aircraft, or known aerial objects that the witnesses did not recognize for some reason. It may not have been the case that military officials were utterly unconcerned about the fireballs. Some unease may have continued in the backs of their minds. But by the middle of 1950, it is fair to say they were far less concerned with the still-unanswered questions about those mystery objects than with other, more immediate, and more pressing things.

One of those things was a startling new, atomic-age war. On June 25, 1950, tens of thousands of North Korean troops surged over the 38th parallel that had divided the Korean peninsula since World War II. Backed by the Soviet Union, the communist North Korean incursion presented the United States with a frightening new situation. It had only been nine months since Mao Zedong had declared the People's Republic of China's foundation. With two communist powerhouses, China and the Soviet Union, in the background, the United States perceived North Korean aggression as a grave new threat.

Acting quickly, the U.S. rounded up allies and a United Nations mandate. Less than five years after the atom bomb has ended World War II, America was now in a new armed conflict. No one knew if the conflict could be contained or whether North Korea's powerful sponsors would directly join the fight. And no one knew if what started as a conventional war might soon lead to nuclear conflict between the world's two superpowers, the United States and the Soviet Union. Stateside, there were still many unanswered questions about the flying saucers and green fireballs. However, in the context of a new war, whatever concerns the military had about UFOs would be moved to the back burner as American leadership looked to the more immediate and potentially catastrophic situation in East Asia.

≡ 26 ≡

Fate

Regardless of any other impact the 1947 wave of UFO sightings had on society, the life of flying-saucer witness Kenneth Arnold would never completely return to normal. For the rest of his days, the amateur pilot would be known to the world as the man who started the so-called modern UFO era. It was not a legacy he ever entirely embraced.

Arnold could do nothing about his fame, but at times, he seemed uncomfortable with it. That feeling began almost immediately after his flying saucer story hit the press in June of 1947. Simple renown was not the worst of it, though. Along with the public attention that came from being at the center of a nationally syndicated news story, there was also the judging that came along with it. Arnold knew that some people were not only skeptical of his report; they regarded him as either an attention-seeker or a crackpot—perhaps both.

From his perspective, that seemed very unfair. The way he saw things, he only reported seeing something unusual. He did not make any grand claims or offer wild theories about the objects over Mount Rainier—at least, not at first. The most he had done was speculate that the unidentified objects might secret military technology. And that suspicion, though strenuously denied by military officials, was hardly outlandish. After all, the government had developed the atom bomb in almost total secrecy and even tested it in the open air of a military range in New Mexico. Given that recent history, why would the idea of an ultra-secret aircraft capable of incredible things be any more amazing?

As time passed, however, Arnold found it increasingly difficult to escape from the UFO controversy. In some respects, his fame from the first press accounts of the Mount Rainier sighting made it difficult to escape from the limelight. In other ways, however, the amateur pilot's actions inadvertently brought more attention his way.

In the months before the Korean War, the Air Force was still trying

163

to convince the public that the UFO sightings of recent months and years were not worth much thought. The plan was not working. Indeed, Americans remained fascinated with the topic, and official declarations did little to dampen enthusiasm for a subject that had already secured a spot in the cultural landscape.

The public's continued interest in UFOs was enough to prompt CBS radio to make the subject the focus of a special report. Hosted by Edward R. Murrow, the report was broadcast nationally in April of 1950.[1]

Murrow was already a well-respected journalist. His radio accounts of events leading up to and during World War II were widely known to the American public. In the postwar years, he assumed an even more prominent role for CBS news, where he would continue to bring investigative reports and context to major news stories for years to come.

The centerpiece of Murrow's radio special, "The Case of the Flying Saucer," was a telephone interview with Arnold. The conversation was recorded in advance and edited. Arnold's comments then were combined with Murrow's narration, which was added later to create the final version of the program.

Unsurprisingly, Murrow retained the role of the skeptical reporter throughout the report. He treated Arnold respectfully and did not attempt to judge the truth of the pilot's recollection of the original 1947 sighting over Mount Rainier. Still, Murrow noted that some people were skeptical from the beginning. "On three different occasions," the reporter says, "Mr. Arnold was questioned by military intelligence. They expressed doubt as to the accuracy of some of his reported observations."[2]

One of the most interesting sections of "The Case of the Flying Saucer" comes in a revealing exchange between Murrow and Arnold. This part of the interview shows the pilot's continued frustration with being the subject of mockery and also his evolving and somewhat surprising thoughts about what the saucers might represent:

> MURROW: Few people realize that Mr. Arnold has reported seeing these same strange objects in the sky on three other occasions. He says that some pilots in the northwest have reported seeing them on eight separate occasions. We asked for his own personal opinion on the nature of what he and the others had seen.
> ARNOLD: I don't know how best to explain that. I more or less have reserved an opinion as to what I think. Naturally, being a natural-born American, if it's not made by our science or our Army Air Forces, I am inclined to believe it's of an extraterrestrial origin.
> MURROW: Extraterrestrial origin? You mean you think there's a possibility

they may be coming out of space from other planets? I suppose that's
pretty hard for people to take seriously.

ARNOLD: Well, I'll tell you this much—all the airline pilots, none of us
have appreciated being laughed at.[3]

No one wants to be the subject of ridicule, and Arnold's annoyance is
understandable. However, it seems likely that some of his decisions
inadvertently added to his credibility problems. One prominent example of a questionable choice was his agreement to become involved in
investigating the so-called Maury Island sighting. Arnold's beliefs about
the incident, which officials and most of the public soon concluded was
a hoax, did not help his reputation.

It may have been details in the backstory of Arnold's Maury Island
investigation of that incident was more damaging in the long run.
This effort was funded by Ray Palmer, a magazine editor who tended
to embrace sensationalism and had no substantial background in news
reporting.

Had Arnold's involvement with Palmer been restricted to just that
one occasion, possibly his reputation would not have eroded as much as
it did. However, it turned out that the Maury Island investigation was
only the beginning. Indeed, in the coming months, the two men became
closely associated. Arnold's continuing involvement with the flying saucer subject became entwined with Palmer's business interests. And that
seems further to have compromised Arnold's credibility with officials.

The connection between Palmer and Arnold became increasingly
apparent in the spring of 1948. At that time, only nine months after
Arnold's newsworthy sighting in June, Arnold's UFO case made a significant leap further into the realm of popular culture. And this turn of
events would bring Palmer and Arnold together once again.

Until then, much (though not all) of the coverage about saucers, pro or con, appeared in traditional newspapers, magazines, and
radio reports. In 1948, however, the story of Kenneth Arnold's strange
encounter was the centerpiece of the inaugural edition of a new pulp
magazine, *Fate*. Significantly, the magazine's editor and co-founder was
none other than Ray Palmer.

Arnold's sighting was the main feature of *Fate*'s first issue, the cover
of which included a painting of the objects based on the amateur pilot's
description. Arnold is listed as the author of the issue's featured story,
although Palmer evidently took a significant role in its writing, as was
his habit.

The article, entitled "The Truth About Flying Saucers," seemed simple enough. However, the wording of that title was also provocatively
and subtly suggestive. Indeed, by saying that this particular article told

readers the "truth," the unstated implication was that perhaps previous accounts had not done so. This way of approaching stories about UFOs would be widely adopted in the years to come when writers and media producers would often give their work titles that implied they were about to reveal hidden truths.

Fate's premier issue also included "many other startling articles and features," as was stated on the cover. Indeed, the magazine seemed designed to thrill and entice its readers. One item was entitled "Twenty Million Maniacs." Another was called "Invisible Beings Walk the Earth."

Overall, readers could be forgiven if their first impressions of *Fate* seemed to resemble pulp publications such as the science-fiction-oriented *Amazing Stories*. Ray Palmer, who co-founded *Fate* with a business partner, was still serving as the editor of *Amazing Stories* for Ziff-Davis publications when the new magazine hit the newsstands. *Fate* aimed at the same type of readership as the science-fiction and adventure-oriented pulps. In other words, telling a good story, especially one that would appeal to the magazine's target audience of young male readers, appears to have been the primary goal.

Ray Palmer was an interesting person and had found success in the pulp magazine world. However, his work in the industry had never relied on bringing the public the news. His was not a world of hard facts. Indeed, that was hardly his interest. He was primarily a storyteller and businessperson, so factual reporting and standard journalistic practices were not his foci. Instead, Palmer made a living by publishing tales that captured the imagination. To do that, Palmer sometimes veered into hyperbole and outright fabrication. In that respect, Fred Nadis, a scholar of popular culture, concludes that Palmer was "ahead of the curve on cultural paranoia and conspiracy theorizing."[4]

It appears likely that Palmer's purposes in promoting Kenneth Arnold's story—and indeed, in promoting UFOs, in general, as subject matter—were very different from Arnold's motives. Arnold wanted to tell his version of events and gain credibility. Palmer wanted to provide readers with compelling subject matters that would garner sales. There is nothing inherently wrong with either goal, but they are very different from each other.

Whether Arnold realized at the outset that his editor and collaborator had a distinctly different agenda is an open question. It only may have dawned on him after the fact. Writer Fred Nadis reports that Arnold later said he did not know much about Palmer when he started communicating with him. It was only later, Arnold said, that he "found out he [Palmer] was connected with the type of publications that I not only never read but had always thought a gross waste of time."[5]

Kenneth Arnold was widely thought to be a sincere person, and it seems clear that his motivation in telling his story through an article in *Fate* was similarly genuine. Even if they were skeptical of his account of the June 1947 sighting, most people seemed to think Arnold honestly believed the story he told. Few people had ever doubted that he was an honest person without pretensions. That, at least, was true until people became aware that he would sell his story to Palmer.

Although Arnold is sometimes described as naïve, people generally have regarded him as a straightforward witness who believed what he said. However, this is not to say that Palmer entirely believed Arnold's account. For him, it may not have mattered if Arnold's recollections were accurate. As someone who was launching a new magazine, Palmer's interests presumably included making the new publication a success. And as a new media venture, that success would depend partially on driving sales and gaining attention.

Palmer already had the skills and experience necessary to convert unusual subject matter into magazine sales. Therefore, in helping Arnold tell his story, Palmer had ample means to shape the tale into something that would win over readers. He had done something somewhat similar before.

In the most well-known example, Palmer had purchased the rambling account that a reader from Pennsylvania sent to *Amazing Stories* several years earlier. The original author of this manuscript, a welder by trade, described strange robotic creatures who lived in caves and attacked humankind with advanced weapons. Despite the unusual nature of his story, the writer evidently regarded this material as a truthful account of actual, albeit bizarre, events. According to one report, he told Palmer that he first learned about these dangerous creatures from "voices in his equipment at a war plant" where he was working.[6]

The welder's unsolicited manuscript would probably have been regarded as unpublishable by most editors, even in the pulp industry. But Palmer saw it as raw material that he could use. So, he paid a nominal sum for the manuscript with the thought it could be the basis of articles for *Amazing Stories.* He then took this material and completely reworked it into an exciting series of articles about hidden creatures called "Deros."

Amazing Stories published Palmer's radical reworking of the material under various fabricated names in 1946, a year before the great UFO wave of 1947. The "Deros" stories proved to be a great success. Although many readers probably enjoyed them while knowing they were fiction, some enthusiastic readers took the stories as truth. A few went so far as to send letters to the magazine attesting to their own, very similar experiences.[7]

One of the people who evidently contacted Palmer at *Amazing Stories* was none other than Fred Crisman. It may be recalled that Crisman was later at the center of the Maury Island sighting.[8] And that was the incident that led Palmer to hire Kenneth Arnold to investigate Crisman's story.

Considering Palmer's role with the "Deros" stories, it is difficult to judge how much he ever actually believed Kenneth Arnold's flying saucer sighting or that UFOs were anything mysterious or otherworldly. Whatever his private thoughts, he could embrace the tale from a business point of view. Palmer seems to have had few misgivings about presenting material he knew was fanciful as though it were fact. The "Deros" articles demonstrated that. But this is hardly an indictment of Palmer. Indeed, such is the nature of many pulp magazines and much of popular culture.

Later readers of supermarket tabloids have often featured sensational, far-fetched headlines and encountered a similar approach in which news and entertainment are blurred. It can be entertaining to take such material, which is certainly—or almost certainly—fictional, as though it were true. But literal truth is not its appeal. In many corners of popular culture, content creators treat the facts loosely, at best. Some publications even signal this fact by employing tongue-in-cheek presentation styles that readers can choose to acknowledge or ignore. It can be similar to a magic show. Most people realize it is an illusion, but at the time, it is fun to pretend otherwise.

Palmer and Arnold collaborated not only in writing for publication in *Fate*. In 1952, they privately published a much-expanded version of Arnold's UFO story in book form under the title, *The Coming of the Saucers.* Again, Palmer seems to have played a significant role in shaping and probably writing the final manuscript. By that time, flying saucers and the extraterrestrial hypothesis were very closely linked in American popular culture. The book cemented Arnold's fame and, to some extent, brought further attention to Arnold's connection with Palmer, at least among some members of the public.

From what he said in interviews, Kenneth Arnold's thinking about UFOs continually evolved. Eventually, he seems to have embraced the idea that these were some sort of alien aircraft. He specifically said as much in conversation with Edward R. Murrow in 1950. In any case, his search for a satisfactory explanation, his perception that other people were judging him negatively, and his frustration with the very thing that made him famous were issues that remained unresolved for the rest of his life.

Meanwhile, it is still not possible to say for sure what Palmer thought about the subject. He continued to publish about UFOs and paranormal topics. He left Ziff-Davis and his job as editor of *Amazing Stories,* and by the mid–1950s, he also departed from *Fate,* the magazine he co-founded. He continued to be interested in occultism, but his private views are somewhat difficult to ascertain reliably.

Writer Joe Nickell has a story that adds to the mystery of Palmer's true beliefs. According to Nickell, a friend of his talked to Palmer in 1965 and asked, "what he thought about flying saucers." According to Nickell, Palmer replied, "What would you say if I told you the whole thing was a joke?"[9] Although this anecdote may or may not reflect anything substantive about him, it does seem consistent with Palmer's life. He was fascinated with unusual events, and he liked a good story. Yet, he may or may not have believed much of what he published.

Regardless of what was yet to come, when Edward R. Murrow interviewed Arnold in 1950, it was clear that the subject of unexplained aerial phenomena was not going away. To the dismay of military and intelligence officials, the matter was as firmly entrenched in the public's imagination as it had ever been.

⇒ 27 ⇐

Going Hollywood

Perhaps the most surprising thing about Hollywood's engagement with the UFO theme was that it did not materialize in any significant way until several years after the 1947 flying saucer craze. Considering that the topic leaped into national headlines within days of the Mount Rainier sighting and retained a strong cultural presence, the U.S. film industry's response time was slow. However, by the fall of 1949, word came that a flying saucer movie was in the works. The film's makers planned a quick production schedule. Within just a few months, a flying-saucer movie would make its way to American movie theaters and the increasingly popular drive-ins that dotted the landscape.

The film in question was a low-budget affair unassumingly called, *The Flying Saucer*. Despite having modest resources at his disposal, the movie's chief architect—a little-known actor-turned-director named Mikel Conrad—did his best to promote it. The first stories about the upcoming release started to appear in the second half of 1949, just as the Air Force's Project Grudge was trying to divert public interest away from the flying-saucer topic.

Publicists took the sensational approach with hopes of building interest in the film before its release. Somehow, Conrad reportedly had obtained "nine hundred feet of top-secret saucer footage," according to author David J. Hogan.[1] What is more, Conrad made other extraordinary claims as he tried to drum up enthusiasm for the upcoming release.

Conrad had been in Alaska as part of another production in 1948. It was there, he said, that he "heard about flying saucers."[2] That was evidently enough to give him the idea for a UFO film and a plan to return to Alaska in 1949 to begin filming background scenery for it.

When speaking to the press about the movie, publicists passed along a remarkable claim from Conrad. "I found a saucer," he reportedly said. "I'm not telling how." It is hard to know if very many people took Conrad at his word. Newspaper writer Aline Mosby suggests that this assertion stretched credulity to the point that it was "not believed even by one of his [Conrad's] press agents."[3]

Conrad's additional statements did not entirely clarify the actor's claims, though he was apparently referring to some sort of earthly, not extraterrestrial, device. "I have scenes of the saucer landing, taking off, flying, and doing tricks," he said. "The saucer is not created in miniature or by trick photography. It is a mechanical man-made object."[4]

The movie's publicists could not verify the claim since they had yet to see the alleged footage. Indeed, when Conrad said, "I'm not showing it to anyone yet,"[5] he evidently included his own team among those who would not be allowed to see it. Still, the publicists could report that this material was "locked in a bank vault" at the time for safekeeping. It is difficult to say whether this was literally true and, if so, whether the reason was really for security rather than a publicity stunt. Regardless of the exact facts, however, it was enough to generate some news coverage.

The Flying Saucer began appearing in U.S. venues by early 1950, just a few months later. Independently made without the financial backing of a major studio, it ended up being picked up by a minor distributor. By the time of its release, public expectations for the movie appear to have been relatively modest. Still, the film generated a few reviews as it opened on a haphazard schedule in various venues over the next few months.

Despite indications that this was a film that safely could be skipped, *The Flying Saucer* somehow came to the attention of *New York Time*'s Bosley Crowther. The venerable critic, whose reviews appeared in the influential paper regularly for many years, wrote about the film for the paper's January 5, 1950, edition. He was not impressed. "Except for some nice Alaskan scenery," he wrote, "it can go right on flying for all we care." The critic described *The Flying Saucer* using such terms as "clumsy," "obviously low-budget," and "awkward." Crowther added, "We hesitate, out of mercy, to fire even a critical shot at it."[6]

Out-of-town newspapers published reviews that were not much better. "It is a safe guess that no one's intelligence about the saucers will be measurably increased by a viewing of the film," wrote Gene Jannuzi in the *Pittsburgh Post-Gazette*. "It is not to Mr. Conrad's credit that he wrote the story and produced and directed the film," he added.[7]

Like the New York Times' critic, Gene Jannuzi was similarly not impressed by the results. One of Jannuzi's main complaints involved the assumptions that Conrad brought to the story. Recent flying saucer reports had "not been uninteresting," the reviewer said, and speculation that the unknown objects might be "interplanetary vehicles" gave the topic inherent interest. However, in Jannuzi eyes, Conrad's "tired little story" failed to take advantage of that potentially fascinating angle. By "making the saucer a man-devised machine" and placing it at the center of a familiar Russian espionage story, Conrad failed to make the most of the source material.[8]

Early in the film, viewers get a good idea about what is to come. One character, a government official, brings up the subject of flying saucers to an agent he plans to send on a mission. "There must be a spark of fire somewhere under all that smoke," the official says, referencing the many UFO reports in the news.

The agent, a skeptical character played by writer-producer-director Mikel Conrad, doubts that the saucers are anything more than "bunk." But the official (the agent's boss) argues that the mysterious objects could be enemy technology. "Russia apparently knows something we don't," he warns. "How would you feel if tomorrow, a flying saucer dropped an atomic bomb?"

From the outset, then, *The Flying Saucer* signals to viewers that they are about to see a story of espionage and international intrigue. And indeed, that is precisely what follows: a tale of spies versus spies in the Alaskan wilderness, a setting evidently chosen because it provided a picturesque backdrop for the otherwise bland and predictable spy story.

A flying saucer does appear in the film, just as Conrad's press agents had foretold in the campaign to drum up interest in the movie before its release. However, it is onscreen for only a minute or two in what appears to be a standard low-budget movie special effect. In one of the quick close-ups of the craft, it seems to be modeled after the circular experimental aircraft that had appeared in newspapers in previous years or perhaps inspired by magazine illustrations from *Popular Mechanics.* In other words, the saucer is familiar and rather unimposing. In the end, despite the film's title implying otherwise, a flying saucer plays a minor role in the movie. Indeed, the saucer could easily have been replaced with any other valuable secret, and it would not have changed the basic outline of the film very much.

The Flying Saucer was the first and possibly one of the least interesting films about flying saucers ever made. At the time, however, it signaled that the floodgates were about to open. Indeed, within a matter of months, numerous UFO-related movies went into production. Unlike *The Flying Saucer,* almost all subsequent films with this theme abandoned the premise that the saucers were human made. Instead, most UFO films in the 1950s based their stories on extraterrestrial alien threats and invasions.

The UFO craze of 1947 eventually helped propel the idea of visitors from other worlds into the mainstream of American culture, even if many—perhaps most—people did not take that thought seriously initially. Still, it was not a new idea. Serialized films had been home to science fiction and extraterrestrial life in the past. Several series featuring the swashbuckling space-hero Flash Gordon were very well known to the American public. The first of these, simply titled *Flash Gordon,* was released in 1936. Due to its popularity, Universal issued a sequel, *Flash Gordon's Trip to Mars,* in 1938 and then another, *Flash Gordon Conquers Mars,* in 1940. Although the heyday of science-fiction movies featuring space-alien themes was yet to come, audiences were already well accustomed to the idea. Indeed, popular culture overall had been selling space aliens as a concept for decades.

At the halfway point of the 20th century, the emergence of the flying saucer phenomenon, coupled with rising public anticipation that advances in rocket science might soon make space flight a reality, brought this theme into the spotlight. As American interest in all things space-related grew in the late 1940s and 1950s, the conditions were right for a rapid increase in stories about extraterrestrials. The American movie business was ready to capitalize on this trend.

In the autumn of 1950, Republic Pictures, a relatively small firm specializing in low-budget movies, released a flying-saucer-oriented serial that somewhat set the tone for many future UFO films. *Flying Disc Man from Mars,* produced on a shoestring budget, was a 12-chapter serialized film primarily aimed at the youth market. It told the story of a malicious Martian, a being named Mota, who plans to invade the earth.

Cheaply made, the film was a minor picture in almost every respect, even in the category of film serials, which hardly had a reputation for high quality. Regardless of these drawbacks, however, *Flying Disc Man from Mars* brought a powerful theme to American cinemas: the notion that UFOs represented extraterrestrial aliens coming with malicious intent. Indeed, the public would almost always associate UFOs with beings from other worlds from around this time forward. This idea, which was very uncommon during the UFO wave of 1947 and some months after, became so dominant that it would usually be taken for granted.

Hollywood did not invent the idea that UFOs were extraterrestrial and could be a threat. Nor, for that matter, did Donald Keyhoe, who championed the idea in his book *The Flying Saucers Are Real* and other writings.[9] But Hollywood and other forms of popular culture took this basic motif, elaborated it in multiple incarnations, and played a crucial role in cementing the association between UFOs and an alien menace in the popular mind. Numerous 1950s films, in particular, took the idea and made it the centerpiece of their stories.

Two films from the following year, 1951, demonstrate this point. Director Robert Wise's classic, *The Day the Earth Stood Still*, brought a flying saucer story to the screen that was far more effective than the entries in the genre from the previous year. And more than that, his film contains many elements of the broader cultural narrative about UFOs that were starting to take hold in the public's mind.

The plot concerns powerful alien beings who possess mind-boggling technology and whose motives are assumed to be vaguely threatening. The U.S. military is also front and center as they seek to keep a lid on disclosures about an alien visitor as much as possible to avoid panic. These facets of *The Day the Earth Stood Still*'s fictional story were similar to the types of things Donald Keyhoe had represented as facts.

Interestingly, *The Day the Earth Stood Still* was based on a short story by Harry Bates in a 1950 issue of the *Astounding Science Fiction* pulp magazine. It was published 12 years before the flying saucer phenomenon beginning in 1947. Yet, Bates' tale and the film adaptation that followed fit congruently with the saucer theories that Keyhoe and others applied to UFO sightings. There were some differences with Keyhoe's ideas in the details. However, in general terms, there was also much overlap.

Another 1951 movie, director Christian Nyby's *The Thing from Another World,* offers a far more secretive and menacing situation than *The Day the Earth Stood Still*. The story involves a flying saucer that crashes in a remote Arctic location. Most of the plot involves military personnel in an isolated military outpost fight for their lives against a deadly alien creature who survived the crash. Still, like *The Day the Earth Stood Still,* flying saucers are associated with something strange, otherworldly, and inherently dangerous.

These science-fiction films, and many that followed, reinforced the rising narrative in which saucers are interpreted as extraterrestrial threats. It was a theme that already was crystalizing in American throughout pop culture, much to the dismay of the Pentagon, which was trying to put the subject to rest. Unfortunately for military officials, lingering unknowns about UFO sightings continued even as popular culture embraced the idea that saucers and threatening aliens made good stories. This presented nearly ideal conditions for fictional UFO stories and official statements about the ongoing mystery to become intertwined in the popular imagination. As time passed, it would sometimes be difficult to sort out which ideas about unidentified aerial phenomena referred to actual events versus those originating in fiction.

≈ 28 ≈

The UFO Myth

Although not anywhere near as often as before, new reports of strange objects continued in the years immediately following 1947. By then, unidentified aerial objects were securely part of the cultural landscape. Thinking about the subject had evolved from the days of the 1947 wave of sightings. The frequent appearance of speculative writings about UFOs, combined with many works of related fiction, created a confusing environment. For the average person, it was difficult to know what to believe.

The sheer volume of UFO material began to crystallize as a cultural narrative, or, as the aerospace historian Curtis Peebles described it, as an "emerging flying saucer myth."[1] The word "myth" often appears in discussions about unidentified aerial phenomena, especially when there is mention of extraterrestrial aliens. Taken uncritically, however, it is an ambiguous, problematic label. It is not always evident what people mean when they use it about this topic.

In everyday language, many people use the word *myth* to refer to something that is not true. However, that is only one way to interpret the word. Traditionally, the term simply refers to a widely shared cultural story that is meaningful to a group, often serving to explain or justify something. Myths of creation, myths about the founding of nations, and myths about the origins of natural phenomena are common examples. These stories may be embellished. They are not necessarily entirely false.

Making things even more complicated, literary theorists, philosophers, and other scholars sometimes use the term in specialized ways that can seem obscure and rarified to the average person. But even within academic circles, it is not always clear what someone means when applying this label to something. Roland Barthes famously used the word in one specific way. Carl Jung used it in another.

The upshot of this is that when someone describes UFOs as a myth, it may not always be apparent what it means in a given context. On a very different matter, Bill Clinton, then president of the United States, once infamously tried to finesse a problematic situation by saying, "It depends upon what the meaning of the word 'is' is." It may have seemed as though he was dodging the subject to many people, but in a way, he had a point. The precise meaning that people take from words can vary dramatically. Similarly, the meaning people take from statements about UFOs being a "myth" greatly depends on exactly how the word is interpreted. On a superficial level, parsing language in this way can seem trivial, but at a deeper level, it is not. The conclusions that people draw are conditioned, at least in part, by the implications that are hidden within the language used to describe a given situation.

Despite these difficulties, there may be some usefulness in thinking about UFOs as myth—providing the term is used carefully. If by "myth," the intended meaning is that something consists of lies, then that adds nothing new to an understanding of the subject, and it is essentially useless. However, if UFOs-as-myth refers to a particular narrative and set of ideas about the alleged objects, the label can be helpful.

It is safe to say that by the early 1950s, a standard set of ideas about UFOs had already gained a foothold in the cultural landscape. UFOs were already the subject of myth, in other words, and as such, they called to mind a specific story, a particular narrative.

Myths do not need to be literally true to be influential. They help shape how things are understood by offering a general framework for interpretation. Indeed, as the eminent anthropologist Claude Lévi-Strauss wrote in a wholly different context many years ago, "myths operate in men's [sic] minds without their being aware of the fact."[2] For anyone with more than a passing interest in UFO as a social phenomenon, this observation suggests that it may be helpful to think about the UFO myth as a story in motion, as something that has meant different things to different people, at times on a subconscious level.

Some of the earliest incarnations of the UFO myth, circa 1950, included some specific core elements. First was the idea that the unknown flying objects were the vehicles of travelers from another world. These spaceships supposedly brought alien visitors who were here to observe or conquer humanity. The second was the notion that the U.S. government knew much more than it was willing to let on. According to the myth, officials intentionally kept Americans in the dark, possibly to avoid causing panic but perhaps because of more sinister motives.[3]

The UFO myth has lurked in the background for the better part of a century. It is present in almost all discussions about the topic. Its strong presence as a familiar narrative has complicated efforts to untangle the original flying saucer story of the late 1940s. Whether or not people take it as an accurate accounting of the phenomenon, this general template is widely known. It is a lens that arguably colors claims and counterclaims, old and new, about the contentious subject.

Yet, the UFO myth has not been static. It slowly changed as a steady stream of new reports, new details, and alleged details of old accounts altered the narrative. For example, months, years, and even decades after the actual events of 1947, statements of alleged witnesses whose stories had never been published before would appear in articles and interviews, often adding some new detail or incident from the past.

In addition, media treatments in print, on-screen, and online have added other layers to the story. From outright fiction to the crossover category of infotainment, many new elements have been added to the original cultural narrative. For instance, numerous documentaries and quasi-documentary screen treatments, including contemporary television series such as *Ancient Aliens*, have blurred the boundaries between the probable and the improbable. Endlessly rehashing old reports with supposedly new and startling revelations about them, many of these productions aim to entertain more than inform.

All of these developments have added new complexities to the myth that first emerged in the mid–20th century. For some, these may have raised more questions than they answered about who knew what, when, and how. Some aspects of the 1947 Roswell case illustrate this point. Although that incident is perhaps the most widely known from the 1947 UFO wave, it has a curious history. To briefly recap this episode, the first reports out of Roswell caused a sensation, but this proved short-lived. Indeed, Air Force officials quickly dismissed the Roswell case as a simple misidentification, and the public soon lost interest. After that, people still talked about unexplained aerial phenomena, but they rarely mentioned Roswell. This cultural amnesia, as it were, persisted for a generation. But then, in the late 1970s, UFO writers and the media resurrected the case. Only then did Roswell gain a secure foothold in the media spotlight, where it has remained ever since.

In an in-depth examination of this incident, anthropologists Benson Saler and Charles A. Zigler and atmospheric physicist Charles B. Moore offer an enlightening dissection of the case's long evolution. Their book, *UFO Crash at Roswell: The Genesis of a Modern Myth*, published in 1997 by the Smithsonian Institution, still remains among the most thoughtful about the subject. Within its pages, the authors trace the development of the Roswell "myth," as they call it, over its first

50 years, identifying at least six different versions of the story in the process.

As they note, accounts about Roswell from 1947 contain no references to authorities discovering extraterrestrial aliens' bodies. By the late 1970s, however, a modified version of the incident surfaced that included this surprising assertion. According to new claims, the Air Force had discovered the corpses of tiny alien beings in 1947. This contention, although coming years after the actual events, soon became woven into the ongoing myth.[4]

The media had never stopped releasing books and articles about UFOs in the years since the mid-century. Such items mainly appealed to a niche market, but they never lacked readers. In this vein, in the late 1970s, UFO researcher Stanton Friedman spoke with Jesse Marcel, a former Air Force officer involved in the Roswell incident. Marcel was one of the few people known to have seen the alleged crash site in New Mexico firsthand in 1947. At that time, there is nothing to suggest that he thought there was anything extraterrestrial about the incident. By the 1970s, however, he had changed his tune. Indeed, his new version of descriptions of what had happened prominently included deceased aliens.[5]

The crux of Marcel's version of events in the late 1970s and 1980s was the claim that he had always known that Roswell involved extraterrestrials but that his superiors ordered him to keep quiet about it. General Roger Ramey, who was deeply involved in the case in 1947 and may have known more details, had died years earlier, and so his side of the story would never be known. In any case, Marcel's revised account of the events was enough to draw significant attention from the popular media.

In short order, the Friedman connection led to Marcel's new claims appearing in a low-budget 1979 documentary called *UFOs Are Real*. The story also appeared in the *Nation Enquirer* tabloid as a major feature. Then, a popular syndicated television series entitled *In Search Of* devoted an episode to the Roswell events and Marcel's claims about it. The refreshed version of the Roswell events quickly picked up steam.

With decades-old events in New Mexico back in the public eye, two writers, Charles Berlitz and William Moore, decided to publish a book about the topic. Berlitz was well-known to readers with interests in the paranormal. He previously had written books based on unusual and paranormal subjects, including *The Bermuda Triangle*. The new book, entitled *The Roswell Incident* (published in 1980), grabbed attention. It further propelled the revised, alien-centric version of the Roswell case into the spotlight, where it has remained ever since that time.

These 1980s era versions of the Roswell story differed profoundly from accounts that appeared in 1947. In addition to claims about alien bodies, there were new assertions about recovered extraterrestrial technology and expanded ideas about government conspiracies. According to the new story, the aliens had died when their flying disc crashed in the Roswell area. The Air Force supposedly whisked the alien corpses away under a veil of secrecy and took them to a secure military installation. In some articulations of the case, a local witness reportedly saw the bodies and examined them.[6] In that variation of the story, officials had ordered the man to stay quiet about his involvement or face serious repercussions.

Somewhat later, in the 1990s, the Air Force re-investigated the Roswell case after much public pressure. Their new detailed report, issued in 1995, refuted the post–1970s version of the Roswell.[7] Indeed, their investigation mostly clung to the original account of the incident from 1947, although the authors did add some new explanations—the formerly secret Project Mogul chief among them.[8] That was enough to send the Roswell story back into the realm of a big misunderstanding for many people. For many of the most committed advocates of the extraterrestrial version of the incident, however, the Air Force's updated explanations made little difference. They still thought the government was lying.

As new cases and alleged details have been added to the Roswell story over the decades, a predictable cycle has emerged. As the story changed, stern denials almost always usually followed each major new claim. The true believers (to borrow Eric Hoffer's label from a different context) and the skeptics both claimed to know the truth throughout. However, they strongly disagree about what that truth is.

Neither side has budged. Perhaps this is not surprising. In the modern world, truth is contested terrain across many subject areas, including this one. Under present conditions, it often seems that truth has become a matter of what people choose to believe.

Three-quarters of a century after the 1947 UFO craze, surveys suggest the public is caught somewhere in the middle, believing some things from each side of the debate. A recent Gallup poll from 2019, for example, indicated that roughly 70 percent of Americans thought U.S. government officials knew "more about UFOs than it is telling us." However, the same poll revealed that only "33 percent of Americans believe alien spacecraft have visited Earth at some point."[9] Meanwhile, a different survey from 2020 indicated that if the officials "had evidence of UFOs," 56 percent of respondents believed the government would "hide it from the public."[10]

Interestingly, the expanded and evolving UFO myth of the late-1970s came on the heels of a massive loss of faith in government and its institutions. By the late 1970s, this breakdown of confidence, precipitated by massive institutional failures of the 1960s and early 1970s, became broadly evident.[11] People were ready to believe that the government was lying to them regularly—not just about UFOs but about many other subjects. For many Americans, the Watergate scandal, the Pentagon Papers, and a host of other issues suggested the government could not be trusted.

In the same era, movies such as 1977's *Star Wars* sparked renewed mainstream interest in science-fiction films and, by extension, in UFOs. Although less discussed, Steven Spielberg's *Close Encounters of the Third Kind,* also released in 1977, brought much of the mythology of UFOs to a broad audience. Complete with a saucer-like spaceship, glimpses of odd-looking aliens, men in black coats, and a government cover-up, it was almost a primer of the so-called "extraterrestrial hypothesis." In the years that followed, aliens and UFOs often appeared on the screen in both movies and television. The intricately plotted television series, *The X-Files,* which premiered in 1993, offered viewers a kaleidoscopic view of UFO mythology presented in a factional guise.

In some ways, the turn of events that thrust Roswell back to center stage in the ongoing and evolving UFO myth was significant. That case, in particular, has become a battleground event, but there is little agreement about UFOs as a broader phenomenon overall. Supporters and debunkers of the so-called extraterrestrial hypothesis have endlessly exchanged barbs and warring assertions.

It is well beyond the scope or purpose of this study to fully evaluate the many new claims or voluminous incarnations of the Roswell story or about UFO sightings, more generally. Despite numerous revelations, hypotheses, and allegations to date, it is possible there are some secrets or overlooked evidence still to be revealed. But even if that proves to be the case, there are enough lingering questions and ambiguities to make speaking in absolutes quite tricky. Although there have been many more experiences and much more analysis since that time, today's understanding is not much different from Carl Jung's conclusions in the late 1950s.

For their part, the Air Force and other government agencies have mostly dismissed new claims and offered explanations. They have continued to support the original contention that they knew nothing about aliens or extraterrestrial technologies. In 2021, a Congressionally mandated report from the Office of National Intelligence indicated that some UFO sightings, including many that were relatively recent, still lacked conclusive explanation.[12] In essence, it was not a very different conclusion from those made by Air Force investigators 70 years earlier.

Meanwhile, for most of the public, the topic of UFOs has not been a central concern. Life has not stopped when new sightings or alleged further details have been added to the constantly evolving UFO myth. Instead, most people go about their business as usual. Only a few have made the UFOs the center of their lives.

Yet, for those deeply committed to one perspective or another, almost no detail has been too small to be a source of controversy. Intricate and passionately argued books, reports, and articles continue to appear, most claiming to offer new insights and new truths. Metaphorically, every tree in the UFO forest has been the subject of intense scrutiny, but a clear view of the whole forest has been hard to find. Meanwhile, the debate rages on. An epic struggle to define the truth continues. Since much of the society no longer agree about what constitutes "truth" or a "fact" in almost any context, it seems unlikely to stop anytime soon.

But perhaps there is another way to look at things. In their compelling stories, myths reveal much about the society in which they thrive. Thinking of myths as right or wrong in absolute terms may be a mistake.

≡ 29 ≡

A Tangled Web

Three centuries before Kenneth Arnold's flying saucer sighting, Church officials hauled Galileo Galilei, then 69 years old, before a tribunal in Rome for the fight of his life. It was September 1632, and the famous scientist had recently published *Dialogues on the Two Chief Systems of the World.* The book caused much trouble for Galileo. Within its pages, he said the Earth is not the center of the solar system but instead that it and other planets revolved around the Sun. It was a simple statement that aligned with observational evidence. Authorities considered it heresy that contradicted official Church doctrine, however. Galileo's claims challenged the prevailing view and, by extension, the Church's authority.

Galileo was hardly the first person to make such claims. Even in the medieval European world, Nicolaus Copernicus, among others, had already figured out that the Earth was not the solar system's center. But previous claims of this sort had not attracted enough attention to elicit the Church's full fury. Galileo's case was different. Officials were not about to let it slide.

At trial, Galileo had little opportunity to convince his accusers that his theories were correct. Instead, the proceedings seemed destined to go only one way—the Church's way. The odds were stacked against him, and authorities threatened severe repercussions, including torture and even death, if he did not relent. Having no real choice, then, Galileo eventually renounced the ideas that had caused his troubles. In the end, he lived under house arrest for the rest of his life.

The Church showed its power with the verdict. Daring to challenge officially sanctioned beliefs would not be tolerated. It did not matter that Galileo knew much more about the planets than Church officials and or that he had evidence to back up his claims. What mattered to the authorities was that Galileo had contradicted them and their teachings. In that situation, power trumped evidence.

Questioning institutional power can be a dicey proposition. During the Renaissance, astronomer Galileo Galilei—like Nicolaus Copernicus and others before him—challenged Church doctrine by asserting that the earth did not lie at the center of the universe. For that transgression, Galileo was placed under house arrest for the remainder of his life (New York Public Library).

According to legend, Galileo muttered, *"E pur si muove"* ("And yet it [the Earth] moves," in English) under his breath at the end of the ordeal. Indeed, renouncing his published ideas did not make them untrue. But the tribunal was not only about truth in the abstract. It was also about *whose* truth would carry the day. The famous astronomer had staked out a position that contradicted Church power, and for that, he paid the price.

As Galileo's case shows, it is not always easy nor safe to question official views. The asymmetry of power can play a significant part in that. Still, the pressure to conform can take many forms. At times, authorities may push a particular perspective openly and without subtlety. In other cases, such efforts can take a low-key and less obvious approach.

In mid–20th-century America, the managers of Project Grudge tried to push public attention away from UFOs as soon as they concluded that continued public scrutiny was problematic. UFO theories that did not square with official conclusions were to be marginalized to achieve that objective. This was a relatively easy and low-cost way to throw cold water on nonconforming perspectives since, in some ways, things were already headed in that direction.

From the beginning, many witnesses to strange occurrences worried if they came forward, they would become objects of ridicule. Even before Project Grudge, for example, the suggestion that the mysterious discs were from another world elicited often raised eyebrows or a smirk from many people. For the most part, all Project Grudge had to do was nudge the public a bit more in that direction.

The framing of UFOs as a fringe topic has not been without ramifications. Indeed, the early marginalization of the UFOs phenomenon surely has not furthered understanding of it. Often treated as a novelty subject, it typically has attracted little serious attention from researchers, academic specialists, and others from outside the committed community of UFO enthusiasts who otherwise might have been able to shed light on some aspects of it.

Take the so-called extraterrestrial hypothesis as an example. Surveys suggest that a substantial number of people give this idea at least some consideration. Yet, many people do not want to be too closely identified with that way of thinking in public. The idea that UFOs are alien spacecraft is still regarded as outside the mainstream in much of the public realm, especially if a person argues too passionately in its favor. The point here is that social pressure, as much as a scientific argument, appears to shape how the subject is presented and interpreted in the everyday world.

Interestingly, the extraterrestrial-focused UFO cultural narrative, though sometimes marginalized in the mainstream, has been embraced fully by a number of media outlets at the margins. One example can be found in a tabloid launched by the publisher of the *National Enquirer* in 1979. Indeed, that publication, *World Weekly News*, consistently adopted an outlandish take on supposed news events and has published many stories about UFOs. Over the years, numerous stories about aliens and "close encounters" have made outrageous claims, most of which are too ridiculous to be taken seriously. That is not to say, however, that such stories have not been widely consumed.

In just one example, a decade after it first appeared in supermarkets and newsstands, an issue *World Weekly News* featured what its editors called "the story the world has been waiting for"—an "exclusive interview with a space alien."[1] According to this piece, an extraterrestrial being named Bertan (supposedly from the planet Det) had come to Earth seeking "cooperation, resources, land and wealth." The article quotes the supposed alien saying that the beings of Det could bring cures to diseases and new technological marvels. If humankind rejected their requests, however, the beings from Det "could also bring you the wrath of hell," the article continued. Bertan also supposedly told the reporter, "I emphasize that we come in peace. We ask you to prepare for us."

As presented in *World Weekly News*, the "space alien" statements seem absurd and possibly even comical. Yet, on one level, there is nothing in the story that differed substantially from some by-then standard parts of the UFO cultural narrative. *World Weekly News* simply presented an exaggerated version of the UFO myth, which many people at least think is possible, as it had developed over the years.

It is difficult to imagine that the standard narrative could be pushed much farther away from respectability than in this type of presentation. Removed from a serious context and instead appearing in a publication specializing in the outlandish, the UFO myth is made to look foolish. It is evident here that context matters. What can look reasonable—or at least worth a second thought—in one context can look completely absurd in another.

Yet, although it is an infrequent occurrence, the marginalized ideas of one era sometimes are accepted as mainstream thought in another. Thus, it is possible that the extraterrestrial hypothesis, which is currently rejected by most institutional authorities and experts, could eventually shed its dubious image and attract more serious consideration. But this would seemingly require a change in mindset and some sort of proof or validation. And for those wanting the extraterrestrial theory to get a broad reconsideration, these, to date, have proven to be imposing hurdles.

For one thing, alleged proof of the extraterrestrial hypothesis tends to be vague, circumstantial, and ambiguous in the eyes of the people who do not share enthusiasm for the extraterrestrial perspective. Although legitimate hints of something out of the ordinary do surface from time to time, there has never been widespread agreement that available evidence or testimony has proven the extraterrestrial case.

Even university professors have run into this problem. For example, when an object from outside the solar system, dubbed Oumuamua, was spotted by astronomers in late 2017, Harvard professor and theoretical physicist Avi Loeb offered bold and controversial speculation. Maybe the object "was artificially made, perhaps a piece of technology or some debris from a faraway alien civilization," he told the press.[2] It was an idea that substantially deviated from what people expected from an academic. Reactions were quick. Loeb had veered from his lane, and for that, he quickly faced a wall of skepticism.

Whatever one makes of competing claims about UFOs, it is clear that three-quarters of a century after the saucer sightings of 1947, the story of UFOs has become immense, complicated, and controversial. It can take significant effort to see through the haze and get a clear view of precisely what happened that summer long ago. And even then, some things remain unclear and hard to understand.

Despite thousands of reports and experiences since 1947, the UFO sightings of that year remain an essential episode. Indeed, it set the stage for the unfolding decades of the UFO phenomenon that were to come. Unexplained objects in the sky had been seen many times before, of course, but it was not until the 1947 flying disc craze that it blossomed into a worldwide phenomenon. For that reason, the original story of those short weeks remains worthy of continuing thought.

Scholar Nassim Nicholas Taleb once observed, "I know that history is going to be dominated by an improbable event. I just don't know what that event will be."[3] While UFOs have not dominated history, the abrupt appearance of so many sightings in 1947 was more than enough to launch an ongoing phenomenon, setting off new speculations about life on other planets, massive government conspiracies, among others.

It would probably be a mistake to regard any of these developments as inevitable. Indeed, there was much about the early UFO story that could have gone another way. When Kenneth Arnold thought he saw nine objects streaking along the horizon near Mount Rainier, no one—including Arnold himself—knew that his experience would become memorable. Earlier sightings of a similar nature seldom made much of a long-term impact. There was no reason to think this one would be any different.

However, things *were* different this time, and Arnold's case did not recede into the background as earlier reports had done. A constellation of circumstances came together in just the right way to transform his sighting into a cultural milestone. He was at just the right place and at the right time to see unusual light in the distance, and he found an eager and willing audience for his story immediately upon landing his plane.

Moreover, journalists of a local paper were in the office the next day and had a hunch that the story would be interesting reading. And then wire services decided it was worth distributing widely. None of these or other details could be taken for granted.

A slight change to even one of these or other related circumstances could have sent the story into oblivion. But that was not what happened. Instead, Arnold's sighting of something—whatever it was—made its way into households across the country and around the world. The story of flying saucers resonated with the public in various ways. Many people soon reported seeing the same kinds of things. Within days, the floodgates opened. UFOs entered the cultural landscape and stayed there.

The Mount Rainier sighting, although possessing some similarities to previous reports of unexplained aerial phenomena, was unique in many ways. Arnold's experience may not have been entirely different from earlier reports at other times and places, but the way it was picked up by the press and widely distributed in the late days of June 1947 was. As presented in the media, Arnold's story attained an almost instant resonance that earlier reports had not. It was front-page news in a very literal sense.

Coming at a pivotal moment in the postwar Atomic Age, the Mount Rainier sighting and UFO stories that followed all fit congruently with the zeitgeist of the era. These accounts came at a time when the public looked out toward wide-open possibilities. In a period of rapid scientific and technological progress, reports of strange objects in the sky struck a chord with much of the American public.

At the same time, the early postwar years were dangerous times. With the atom bomb lurking in the background and advances in rocketry—hence, missile technology—coming at a breakneck speed, the skies probably potentially menacing to many people. Unusual and inexplicable objects in the air were bound to capture public interest given those conditions. The foreboding mood of the developing Cold War assured that. Under the circumstances, news stories about flying saucers in the Pacific Northwest had an outsized impact.

Yet, the unknowns in Arnold's account may have had the most influence in pushing his flying saucer story from something personal to something of national consequence. His description of the incident was tantalizing. It possessed just enough odd details to make it noteworthy, but it left enough open questions to make it ripe for speculating and wondering what it all meant. The many conjectures, which people took in various and sometimes opposite directions, attempted to somehow convert the unknown into the known—to make something potentially problematic because it was not understood into something that could be tamed.

By mid–July, the astonishing scope and scale of flying saucer sightings throughout the country made an impression too big to ignore. The 1947 UFO wave presented all the necessary elements for mythmaking. It also set the stage for numerous attempts to rationalize the episode's oddities and reconcile the strange events with the anxieties of the age.

≋ 30 ≋

Project Blue Book

Five years after Roswell and the 1947 flurry of UFO reports, another series of sightings surprised the nation. It may have looked like a case of art imitating life. The location of these latest reports was far removed from remote regions such as Mountain Rainer or Roswell, New Mexico. Indeed, the new sightings involved the skies over Washington, D.C. It was the same setting as the popular movie, *The Day the Earth Stood Still*, released just ten months earlier.

In the classic film, an alien spacecraft lands on a baseball field in the middle of the city. In real-life cases, no one claimed a flying saucer touched down in Washington. Yet, the appearance of unknown objects in the capital region's airspace was enough to cause concerns. That was especially the case because the latest reports did not come from untrained observers or people without expertise about objects in the sky—far from it. Instead, the witnesses were experienced air traffic controllers whose radar screens showed something very unusual on the afternoon of July 19, 1952.

A subsequent wire story reported that the Air Force had quickly launched an investigation of this incident that occurred "virtually in its own back yard."[1] According to published reports, adding weight to the mystery, "two airline pilots and a newsman saw eerie lights" only a few hours later. Something did not seem right. Journalist Jack Rutledge said that authorities were initially unsure if they should classify the sightings as "flying saucers." Whatever label they used, however, "all agreed it was unusual."[2]

At that period in the Cold War, it was always true that the slightest hint of an unknown aerial intrusion over the free world's center would be examined thoroughly. Officials needed to be entirely sure that the capital remained secure. Therefore, it was not surprising that the Air Force's Air Technical Intelligence Center at Ohio's Wright-Patterson base quickly became involved in the investigation, just as it had done in many cases before.

In addition to having first-rate witnesses and radar evidence, these new Washington-area reports somewhat stood apart from many previous incidents. For one thing, the objects appeared to travel at "a relatively slow speed" much of the time. Indeed, official estimates were in the range of only 100 to 120 miles per hour. Yet, at other times the objects quickly sped up, reaching a velocity that was far beyond that of "normal airplanes."[3] It all seemed very odd.

As would be expected, military officials were not happy about these incidents and the resulting public attention. They had been trying to downplay UFOs for months, and new sightings in the capital region were an added complication. Unfortunately for them, however, after the first reports, further capital region sightings were to come.

A week later, for instance, radar at the civilian control center at National Airport (now Ronald Reagan Washington National Airport) tracked new unknown objects. That incident lasted about four hours. At some points, the number of unidentified objects reached as many as 12 in that sighting, which prompted the Air Force to send Lockheed F-94 fighter jets to investigate. No answers were forthcoming, however. Indeed, the mission quickly turned into "a futile attempt to intercept [the] mysterious glowing objects."[4] Reports indicated that the Air Force pilots spotted the objects but could not catch up to them.

These and other sightings briefly brought UFOs back into the news at a level that had been seen for a while. The Washington angle was probably the most disturbing development for officials. After all, the Cold War was still raging, and suspicions of all sorts were running high. The author of a later study published in an internal CIA peer-reviewed journal—hardly a publication prone to siding with the UFO community—concludes that the Washington sightings "alarmed the Truman administration" and that these incidents led the CIA to create "a special study group ... to review the situation."[5] The members of that group mainly worried about earthly threats from America's Cold War enemies. In that context, the potential danger they saw in UFOs was that the strange objects might "touch off mass hysteria and panic" throughout the country. More than that, they were uneasy about the possibility that "the Soviets might use UFO sightings to overload the U.S. air warning system so that it could not distinguish read largest from phantom UFOs."[6]

Unknown to the general public, Air Force officials had remained wary of the unexplained phenomena even after announcing the closure of Project Grudge. Indeed, well before the capital sightings, authorities realized that 1952 was shaping up to be a banner year in the persisting UFO phenomenon. By late 1951, they already decided that a renewed effort to get to the bottom of the most perplexing incidents was warranted. Quietly, the head of Air Force intelligence operations, Major General C.B. Cabell, authorized a new push to investigate the phenomenon.[7] By the spring, that new program, Project Blue Book, was at work, trying to make sense of the latest cases and older ones that remained hard to understand.[8]

Throughout 1952 and by the Air Force's own reckoning, there were more than 1500 UFO sightings. Compared to the years before, it was a massive number. What is more, of this considerable total, more than 300 of them—including some of the sightings around the capital—could not be explained. The highest number of unexplained sightings in recent years had been 22. Something was going on in 1952, though officials did not know what that was.

The Cold War does not necessarily explain why there was such a big jump in reports in 1952. Still, that context does shed light on the urgency the military placed on investigating the phenomenon. At the time, Americans were stuck in the Korean War. The United States and its allies initially met with much success in that conflict. However, the U.S. faced increasing difficulties after Chinese troops unexpectedly joined the fight in support of the North Korean communists in October of 1950. For months, the situation threatened to get out of hand. As the war dragged on, General Douglas MacArthur, a seasoned veteran with a somewhat grandiose manner, sought authorization to use nuclear weapons against the North Korean and Chinese troops. President Truman strongly disagreed and fired him in the spring of 1951. That move proved to be controversial with the American public. But by raising the potential for atomic warfare in an era when the Soviets also possessed nuclear capabilities, it was clear that the times were indeed dangerous.

Moreover, in the early 1950s, Americans were still reeling from the Soviet Union's acquisition of atomic bomb technology a few years earlier. Many still did not believe that the USSR could have developed that capability so quickly on its own. In some ways, those suspicions were reasonable.

Americans had been surprised when the United States unveiled the atom bomb in 1945. The Soviet leadership, however, was not. In fact, Moscow quietly had been working on atomic weapons development for several years. Stalin had initiated a home-grown atomic weapon development project as early as 1943, although this was not widely known, even to American leaders.

As Americans later suspected, throughout the development process, the Soviets aimed to augment their in-house research with information that could be obtained via espionage activities. When it became clear that the USSR had succeeded in obtaining atomic weapons in the summer of 1949, many people in the United States felt that this was so fast that their nation must have been betrayed. Soon, the search was on for Americans who might have turned on their country and slipped secrets to Russian spies.

The following year, officials had investigated possible atomic espionage and were ready to make arrests. Of those detained, it was the cases of Julius Rosenberg and his wife Ethel Rosenberg that captured the nation's attention. Charged with wartime espionage, they were tried, convicted, and sentenced to death in 1951 to much public fanfare.

The 1952 flurry of UFO reports occurred against the background of these and other tense conditions. Indeed, given that environment, it is understandable why Air Force officials determined that they should make additional efforts to deal with the many unresolved UFO cases. This context, in which suspicion and extreme anxiousness about potential communist threats were all around, also might shed some light on why so many reports were filed that year, as well. America was on high alert, possibly even hypervigilant, and anything out of the ordinary drew attention. Unexplained aerial phenomena fit that bill. Still, these background factors may not completely clear up the situation. Context probably was a major contributing factor to the new wave of sightings, but it does not seem to be the only one. Considering all this, the Air Force's decision to breathe new life into UFO investigations seems sensible.

In 1951, the remnants of Project Grudge only had a single investigator, Edward J. Ruppelt.[9] That was nowhere near enough personnel to attempt the sort of study and analysis the Air Force envisioned. However, although he was only one person, Ruppelt was open-minded, well organized, and competent. When his superiors decided to reinvigorate Grudge (which was renamed Project Blue Book in 1952), Ruppelt was a logical choice to lead the new effort.

Over the months of 1952, undoubtedly hastened by the high-profile reports from Washington in July, officials increased Project Blue Book's budget and gave it more resources. Through it all, Ruppelt generally brought an attitude and a concerted effort to the investigations. He later wrote about his strong desire to be objective, which to him meant not deciding in advance what the UFOs were or were not.[10]

Regardless of their allegiances on the controversial subject, most observers seem to regard Ruppelt as a thoughtful, dutiful investigator determined to discover what the facts were and what could be said about them. To his credit, he navigated the earliest days of Project Blue Book through a brief period when sightings spiked, and the public suddenly wanted to know everything there was to know about UFOs.

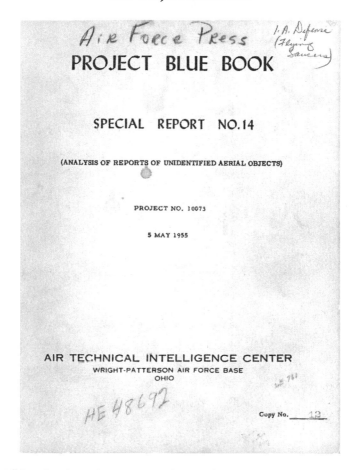

Project Blue Book took over UFO data collection and investigatory functions for the Air Force in the early 1950s. Although it is more remembered
than its predecessors, it was only the latest of several Air Force groups to
serve that function. Project Blue Book remained officially active until 1969
when the program was terminated (National Archives).

In the end, the Washington, D.C., rash of sightings came and went.
By 1953, the Air Force's attitude about Project Blue Book noticeably
changed. Historian David Michael Jacobs concludes that by that time,
the project was already unable to "adequately investigate or analyze
UFO reports." Instead, it became mainly a "public relations and collecting office,"[11] functioning much as Project Grudge had before. Some of
this change appears to coincide with the CIA's rising interest in UFOs.
That interest led to creating a study group called the Robertson Panel, a
secret commission that first convened in early 1953. However, other reasons were likely in play, too.

In the end, Ruppelt's tenure at Project Blue Book was relatively brief. He did have some success. At first, he was successful in upgrading the UFO investigation process with Project Blue. He professionalized the process and even brought astronomer J. Allen Hynek back into the fold as a consultant.

When the secret Robertson Panel concluded the unexplained aerial phenomenon presented no threat and public interest in it should be discouraged, the Air Force's priorities appeared to shift. The situation largely reverted to where it had been some months earlier, essentially undoing much of the progress Ruppelt had made.

Edward Ruppelt left Project Blue Book in 1953, apparently somewhat discouraged about the situation. He left the Air Force entirely not long after that. Afterward, he remained interested in UFOs and published his famous book, *The Report on Unidentified Flying Objects*, in 1956.

If things had been different, Ruppelt might have been a voice with something substantive to add to the increasingly complicated debate about UFOs in American society, but it was not to be. Only a few years later, in September 1960, he died after suffering a heart attack. He was only 37 years old at the time. With his death, his voice and perspective were lost in the ongoing UFO debate.

In the meantime, officials had long since concluded that the famous UFO radar blips at the heart of the 1952 Washington sightings were nothing major. According to their analysis, these were the result of a phenomenon known as "temperature inversions."[12] Experts in such things reported it is a common occurrence well known to interfere with radar.

Unsurprisingly, many in the UFO community refused to believe that was the real explanation. Suspicions that the CIA and military were trying to shove the whole topic off the stage and gloss over UFO questions had fed such skepticism. In the long run, U.S. officials' somewhat clumsy attempts to change the subject most likely worked against government objectives, adding fuel to the fire instead of dousing it with water. Constantly appearing to avoid the topic and repeatedly dismissing concerns as though only crackpots or severely underinformed people could possibly take them seriously, authorities tied their fortunes to trust in their own and other American institutions. As that trust slowly eroded in future years, many people came to believe that the government was hiding something, whether it was doing so or not.

On a more general level, the UFO events of the early 1950s, like those that would come later, were tied to perceptions, understandings, and misunderstandings from the UFO craze that surprised Americans in the summer of 1947. At one level, many cases safely could be chalked up to fairly obvious explanations. However, the percentage of incidents that could not be explained so easily were, and remain, a source of disagreement and confusion. The unresolved adventures continue to be the crux of the problem. What should be made of such cases? Are they aberrations that will prove to be insignificant? Or are they evidence of something else? The answers to these and many other questions still seem distant.

Regardless of unsettled dimensions of the phenomenon, the stage was set for much of what followed. Already, by the end of summer 1947, the themes, presumptions, and interpretative frameworks that people used as they tried to make sense of UFOs were in place. They would cast a long-lasting shadow over the continually unfolding UFO story.

Postscript

The overarching storyline of the long-running television series, *The X-Files*, involved UFOs, extraterrestrials, and a global conspiracy. With its famous tagline, "The Truth is out there," the popular 1990s television series reveled in tales of the paranormal and bizarre.

Two characters, FBI agents Fox Muller and Dana Scully, were at the heart of the show for most of its run. Mulder is on a quest to find out what happened to his sister. He believes aliens abducted her, and quasi-governmental conspirators know all about it. By contrast, Dana Scully is skeptical of Mulder's unorthodox beliefs. As a physician by training, she brings a traditionally scientific perspective to the situation and looks for concrete evidence and traditional explanations for the mysteries the characters encounter.

Throughout the series, *The X-Files'* writers often mined actual UFO reports for ideas and source material. The show inserts many real-world UFO theories into its storylines, weaving them into a complex, crazy-quilt science fiction narrative. *The X-Files* often shows UFO true believers, embodied primarily in the character of Fox Mulder, facing off against skeptics, chief of whom is Dana Scully. Indeed, it is a fascinating portrayal of UFO mythology.

The series' main storyline is based on the premise that sinister human forces know of an impending disaster involving extraterrestrials. But the conspirators work in secret and hide humankind's dark future from ordinary people. With that background, *The X-Files* builds narratives on the idea that the main characters' primary purpose is to expose the hidden truth and shine a light on the previously unknown.

The "Truth is out there" tagline concisely sums up that idea, which is at the center of the show's multi-season story arc. In Agent Mulder's quest to unravel incompletely understood events about his sister and UFOs, he is confident that a missing explanation truly is "out there." He believes the critical evidence lies hidden or unnoticed somewhere and that once he finds it, all his questions will be answered. In that respect, Mulder's viewpoint is very much like the perspective that many real people have about unexplained aerial phenomena.

In the modern world, many people presume that all things ultimately are knowable. If something is not understood, many assume that all will be revealed as long as people keep searching. Tremendous strides in science and the march of human progress have reinforced such beliefs. Indeed, it can be alluring to believe missing evidence must exist and that by simply finding it will clear up any kind of vexing question.

The idea that some things may *not* be knowable is far less common. That judgment seems both overly pessimistic and short-sighted to most Americans. Yet, in the real world, some things truly do remain stubbornly beyond understanding. Extra effort does not always reverse this situation, either. Even when new clues to some enigma come to light, new evidence still can be incomplete, conflicting, and potentially misleading. Some mysteries remain mysteries despite tremendous efforts to unravel them.

The modern UFO era is only about 75 years old, but these kinds of issues have hampered a coherent understanding of the topic from the beginning. At the start, things were pretty simple. From the moment he witnessed nine objects in the sky near Mount Rainier in 1947, Kenneth Arnold just wanted to know what he had seen. But the simplicity of that desire was misleading. The amateur pilot saw enough to offer a fascinating account of his sighting, and he even had time to make some careful observations. But many details in his case were missing or ambiguous. And in the end, although he eventually reached some conclusions, he never found wholly satisfying answers to all his questions about the incident.

Kenneth Arnold's frustration would become a hallmark of the UFO phenomenon. A similar experience—looking for answers but not finding them—would be shared by many people over the decades. Indeed, although many UFO sightings ultimately have been explained after some digging and piecing together of evidence, a substantial number of cases continue to defy not only easy explanation but any sort of convincing explanation at all. In many instances, there is simply not enough known from which to draw a solid conclusion. This, of course, is wholly unacceptable to many people, especially in the United States, where the culture favors swift and confident judgment. *Some* evidence is *enough* evidence for much of the American population. In a society that distains uncertainty and ambiguity, perhaps this is not surprising.

Today, many Americans have strong opinions about UFOs. Like the fictional Fox Mulder character, many want to believe UFOs represent some form of extraterrestrial life. However, others want no part of such presumptions. And still others are not sure what to think.

Yet, the topic remains fascinating for many people. As was true in the late 1940s, the subject still reliably draws public interest. The UFO story has remained a staple of conversation in media outlets that run the gamut from self-published newsletters and small-time websites to mainstream material from corporate powerhouses.

Something akin to a "hidden-truth industry" complicates matters and adds much haze to this already foggy situation. Indeed, as the marketplace for UFO material has become ever more crowded, new content creators have looked for ways to capture the public's attention. This has led to a tendency for creators—authors, filmmakers, television producers, etc.—to claim they have discovered new evidence or that they have found something startling that was previously overlooked. Indeed, many creators and marketers have turned to hyperbolic rhetoric and sensational claims. Voluminous UFO material available today claims to expose "secrets," "cover-ups," "conspiracies," and bring the public the "truth." Despite numerous such claims, however, there is a familiar sameness to much of this material.

Meanwhile, witnesses continue to file new reports of unexplained aerial phenomena. These recent reports sometimes draw public attention, but at the same time, there has been little let-up in the trend of revisiting material about older cases. For example, as a symbol of the UFO phenomenon in general, Roswell is as well known for that today as it was in the late 1940s. Through it all, the essential UFO myth—the narrative of extraterrestrial aliens in the skies and a U.S. government conspiracy—continues to provide a readymade and widely recognized template for the popular culture of many types.

It is legitimately possible that some unforeseen blockbuster revelation about UFOs will arrive at some point. And indeed, such new disclosures—or more thorough research by the scientific community than has been conducted to date—could change perceptions and further understanding of the topic. To date, however, the available evidence remains inconclusive, at best. It sometimes offers hints of something extraordinary and suggests intriguing possibilities, but it is not sufficient to substantially change the overall uncertainty of the situation. At the end of the day, many unexplained sightings and encounters remain unexplained. They have been neither refuted nor affirmed in a way that satisfies all. There is little that seems capable of convincing people who have chosen sides—whether as believers or skeptics—to change their minds.

What, then, are people to make of the 1947 flying saucer sightings and later UFO incidents? For such questions, the best response may not be much different from Carl Jung's answer in 1959. Many sightings still officially categorized as unsolved were possibly misidentifications, optical illusions, or other straightforward observational errors. A few cases were likely hoaxes. And some were perhaps cases of still-classified military programs. Evidence of a kind that would allow for more certain judgments is just not there at the moment. Wishing it to be otherwise has had no effect on that situation.

The U.S. government sometimes indicates it wants to help shed light on UFOs. However, if sincere, such stated intentions are hampered by its long-standing tendency to dodge questions and its somewhat lackadaisical interest in transparency and forthrightness. Government candor remains a rare commodity. Unsurprisingly, therefore, skepticism about the government UFO statements still runs deep. So, when federal authorities claim they do not know any more than they have publicly stated, many people simply do not believe them. That is lamentable but wholly unsurprising. After all, the United States government's cult of secrecy has mostly remained intact over the years. Given its checkered history with truth-telling and forthrightness, it is easy to understand why some people might have that attitude.

Given all of this, theories about extraterrestrial origins and government conspiracies, which remain popular and in wide circulation, also continue to complicate the situation. Many people are convinced that the unknown things are unknown simply because officials deliberately hide them from the public. The conspiratorial angle implies that there has been much going on beneath the surface in secret. Considering the scope and scale of the UFO phenomenon, this suggests the complicity, willing or not, of hundreds or even thousands of people, stretched out over 75 years. That may stretch credulity in the eyes of many people. Still, it must be admitted that such theories are technically possible even if they strike many as extremely unlikely.

Despite numerous efforts to unravel the UFO story, then, much of it, from 1947 onward, continues to defy any sort of explanation that will satisfy everyone. Incomplete data, hazy witness statements, and other problems with evidence mean it is not yet possible—and it may never be possible—to fully understand the most puzzling cases.

The medieval principle of Occam's Razor is sometimes mentioned as a way to deal with this conundrum. That idea suggests that "the simplest explanation for a phenomenon is most likely to be correct."[1] In other words, when there seems to be more than one plausible answer to the same question, the most straightforward one is often better than those that are more complicated.

A person adopting this approach might conclude that the UFO

events of the late 1940s—and indeed, in the modern era, overall—
may not be very extraordinary, after all. The unexplained aspects of
UFO cases could simply result from mundane things that people failed
to notice or piece together. That is also possible. To take that position
would mean accepting that some unknowns are and will likely remain
unknown, however. And this way of dealing with the issue would hardly
satisfy everyone. Indeed, many people demand answers even if the evidence does not lead to a clear explanation. Leaving big questions about
UFOs as grey areas about which bullet-proof certainty is not yet possible is simply not acceptable for some. People with strong beliefs, pro or
con, often want their views validated sooner rather than later.

In the end, the verdict people draw about UFOs likely will depend
on their thoughts about what constitutes conclusive evidence and about
their feelings about the integrity and reliability of government and other
institutional entities. That is hardly encouraging, however. Indeed, these
are things about which Americans strongly disagree, not only on the
subject of UFOs but also on a wide range of subjects and issues.

Whatever role it ultimately plays in U.S. society and culture, the
long-simmering UFO debate exposes a fundamental concern that many
Americans harbor but may not consider explicitly. That issue is control, or more precisely, the perceived lack of it. Indeed, as mysteries that
turn up at random times and places without warning, unexplained aerial
phenomena pointedly suggest that some things lie beyond America's—
or humankind's—ability to control them.

Control is a significant issue for most Americans, and residents of
the United States like to think their country possesses it. In the post–
World War II era, the United States metaphorically reached for the stars
in many ways. At the same time, it has consistently projected the idea
that it controls its destiny and that of the world at large. The baffling
UFOs are an unpleasant reminder that, despite the optimistic trium-
phalism of American politics and culture, there are still things Americans can neither comprehend nor control. Even in a time of unrivaled
scientific progress, some things remain bewildering and defy American attempts to tame them. It is a situation that many Americans would
rather not accept.

All this leads up to the thought that there may not be definitive
answers to every UFO question anytime soon—if, indeed, such solu-
tions ever come. The state of affairs, as it stands, is reminiscent of what
Arthur Eddington, a well-known astronomer-physicist in the early 20th
century, once said about the atomic world: "Something unknown is
doing we don't know what."[2]

Without the introduction of substantial and agreed-upon new

evidence, there is probably no set of arguments that will persuade people who have made up their minds to change their attitudes. In the future, some new evidence may become available, and some incidents could be settled. Increased involvement of scientists and other researchers may also help, though the subject would need to be mainstreamed and destigmatized as a topic of inquiry for that to happen. But still, however, it seems likely that not every case will be resolved to everyone's satisfaction. Too much time may have passed to fully settle some cases, especially those from the late 1940s. And as long as a single incident remains unresolved, disagreement about UFOs—about what they are, where they came from, and what they represent—may persist for some time to come.

Chapter Notes

Introduction

1. The terms "unidentified flying objects" and "UFOs" were not coined until several years after 1947. Although this book primarily looks at events that occurred before this language came into use, these terms, which are widely used today, are used throughout the following pages.

2. Daniel L. Schacter and Scott D. Slotnick, "The Cognitive Neuroscience of Memory Distortion," *Neuron* 4, no. 1 (September 30, 2004): 149.

3. John E. Kiat and Robert F. Belli, "An Exploratory High-Density EEG Investigation of the Misinformation Effect: Attentional and Recollective Differences Between True and False Perceptual Memories," *Neurobiology of Learning and Memory* 141 (May 2017): 199.

Chapter 1

1. Jung made this statement in a memorandum to the Aerial Phenomena Research Organization, a private UFO investigative organization that was founded in 1952. The statement is reprinted in Carl G. Jung, *Flying Saucers: A Modern Myth of Things Seen in the Sky* (New York: MJF Books, 1978), 136.

2. Jung's letter to the Swiss magazine *Weltwoche*, dated July 9, 1954, is reproduced in *Ibid.*, 131.

3. "A Quarter of Americans Believe that Crashed UFO Spacecrafts Are Held at Area 51 in Southern Nevada," Ipsos Press press release (October 3, 2019).

https://www.Ipsos.com/en-us/news-polls/americans-believe-crashed-ufo-spacecrafts-held-at-area-51.

4. Carl Jung, *Flying Saucers*, vii.

5. *Ibid.*

6. *Ibid.*, 3.

7. *Ibid.*, 136.

8. *Ibid.*, 3.

9. *Ibid.*, 136.

10. *Ibid.*

11. *Ibid.*, 107.

Chapter 2

1. "Radio Listeners Panic, Taking War Drama as Fact," *New York Times*, October 31, 1938.

2. "Fake Radio 'War' Stirs terror Through U.S.," *Daily News*, October 31, 1938.

3. Jefferson Pooley and Michael J. Socolow, "The Myth of the War of the Worlds Panic," *Slate*, October 28, 2013. https://slate.com/culture/2013/10/orson-welles-war-of-the-worlds-panic myth-the-infamous-radio-broadcast-did-not-cause-a-nationwide-hysteria.html.

4. "Flying Saucers Still Evasive 70 Years After Pilot's Report," *The Spokesman-Review*, June 25, 2017.

5. Details of flight are recorded in Charles Apple, "UFOs Over Washington," *The Spokesman-Review*, June 23, 2020.

6. Wesley Frank Craven and James Lea Cate, *The Army Air Forces in World War I: Services Around the World* (Chicago: University of Chicago Press, 1948), 35.

7. The flight details are described in

Daryl C. McClary, "A Curtis Commando R5C Transport Plane Crashes into Mount Rainier, Killing 32 U.S. Marines, on December 10, 1946," *HistoryLink.org* (July 29, 2006). https://www.historylink.org/File/7820/.

8. "Storm Delays Plane Search," *The Windsor Daily Star*, December 13, 1946.

9. This account and quotation appear in Kenneth Arnold and Raymond Palmer, *The Coming of the Saucers* (Boise: [Privately published by the authors], 1952), 9–13.

10. *Ibid.*

11. "Salesman Launched UFO Age: A Portland Man's Innocent Question Sparked 50-Year Search for Flying Saucer," *The Spokesman-Review,* June 22, 1997.

12. "Flying Saucers Still Evasive 70 Years After Pilot's Report," *The Spokesman-Review,* June 25, 2017.

13. These details are reported in "Salesman Launched UFO Age: A Portland Man's Innocent Question Sparked 50-Year Search for Flying Saucers," *The Spokesman-Review,* June 22, 1997.

Chapter 3

1. Arnold explained his calculations in Kenneth Arnold and Ray Palmer, *The Coming of the Saucers,* 13–14.

2. Jack Hauptli, "Rocket Plane Given Tests," *San Jose Evening News,* December 11, 1946.

3. *Ibid.*

4. Robert Van Der Linden, *Milestones of Flight: The Epic of Aviation* (Washington, D.C. : National Air and Space Museum, 2016), 139.

5. Gareth Hector, Jim Laurier, and Peter E. Davies, *Bell X-1* (New York: Bloomsbury, 2016), 41.

6. "Conjecture Over mystery 'Disc' Craft grows," *Lewiston Daily Sun,* June 27, 1946.

7. "'Flying Discs' Reported in Many States," *Tuscaloosa News,* July 6, 1947.

8. "Veteran Pilot Clings to Flying Saucer Story," *Lodi News-Sentinel,* June 27, 1947.

9. "Impossible! Maybe, But Seein' is Believin', Says Flyer," *East Oregonian,* June 25, 1947.

10. "Veteran Pilot Clings to Flying Saucer Story," *Lodi News-Sentinel,* June 27, 1947.

11. A transcription of section from Murrow's interview with Kenneth Arnold appears in Megan Garber, "The Man Who Introduced the World to Flying Saucers," *The Atlantic* (June 15, 2014). https://www.theatlantic.com/technology/archive/2014/06/the-man-who-introduced-the-world-to-flying-saucers/372732/.

12. The origin of the "flying saucer" label has been much discussed. One of the more enlightening discussions appears in Hilary Evans and Robert E. Bartholomew, eds., *Outbreak! The Encyclopedia of Extraordinary Social Behavior* (New York: Anomalist Books, 2009), 179.

Chapter 4

1. "Oklahoma Man Saw Them Too," *Ellensburg Daily Record,* June 26, 1947.

2. *Ibid.*

3. *Ibid.*

4. "Hundreds in 31 States Report Seeing Weird 'Flying Saucers," *Evening Star,* July 6, 1947.

5. *Ibid.*

6. *Ibid.*

7. This quotation appears in Emil Earl Wennergren, "The 'Flying Saucers' Episode," Master's Thesis (University of Iowa, 1948), 6.

8. *Ibid.,* 8.

9. *Ibid.*

10. "Hundreds in 3 States Report Seeing Weird 'Flying Saucers,'" *Evening Star,* July 6, 1947.

11. Emil Wennergren, "The 'Flying Saucers' Episode," 7.

12. *Ibid.*

13. *Ibid.,* 9.

14. *Ibid.*

15. *Ibid.*

16. "Officials Skeptical of Story of Fast-flying 'Objects" in Air," *Evening Star,* June 26, 1947.

17. *Ibid.*

18. *Ibid.*

19. *Ibid.*

20. *Ibid.*

Chapter 5

1. John Waller, "A Forgotten Plague: Making Sense of Dancing Mania," *Lancet* 21, no. 373 (February 29, 2009): 624–5.

2. "Some Old-Time Epidemics," *The Sanitary News* 7, no. 95 (November 28, 1885), 34–35.

3. M.J. Colligan and L.R. Murphy, "A Review of Mass Psychogenic Illness in Work Settings," in *Mass Psychogenic Illness: A Social Psychological Analysis,* edited by M.J. Colligan, J.W. Pennebaker and L.R. Murphy (Mahwah, NJ: Erlbaum, 1982), 35.

4. John Waller, *A Time to Dance, a Time to Die: The Extraordinary Story of the Dancing Plague of 1518* (Cambridge: Icon, 2008).

5. John Waller, "A Forgotten Plague: Making Sense of Dancing Mania."

Chapter 6

1. Les Barnard, "'Flying Saucers' May Be This or That; Speculation Rife," *The Tennessean Sun,* June 29, 1947.

2. *Ibid.*

3. Quoted in Emil Wennergren, "The 'Flying Saucers' Episode," 81.

4. "Psychiatrist Rules Out Hysteria as Answer to Reports of Saucers," *Boston Globe,* July 7, 1947.

5. Les Barnard, "Flying Saucers May Be This or That; Speculation Rife."

6. "Harassed Saucer-Sighter Would Like to Escape Fuss," *Boise Statesman,* June 27, 1947.

1. This quotation is reprinted in William C. Berman, *The Politics of Civil Rights in the Truman Administration* (Columbus: Ohio State University Press, 1970), 64.

2. George Marshall, Address at Harvard University, June 5, 1947.

3. Ted Bloecher, *Report on the UFO Wave of 1947* (Washington, D.C.: [Privately published by the author], 1967). An updated version of this report was privately circulated by Jean Waskiewicz and Francis Ridge in 2005.

4. By that time, the Air Force's UFO investigations were conducted under the auspices of Project Blue Book. The report referenced here was issued as Air Technical Intelligence Center, *Project Blue Book,* Special Report No. 14, "Analysis of Unidentified Flying Objects" (Wright-Patterson Air Force Base, OH: U.S.A.F., 1955).

5. See Table A5, "Evaluation of All Sightings by Month and Year, 1947," in *Ibid.*

6. Data sources for the report are detailed in Air Technical Intelligence Center, *Project Blue Book,* "Special Report No. 14," 3.

7. *Ibid.*

8. *Ibid.*

9. *Ibid.*

Chapter 8

1. United States Air Force, *The Roswell Report: Fact Versus Fiction in the New Mexico Desert* (Washington, D.C.: GPO, 1995), 2.

2. *Ibid.*

3. Detailed accounts of the B-52's development, as well as Twining role in it, can be found in Mark D. Mandeles, *The Development of the B-52 and Jet Propulsion: A Case Study in Organizational Innovation* (Maxwell Air Force Base, AL: Air University Press, 1998), and Lori S. Tagg, *Development of the B-52: The Wright Field Story* (Wright Patterson Air Force Base, OH: Air Force Materiel Command, 2004).

4. This letter, listed under the subject of "Issuance of Orders," is reproduced in United States Air Force, *The Roswell Report,* Appendix 14.

5. "Army Plans Probe into Flying Discs," *Deseret News,* July 3, 1947.

6. *Ibid.*

7. Some UFO writers argue that Twining was a member of a purported top-secret group that was allegedly called the Majestic 12 (sometimes simply called MJ-12). Government researchers have written that such a group never existed and that the materials purporting to show otherwise are the result of a hoax. An overview of the Majestic-12 theories and the debunking of them can be found in Eric Grundhauser, "The FBI Debunked These UFO Documents in the Most Childish Way Possible," *Slate* (December 6, 2016). https://

slate.com/human-interest/2016/12/
the-fbi-debunked-the-majestic-12-ufo-
documents-in-the-most-childish-way-
possible.html.

8. Military efforts to analyze this background were evidently earnest. The Air Force's methodology in reconstructing the Roswell case for its 1994 study documented in its publication, United States Air Force, *The Roswell Report*, 13–19.

9. *Ibid.*, 21.

10. These percentages do not add up to exactly 100 due to rounding. The statistics here are derived from data reproduced in "Table A5—Evaluation of All Sightings by Month of Year, 1947" in Air Technical Intelligence Center, *Project Blue Book*, "Special Report No. 14," Appendix, 110.

11. *Ibid.*, 12.

12. *Ibid.*

13. The categories are described in *Ibid.*, 11–12.

14. *Ibid.*, 94.

Chapter 9

1. "Harassed Rancher Who Located 'Saucer' Sorry He Told About It," *Roswell Daily Record*, July 9, 1947.

2. This account, including the quotations, draws on Benson Saler, Charles A. Ziegler, and Charles B. Moore, *UFO Crash at Roswell* (Washington, D.C.: Smithsonian Institution, 1997), 5–7.

3. This detail is recorded in Emil Wennergren, "The 'Flying Saucers' Episode," 58.

4. *Ibid.*

5. See United States Air Force, *The Roswell Report*, 12, and also Benson Saler, et al., *UFO Crash at Roswell*, 6.

6. Emil Wennergren, "The 'Flying Saucers' Episode," 58.

7. "RAAF Captures Flying Saucer on Ranch in Roswell Region," *Roswell Daily Record*, July 8, 1947.

8. *Ibid.*

9. *Ibid.*

10. *Ibid.*

11. Emil Wennergren, "The 'Flying Saucers' Episode," 59.

12. Benson Saler, et al., *UFO Crash at Roswell*, 8.

13. "Harassed Rancher Who Located 'Saucer' Sorry He Told About It," *Roswell Daily Record*, July 9, 1947.

14. Benson Saler, et al., *UFO Crash at Roswell*, 8.

15. These quotations appear in "Harassed Rancher Who Located 'Saucer' Sorry He Told About It."

16. *Ibid.*

17. *Ibid.*

18. Both statements appear in "RAAF Captures Flying Saucer on Ranch in Roswell Region."

19. "Military Planes Hunt Sky Discs with Cameras in Vain on Coast," *New York Times*, July 7, 1947.

20. *Ibid.*

21. *Ibid.*

Chapter 10

1. The story of William Bonney, the legendary outlaw more commonly known as Billy the Kid, was recounted in Sheriff Pat Garrett's well-known 1882 book, *The Authentic Life of Billy, the Kid*. It since has been reprinted several times, including this edition: Pat Garrett, *The Authentic Life of Billy, the Kid* (Norman: University of Oklahoma, 1954).

2. Before that, officials considered the town for one of the controversial Japanese American internment camps that the government placed in several areas of the Southwest. However, after vocal opposition, much of which appears racially motivated, it was dropped as a potential site for a "relocation center," as the internment camps were called euphemistically.

3. R. Douglas Hurt, *The Great Plains During World War II* (Lincoln: University of Nebraska Press, 2008), 285.

4. A general history of the United States' World War II prisoner of war camps can be found in Arnold Krammer, *Nazi Prisoners of War in America* (New York: Stein & Day, 1979).

5. "One of 3 Killed Escaping from Internment Camp," *Evening Star*, January 14, 1943.

6. R. Douglas Hurt, *The Great Plains During World War II*, 245.

7. Alan Armstrong, "The Legacy of Walker Air Force Base," *Warbirds News*, December 31, 2013. http://warbirdsnews.

com/aviation-museum-news/legacy-walker-air-force-base.html.

8. These details are included in "RAAF Captures Flying Saucer," *Roswell Daily Record*, July 8, 1947.

9. *Ibid.*

10. *Ibid.*

11. *Ibid.*

1. "Army Whips Up Saucer Flurry, However 'Find' Finally Fizzles," *Wilmington Morning Star*, July 9, 1947.

2. "Ramey Empties Roswell Saucer," *Roswell Daily Record*, July 9, 1947.

3. The details are documented in Benson Saler, et al., *UFO Crash at Roswell*, 9.

4. Murray Schumach, "'Disk' Near Bomb Test Site Is Just a Weather Balloon," *New York Times*, July 9, 1947.

5. *Ibid.*

6. Ramey's remark originally appeared in a July 9, 1947, *San Francisco Chronicle* story quoted in Benson Saler, et al., *UFO Crash at Roswell*, 9.

7. *Ibid.*

8. "Find 'Flying Saucer' Was Just Weather Balloon," *Ottawa Citizen*, July 9, 1947.

9. *Ibid.*

10. Bud Kennedy, "What Actually Crashed Near Roswell? This Photo May Hold a Crucial Clue," *Charlotte Observer*, July 17, 2017.

11. These photographs are available for online inspection at the University of Texas website: https://library.uta.edu/roswell/images.

12. "'Disk-overy' Near Roswell Identified as Weather Balloon by FWAAF Officer," *Fort Worth Star-Telegram*, July 9, 1947.

13. This memorandum, dated July 8, 1947, is preserved by the FBI among publicly available materials collected at https://vault.fbi.gov/Roswell%20UFO/Roswell%20UFO%20Part%201%20of%201/view.

14. *Ibid.*

Chapter 12

1. James McAndrew, "Report on Project Mogul: Synopsis of Balloon Research Findings," Muller's Group, Lawrence Berkeley Laboratory (September 21, 1995). https://muller.lbl.gov/teaching/ physics10/Roswell/USMogulReport.html.

2. United States Air Force, *The Roswell Report: Fact Versus Fiction in the New Mexico Desert* (Washington, D.C.: GPO, 1995), 45.

3. *Ibid.*, 2.

4. *Ibid.*

5. James Michael Young, "The U.S. Air Force's Long Range Detection Program and Project MOGUL," *Air Power History* 67, no. 4 (Winter 2020): 27.

6. *Ibid.*

7. United States Air Force, *The Roswell Report*, Appendix 21.

8. *Ibid.*, 3.

9. *Ibid.*

10. *Ibid.*

11. James Michael Young, "The U.S. Air Force's Long Range Detection Program and Project MOGUL," 27.

United States Air Force, *The Roswell Report*, 3.

12. *Ibid.*, 27.

13. *Ibid.*, 30.

Chapter 13

1. See, for example, Karl T. Pflock, *Roswell: Inconvenient Facts and the Will to Believe* (Amherst, NY: Prometheus Books, 2001).

2. United States Air Force, *The Roswell Report*, 27.

3. *Ibid.*, 12.

4. The offer of a reward continued to appear on the University's website at the time of this writing in 2021. See University of Texas at Arlington, Ramey Memo, High Resolution Microfiche Scans at https://library.uta.edu/roswell/ramey-memo.

5. Kathryn Schulz, "The Rabbit-Hole Rabbit Hole," *New Yorker*, June 4, 2015. https://www.newyorker.com/culture/cultural-comment/the-rabbit-hole-rabbit-hole.

Chapter 14

1. Emil Wennergren, "The 'Flying Saucers' Episode," 86–102.

2. *Ibid.*, 86.

3. Henry McLemore, "Unable to Break a Flying Saucer," *Evening Star*, July 17, 1947.

4. Walter Winchell, [untitled column], *St. Joseph Gazette*, July 11, 1947.

5. "Speaking of Pictures: A Rash of Flying Disks Breaks Out Over the U.S." *Life*, July 21, 1947, 14–15.

6. David Riesman, Nathan Glazer, and Reuel Denney, *The Lonely Crowd A Study of the Changing American Character* (New Haven: Yale University Press, 2020), xxxvi.

7. *Ibid.*

8. Rod A. Martin and Thomas Ford, *The Psychology of Humor: An Integrative Approach* (London: Academic Press, 2018), 262.

9. *Ibid.*

10. Leslie Janes and James Olson, "Jeer Pressure: The Behavioral Effects of Observing Ridicule of Others," *Personality and Social Psychology Bulletin* 26 (2000): 474–485.

11. Anna Freud, *The Writings of Anna Freud: The Ego and the Mechanisms of Defense* (New York: International Universities Press, 1967), 37.

12. [Classified advertisement], *Evening Star*, July 13, 1947.

Chapter 15

1. "Where Are the Saucers?" *Key West Citizen*, July 24, 1947.

2. *Ibid.*

3. "Flying Disc Tales Decline as Army, navy Crack Down," *Las Vegas Review-Journal*, July 9, 1947.

4. Carlyle Holt, "Flying Saucers Old Stuff to U.S. Flyers During War," *Daily Boston Globe*, July 13, 1947.

5. "AAF Flyers Reported 'Foo Fighters' in War Like "Flying Saucers,'" *Evening Star*, July 6, 1947.

6. "Reports from Experts lend More Serious View to 'Discs,'" *Evening Star*, July 8, 1947.

7. *Ibid.*

8. *Ibid.*

9. "Top Secret War Project Is Told," *Pentwater News*, July 13, 1947.

10. "Flying Wing," *Arizona Sun*, January 31, 1947.

11. "AERIAL: New Sky Weapons," *Wilmington Morning Star*, February 16, 1947.

12. See, for example, "Year of Achievement," *Wilmington Morning Star*, January 4, 1947.

Chapter 16

1. An overview of the Act's history can be found in Charles A. Stevenson, "The Story Behind the National Security Act of 1947," *Military Review* (May-June 2008): 13–20.

2. "Score Importation of Nazi," *Arizona Post*, March 21, 1947.

3. "Ten in State Department Fired on Suspicion of Disloyalty," *Evening Star*, June 27, 1947.

4. "Marzini Gets Term of 1 to 3 Years, to Start Immediately," *Evening Star*, June 27, 1947.

5. Joseph Alsop and Stewart Alsop, "The Flying Sauces Serve Up One Lesson Vital to Americans: No Warning System Developed Against Surprise Attack," *Boston Globe*, July 13, 1947.

6. *Ibid.*

7. "Russia Near Atomic Secret," *Wilmington Morning Star*, March 30, 1947.

8. Murray Schumach, "'Disk' Near Bomb Test Site Is Just a Weather Balloon," *New York Times*, July 9, 1947.

9. Thomas R. Henry, "Flying Discs Not U.S. Weapon, Declare Physicists," *Daily Boston Globe*, July 11, 1947.

10. Quoted in "Insufficient Evidence Ends AAF's Probe of Flying Saucers," *Daily Boston Globe*, August 9, 1947.

Chapter 17

1. "Lost Marine transport Discovered," *Lodi News-Sentinel*, July 25, 1947.

2. *Ibid.*

3. Committee on Interstate and Foreign Commerce, "Safety in Air Navigation: Hearings Before the Committee on Interstate and Foreign Commerce, House of Representatives," Eightieth Congress, First Session (Washington, D.C.: U.S. Government Printing Office, 1947), 1.

4. "Stepped Up operations held Cause of Flurry of Air Force Accidents," *Meriden Daily Journal*, August 30, 1948.

5. *Ibid.*

6. *Ibid.*

7. "'Chutes Save Two in Bomber Crash," *Altus Times-Democrat,* August 1, 1947.

8. "Identify Fliers Killed in Crash of B-25 Bomber," *Ellensburg Daily Record,* August 2, 1947.

9. "Crashed Plan Pilots Believed Carrying 'Disc Pieces,'" *Lewiston Morning Tribune,* August 3, 1947.

10. This incident is recounted in any sources. This summary draws upon a recent summary produced for KNKX radio. Jennifer Wing, "Before UFOs In Roswell, There Was the Maury Island Incident," KNKX.com (October 15, 2013). https://www.knkx.org/post/ufos-roswell-there-was-maury-island-incident.

11. *Ibid.*

12. Walt Crowley, "Maury Island UFO Sighting Predated Mount Rainier's," *Nisqually Valley News,* January 25, 2018.

13. "Saucer Reports Increase as Sky Is Search in Vain," *Spokesman-Review,* July 7, 1947.

14. Kenneth Arnold and Ray Palmer, *The Coming of the Saucers* (Boise: [Privately published by the authors], 1952), 45.

15. The quotations appear in "Crashed Plan Pilots Believed Carrying 'Disc Pieces,'" *Lewiston Morning Tribune,* August 3, 1947.

16. Many years after the fact, in 2007, the Seattle Museum of Mysteries, a small storefront operation dedicated to the paranormal, paid for a scientific analysis of debris said to have been from the B-25 crash site. According to subsequent findings, the samples, presumably including some of the material Brown and Davidson loaded aboard the aircraft, was "ordinary igneous rocks or, possibly, fragments of a meteor." See Walt Crowley, Dahl and Crissman [sic] report a June 21, 1947, explosion of a flying saucer over Maury Island on or after June 26, 1947," HistoryLink.org (January 1, 2000; updated 2007). https://www.historylink.org/File/2068 .

17. "'Flying Disk' Pilot in Air Crash; Unhurt," *Spokesman-Review,* August 6, 1947.

18. "Army Find No Evidence 'Saucers' Ever Existed," *St. Petersburg Times,* August 10, 1947.

Chapter 18

1. "F.B.I. Aid Army in Disk Probes," *Spokane Daily Chronicle,* August 6, 1947.

2. Memorandum to D.M. Ladd from [redacted], "Subject: Flying Saucers," August 6, 1947. This memorandum and others cited in this chapter was released in redacted form under provisions of the Freedom of Information Act. An electronic copy of this particular memorandum is preserved at the Black Vault website. https://documents.theblackvault.com/documents/ufos/fbi/ufo1.pdf.

3. Memorandum to D.M. Ladd from [redacted], [Subject not indicated], August 18, 1947. This memorandum, released under provisions of the Freedom of Information Act, is preserved by the FBI at https://vault.fbi.gov/UFO/UFO%203%20of%2016/view.

4. *Ibid.*

5. *Ibid.*

6. Memorandum to D.M. Ladd from [redacted], "Subject: Flying Saucers and Flying Discs," August 8, 1947. This memorandum is preserved at https://vault.fbi.gov/UFO/UFO%20Part%203%20of%2016/view.

7. Memorandum to D.M. Ladd from [redacted], "Subject: Flying Discs," August 19, 1947. This memorandum is preserved at https://vault.fbi.gov/UFO/UFO%20Part%203%20of%2016/view.

8. *Ibid.*

9. *Ibid.*

10. *Ibid.*

11. "200 Magazine Beach Bathers Spot Flying Sauce Over Braves Field," *Daily Boston Globe,* July 11, 1947.

12. *Ibid.*

Chapter 19

1. "Planes to Chase 'Flying Saucers'; 'Something to This,' AAF Feels," *Evening Star,* July 7, 1947.

2. "Sky Seems Normal After 'Saucer' Scare; Publicity Agents Strive to Utilize the Idea," *New York Times,* July 12, 1947.

3. Kate Dorsch, "Reliable Witnesses, Crackpot Science: UFO Investigations in Cold War America, 1947–1977," Ph.D. diss., University of Pennsylvania, 2019, 35.

4. "Planes to Chase 'Flying Saucers';
'Something to This,' AAF Feels," *Evening
Star,* July 7, 1947.

5. A well-documented account of
these efforts appears in Michael D.
Swords and Robert Powell, *UFOs and
Government* (San Antonio: Anomalist
Books, 2012).

6. Nathan Twining to Commanding General (Brigadier General George
Schulgen, AC/AS-2), Army Air Forces,
"Subject: AMC Opinion Concerning
'Flying Discs,'" September 23, 1947. This
document, which has since been declassified under provisions of the Freedom
of Information Act), can be found in
reproduced form in multiple sources. A
good-quality electronic reproduction is
available at https://medium.com/on-the-
trail-of-the-saucers/twining-memo-ufo-
c719bed1d287.

7. *Ibid.*
8. *Ibid.*
9. *Ibid.*
10. *Ibid.*
11. *Ibid.*
12. *Ibid.*
13. *Ibid.*
14. *Ibid.*
15. Kate Dorsch, "Reliable Witnesses,
Crackpot Science," 35–36.
16. *Ibid.*
17. Memorandum to D.M. Ladd from
[redacted], "Subject: Flying Discs," September 16, 1947. This memorandum was
declassified under provisions of the Freedom of Information Act and is preserved
in electronic form at https://vault.fbi.gov/
UFO/UFO%20Part%203%20of%2016/view.
18. *Ibid.*
19. This language is taken from the
National Archives' administrative note
to the page "Department of Defense.
Department of the Air Force. Air Force
Systems Command. Foreign Technology Division. Project Blue Book Office.
(7/1/1961–12/17/1969), Organization
Authority Record." (n.d.) Web. https://
catalog.archives.gov/id/10455222.

Chapter 20

1. Good Evening, Mars!" *Coconino
Weekly Sun,* August 6, 1896.
2. *Ibid.*

3. Percival Lowell, *Mars and Its
Canals* (New York: Macmillan, 1906),
376.
4. *Ibid.,* 377, 378.
5. As early as 1899, for example, some
scientist expressed doubt about the use
of the word *canals* in descriptions of the
Martian surface. See, for example, "New
Theories of Mars' Canals; Astronomer
Burnham Thinks That They Have Been
Misnamed," *Cook County Herald,* April
15, 1899.
6. "The Riddle of Mars," *Scientific
American,* July 13, 1907, 25–26.
7. "Aerial Houseboats and Villages
of Mars," *San Francisco Call,* October 3,
1909.
8. "Is Mars Trying to Signal Our
Earth?" *Times-Dispatch,* November 9,
1913.
9. "Mars Peopled by One Vast Thinking Vegetable!" *Omaha Sunday Bee,*
October 6, 1912.
10. H. Gernsback, "Life on Mars," *Science and Invention* 9, November 1921,
586.
11. George W. Gray, "The Riddle of
Mars," *Popular Mechanics,* April 1933,
548.
12. Donald H. Menzel, "New Light on
the Mystery of Mars," *Popular Science,*
October 1943, 125.
13. *Ibid.*
14. William Cecil Dampier Whetham,
A Shorter History of Science (Cambridge:
Cambridge University Press, 1944), 162.

Chapter 21

1. "Plane Crash Ends Sky Object
Chase," *The Bulletin,* January 8, 1948.
2. News accounts of the era identify
the aircraft as a P-51, although the Air
Force officially renamed it the F-51 in
1947.
3. "Airman Killed Chasing 'Flying
Disc'; Flaming Red Cone Seen By Ohioans," *St. Petersburg Times,* January 9,
1948.
4. "Pilot Dies Trying to Follow 'Flying
Disk' in Kentucky," *Spokane Daily Chronicle,* January 9, 1948.
5. "'Ball of Fire in Skies Excites Southern Ohioans," *Painesville Telegraph,* January 9, 1948.

6. "Pilot Dies Trying to Follow 'Flying Disk' in Kentucky."

7. 'Ball of Fire in Skies Excites Southern Ohioans."

8. "Surprise: Back Again," *Laurel Outlook*, January 14, 1948.

9. *Ibid.*

10. *Ibid.*

11. "Airman Killed Chasing 'Flying Disc.'"

12. "Ball of Fire in Skies Excites Southern Ohioans."

13. *Ibid.*

14. "Surprise: Back Again."

15. "Airman Killed Chasing 'Flying Disc.'"

16. Kate Dorsch, "Reliable Witnesses, Crackpot Science," 38–39.

17. L.H. Truettner and A.B. Deyarmond, "Unidentified Aerial Objects, Project 'Sign,'" Air Material Command, United States Air Force, Wright-Patterson Air Force Base, Dayton, Ohio, 1949. https://apps.dtic.mil/dtic/tr/fulltext/u2/311102.pdf.

18. *Ibid.*

19. *Ibid.*

20. *Ibid.*

21. *Ibid.*

22. *Ibid.*

23. Kate Dorsch, "Reliable Witnesses, Crackpot Science," 40.

24. L.H. Truettner and A.B. Deyarmond, "Unidentified Aerial Objects, Project 'Sign,'" 26.

25. *Ibid.*, 35.

26. The letter from RAND is included as Appendix D in Project Sign's 1949 report. See L.H. Truettner and A.B. Deyarmond, "Unidentified Aerial Objects, Project 'Sign,'" 35.

27. Mark O'Connell, *The Close Encounters Man* (New York: Dey Street, 2017), 48–49.

28. "'Mystery Plane' Initiates Reports of Flying Discs," *The Free Lance-Star*, July 27, 1948.

29. *Ibid.*

Chapter 22

1. Robert W. Rieber and Robert J. Kelly, *Film, Television and the Psychology of the Social Dream* (New York: Springer, 2013), 22.

2. Richard Hofstadter, *The Paranoid Style in American Politics* (New York: Knopf, 1965).

3. See L.H. Truettner and A.B. Deyarmond, "Unidentified Aerial Objects, Project 'Sign,'" [unpaginated appendices].

4. David Michael Jacobs, *The UFO Controversy in America* (Bloomington: Indiana University Press, 1975), 47.

5. Carl Jung, *Flying Saucers: A Modern Myth of Things Seen in the Sky.*

6. Edward J. Ruppelt, *The Report on Unidentified Flying Objects* (Garden City, NY: Doubleday, 1956), n.p. An electronic copy of this book is preserved by Project Gutenberg: https://www.gutenberg.org/cache/epub/17346/pg17346.html.

7. *Ibid.*

8. *Ibid.*

9. *Ibid.*

Chapter 23

1. David Michael Jacobs, *The UFO Controversy in America*, 44.

2. Office of Public Information, National Military Establishment, "Project Saucer" [memorandum to the press], Washington, D.C., April 27, 1949.

3. Sidney Shalett, "What You Can Believe About Flying Saucers," *Saturday Evening Post*, April 30, 1949, 20.

4. *Ibid.*

5. *Ibid.*, 137.

6. *Ibid.*, 139.

7. *Ibid.*

8. *Ibid.*, 138.

9. Sidney Shalett, "What You Can Believe About Flying Saucers: Conclusions," *Saturday Evening Post*, May 7, 1949, 36.

10. *Ibid.*, 185.

11. *Ibid.*, 186.

12. Curtis Peebles, *Watch the Skies! A Chronicle of the Flying Saucer Myth* (Washington, D.C.: Smithsonian Institution Press, 1994), 35.

13. *Ibid.*

14. *Ibid.*, 42.

15. Gerald K. Haines, "CIA's Role in the Study of UFOs, 1947–90 : A Diehard Issue, " *Intelligence and National Security* 14 (Summer 1999). https://fas.org/sgp/library/ciaufo.html.

16. "Bomb to Bomb," *Life*, October 3, 1949, 22.

Chapter 24

1. Curtis Peebles, *Watch the Skies!*, 43.
2. *Ibid.*, 45.
3. *Ibid.*, 39.
4. David Michael Jacobs, *The UFO Controversy in America*, 56.
5. Curtis Peebles, *Watch the Skies!*, 39.
6. *Ibid.*
7. Donald E. Keyhoe, "The Flying Saucers Are Real," *True*, May 1949, 11.
8. "Around Our Town and Country; the Saucer Book," *Warsaw Times-Union*, May 27, 1950.
9. Donald E. Keyhoe, "The Flying Saucers Are Real," 13.
10. *Ibid.*, 13.
11. *Ibid.* 12–13.
12. *Ibid.*, 12.
13. "U.S. Ban Hinted on New Flying Saucer Book," *The Telegraph-Herald*, May 25, 1950.
14. *Ibid.*
15. "School Children in Every State Told Flying Saucers Are Real," *Evening Star*, October 1, 1950.
16. *Ibid.*

Chapter 25

1. "'Flying Saucer' Chased by National Guard Flier While Three Men Watch," *St. Petersburg Times*, October 3, 1948.
2. Edward U. Condon, *Scientific Study of Unidentified Flying Objects* (Boulder: University of Colorado, 1969), 848–849.
3. Curtis Peebles, *Watch the Skies!*, 27.
4. *Ibid.*, 27–28.
5. "Brilliant Fireball Streaks Over Southwestern States," *The Bulletin*, October 15, 1948.
6. "Meteor tracers Say Campsite Possible Scene of Landing," *Eugene Register-Guard*, January 27, 1948.
7. "Meteor Seen Over Arizona," *Toledo Blade*, April 18, 1949.
8. U.S. Air Force, Office of Special Investigations, *The Air Force Office of Special Investigations, 1948–2000* (Andrews Air Force Base, MD: United States Air Force, 2008), 70.
9. *Ibid.*, 71.
10. Curtis Peebles, *Watch the Skies!*, 28.
11. *Ibid.*
12. U.S. Air Force, Office of Special Investigations, *The Air Force Office of Special Investigations, 1948–2000*, 71.
13. "Have We Visitors from Space?" *Life*, April 7, 1952, 92.
14. *Ibid.*
15. *Ibid.*
16. These details are recounted in Annie Jacobsen, *Area 51: An Uncensored History of America's Top Secret Military Base* (New York: Little, Brown, 2011), 70.
17. *Ibid.*
18. *Ibid.*
19. David Michael Jacobs, *The UFO Controversy in America* (Bloomington: Indiana University Press, 1975), 55.

Chapter 26

1. Edward R. Murrow, "The Case of the Flying Saucer," [CBS Radio Special Report], April 7, 1950. Audio archived at https://www.albany.edu/talkinghistory/arch2004jan-june.html.
2. *Ibid.*
3. *Ibid.*
4. Fred Nadis, *The Man from Mars: Ray Palmer's Amazing Pulp Journey* (New York: Tarcher, 2013), 104.
5. *Ibid.*, 125.
6. Kenn Thomas, *JFK and UFO: Military-Industrial Conspiracy and Cover-Up from Maury Island to Dallas* (Port Townsend, WA: Feral House, 2011), 32.
7. Joe Nickell, "Creators of the Paranormal," *Skeptical Inquirer* 40, no. 3 (May/June 2016): 34.
8. Thomas, *JFK and UFO*, 32.
9. Joe Nickell, "Creators of the Paranormal," 34.

Chapter 27

1. David J. Hogan, *Invasion U.S.A.: Essays in Anti-Communist Movies of the 1950s and 1960s* (Jefferson, NC: McFarland, 2017), 75.

2. Aline Mosby, "Hollywood Now is Starring, of All Things, a Flying Saucer," *Washington Reporter,* September 15, 1949.

3. *Ibid.*

4. *Ibid.*

5. *Ibid.*

6. Bosley Crowther, "The Screen" [Review of *The Flying Saucers*], *New York Times,* January 5, 1950.

7. Gene Jannuzi, "The Flying Saucer; Cry Murder," *Pittsburgh Post-Gazette,* March 27, 1950.

8. *Ibid.*

9. Curtis Peebles, *Watch the Skies!,* 51–52.

Chapter 28

1. Curtis Peebles, *Watch the Skies!,* 50.

2. Claude Lévi-Strauss, *The Raw and the Cooked: Mythologiques, Volume 1* (Chicago: University of Chicago Press, 1983), 12.

3. Donald E. Keyhoe, *The Flying Saucers Are Real* [book], 83.

4. United States Air Force, *The Roswell Report,* 9.

5. *Ibid.,* 9–10.

6. See *Ibid.,* Appendix 6 [unpaginated], "Synopsis of Roswell Incident."

7. *Ibid.*

8. *Ibid.*

9. Lydia Saad, "Americans Skeptical of UFOs, but Say Government Knows More," Gallup (September 6, 2019). Web. https://news.gallup.com/poll/266441/americans-skeptical-ufos-say-government-knows.aspx.

10. Jamie Ballard, "Most Americans Believe the U.S. Government Would Hide Evidence of UFOs," YouGov.com (July 7, 2020). Web. https://today.yougov.com/topics/science/articles-reports/2020/07/07/us-government-ufos aliens-poll-data.

11. Gordon Arnold, *The Rise and Fall of the Future: America's Changing Vision of Tomorrow, 1939–1986* (Jefferson, NC: McFarland, 2020), 139–140.

12. Office of the Director of National Intelligence, *Preliminary Assessment: Unidentified Aerial Phenomena* (Washington, D.C.: Office of National Intelligence, 25 June 2021).

Chapter 29

1. Ragan Dunn, "World's First Space Alien Interview," *World Weekly News,* January 24, 1989.

2. Loeb is quoted in Eve Peyser, "Let This Harvard Professor Convince You That Aliens Exist," *New York Magazine Intelligencer,* January 24, 2021. https://nymag.com/intelligencer/2021/01/harvard-astrophysicist-avi-loeb-on-oumuamua-and-aliens.html.

3. Nassim Nicholas Taleb, *The Black Swan: The Impact of the Highly Improbable* (New York: Random House, 2010), 154.

Chapter 30

1. Jack Rutledge, "AF Investigating Reports of Radar Spotted Flying Saucers," *Key West Citizen,* July 22, 1952.

2. *Ibid.*

3. *Ibid.*

4. "Strange Objects Are Seen Over Washington, D.C.," *The Bulletin,* July 26, 1952.

5. Gerald K. Haines, "CIA's Role in the Study of UFOs, 1947– 1990," *Studies in Intelligence* 1, no. 1 (1997), 68.

6. *Ibid.*

7. David Michael Jacobs, *The UFO Controversy in America,* 64–65.

8. *Ibid.*

9. *Ibid.,* 62.

10. *Ibid.,* 65.

11. *Ibid.,* 89.

12. Gerald K. Haines, "CIA's Role in the Study of UFOs, 1947–90."

Postscript

1. The articulation of the Occam's Razor concept appears in Konrad Bates Krauskopf and Arthur Beiser, *The Physical Universe,* 16th ed. (New York: McGraw-Hill Higher Education, 2016), 14.

2. Arthur Eddington, *The Nature of the Physical World* (Cambridge: Cambridge University Press, 1948), 146.

Bibliography

Air Technical Intelligence Center (United States) *Project Blue Book* "Special Report No. 14" (Analysis of Unidentified Flying Objects). Wright-Patterson Air Force Base, OH: U.S.A.F., 1955.

Armstrong, Alan. "The Legacy of Walker Air Force Base." *WarBirds News*. December 31, 2013. http://warbirdsnews.com/aviation-museum-news/legacy-walker-air-force-base.html.

Arnold, Gordon. *The Rise and Fall of the Future: America's Changing Vision of Tomorrow, 1939–1986*. Jefferson, NC: McFarland, 2020.

Arnold, Kenneth, and Raymond Palmer. *The Coming of the Saucers*. Boise: [Privately published by the authors], 1952.

Berman, William C. *The Politics of Civil Rights in the Truman Administration*. Columbus: The Ohio State University Press, 1970.

Bloccher, Ted. *Report on the UFO Wave of 1947*. Washington, D.C.: [Privately published by the author], 1967.

Colligan, M.J., and L.R. Murphy, "A Review of Mass Psychogenic Illness in Work Settings." In *Mass Psychogenic Illness: A Social Psychological Analysis*, edited by M.J. Colligan, J.W. Pennebaker and L.R. Murphy, 33–52. Mahwah, NJ: Erlbaum, 1982.

Committee on Interstate and Foreign Commerce. "Safety in Air Navigation." Hearings Before the House of Representatives, Eightieth Congress, First Session, on Safety in Air Navigation. Washington, D.C.: U.S. Government Printing Office, 1947.

Condon, Edward U. *Scientific Study of Unidentified Flying Objects*. Boulder: University of Colorado, 1969.

Craven, Wesley Frank, and James Lea Cate. *The Army Air Forces in World War II: Services Around the World*. Chicago: University of Chicago Press, 1948.

Dorsch, Kate. "Reliable Witnesses, Crackpot Science: UFO Investigations in Cold War America, 1947–1977." Ph.D. diss. University of Pennsylvania, 2019.

Evans, Hilary, and Robert E. Bartholomew, eds. *Outbreak! The Encyclopedia of Extraordinary Social Behavior*. New York: Anomalist Books, 2009.

Freud, Anna. *The Writings of Anna Freud: The Ego and the Mechanisms of Defense*. New York: International Universities Press, 1967.

Garber, Megan. "The Man Who Introduced the World to Flying Saucers." *The Atlantic*, June 15, 2014. https://www.theatlantic.com/technology/archive/2014/06/the-man-who-introduced-the-world-to-flying-saucers/372732/.

Gareth, Hector, Jim Laurier, and Peter E. Davies. *Bell X-1*. New York: Bloomsbury, 2016.

Grundhauser, Eric. "The FBI Debunked These UFO Documents in the Most Childish Way Possible." *Slate*. December 6, 2016. https://slate.com/human-interest/2016/12/the-fbi-debunked-the-majestic-12-ufo-documents-in-the-most-childish-way-possible.html.

Haines, Gerald K. "CIA's Role in the Study of UFOs, 1947–1990: A Diehard Issue." *Intelligence and National Security* 14 (Summer 1999). https://fas.org/sgp/library/ciaufo.html.

Hofstadter, Richard. *The Paranoid Style in American Politics.* New York: Knopf, 1965.

Hogan, David J. *Invasion U.S.A.: Essays in Anti-Communist Movies of the 1950s and 1960s.* Jefferson, NC: McFarland, 2017.

Hurt, R. Douglas. *The Great Plains During World War II.* Lincoln: University of Nebraska Press, 2008.

Jacobs, David Michael. *The UFO Controversy in America.* Bloomington: Indiana University Press, 1975.

Janes, Leslie, and James Olson. "Jeer Pressure: The Behavioral Effects of Observing Ridicule of Others." *Personality and Social Psychology Bulletin* 26 (2000): 474–485.

Jung, Carl G. *Flying Saucers: A Modern Myth of Things Seen in the Sky.* New York: MJF Books, 1978.

Keyhoe, Donald. *The Flying Saucers Are Real.* New York: Fawcett, 1950.

Kiat, John E., and Robert F. Belli. "An Exploratory High-Density EEG Investigation of the Misinformation Effect: Attentional and Recollective Differences Between True and False Perceptual Memories." *Neurobiology of Learning and Memory* 141 (May 2017): 199–208.

Krammer, Arnold. *Nazi Prisoners of War in America.* New York: Stein & Day, 1979.

Lévi-Strauss, Claude. *The Raw and the Cooked: Mythologiques.* Vol. 1. Chicago: University of Chicago Press, 1983.

Lowell, Percival. *Mars and Its Canals.* New York: Macmillan, 1906.

Mandeles, Mark D. *The Development of the B-52 and Jet Propulsion: A Case Study in Organizational Innovation.* Maxwell Air Force Base, AL: Air University Press, 1998.

McAndrew, James. "Report on Project Mogul: Synopsis of Balloon Research Findings." Muller's Group, Lawrence Berkeley Laboratory, September 21, 1995. https://muller.lbl.gov/teaching/physics10/Roswell/USMogulReport.html.

McClary, Daryl C. "A Curtis Commando R5C Transport Plane Crashes into Mount Rainier, Killing 32 U.S. Marines, on December 10, 1946." *HistoryLink.org.* July 29, 2006. https://www.historylink.org/File/7820/.

Nadis, Fred. *The Man from Mars: Ray Palmer's Amazing Pulp Journey.* New York: Tarcher, 2013.

Nickell, Joe. "Creators of the Paranormal." *Skeptical Inquirer* 40, no. 3 (May/June 2016). https://skepticalinquirer.org/2016/10/creators-of-the-paranormal/.

O'Connell, Mark. *The Close Encounters Man.* New York: Dey Street, 2017.

Office of the Director of National Intelligence. *Preliminary Assessment: Unidentified Aerial Phenomena.* Washington, D.C.: Office of National Intelligence, 25 June 2021.

Peebles, Curtis. *Watch the Skies! A Chronicle of the Flying Saucer Myth.* Washington, D.C.: Smithsonian Institution Press, 1994.

Pflock, Karl T. *Roswell: Inconvenient Facts and the Will to Believe.* Amherst, NY: Prometheus Books, 2001.

Pooley, Jefferson, and Michael J. Socolow. "The Myth of the War of the Worlds Panic." *Slate.* October 28, 2013. https://slate.com/culture/2013/10/orson-welles-war-of-the-worlds-panic-myth-the-infamous-radio-broadcast-did-not-cause-a-nationwide-hysteria.html.

Rieber, Robert W., and Robert J Kelly. *Film, Television and the Psychology of the Social Dream.* New York: Springer, 2013.

Ruppelt, Edward J. *The Report on Unidentified Flying Objects.* Garden City, NY: Doubleday, 1956.

Saler, Benson, Charles A. Ziegler, and Charles B. Moore. *UFO Crash at Roswell.* Washington, D.C.: Smithsonian Institution, 1997.

Schacter, Daniel L., and Scott D. Slotnick. "The Cognitive Neuroscience of Memory Distortion." *Neuron.* 4, no. 1 (September 30, 2004): 149–60.

Schulz, Kathryn. "The Rabbit-Hole Rabbit Hole." *New Yorker,* June 4, 2015. https://www.newyorker.com/culture/cultural-comment/the-rabbit-hole-rabbit-hole.

Stevenson, Charles A. "The Story Behind the National Security Act of 1947." *Military Review,* May–June 2008: 13–20.

Swords, Michael D., and Robert Powell. *UFOs and Government*. San Antonio: Anomalist Books, 2012.

Tagg, Lori S. *Development of the B-52: The Wright Field Story*. Wright Patterson Air Force Base, OH: Air Force Materiel Command, 2004.

Taleb, Nassim Nicholas. *The Black Swan: The Impact of the Highly Improbable*. New York: Random House, 2010.

Thomas, Kenn. *JFK and UFO: Military-Industrial Conspiracy and Cover-Up from Maury Island to Dallas*. Port Townsend, WA: Feral House, 2011.

Truettner, L.H., and A.B. Deyarmond. "Unidentified Aerial Objects, Project 'Sign.'" Air Material Command, United States Air Force, Wright-Patterson Air .Force Base, Dayton, Ohio, 1949. https://apps.dtic.mil/dtic/tr/fulltext/u2/311102.pdf.

United States Air Force. *The Roswell Report: Fact Versus Fiction in the New Mexico Desert*. Washington, D.C.: GPO, 1995.

U.S. Air Force, Office of Special Investigations. *The Air Force Office of Special Investigations, 1948–2000*. Andrews Air Force Base, MD: United States Air Force, 2008.

Van Der Linden, Robert. *Milestones of Flight: The Epic of Aviation*. Washington, D.C. : National Air and Space Museum, 2016.

Waller John. "A Forgotten Plague: Making Sense of Dancing Mania." *Lancet* 21, no. 373 (February 29, 2009): 624–5.

_____. *A Time to Dance, a Time to Die: The Extraordinary Story of the Dancing Plague of 1518*. Cambridge: Icon, 2008.

Wennergren, Emil Earl. "The 'Flying Saucers' Episode." Master's thesis. University of Iowa. (1948).

Whetham, William Cecil Dampier. *A Shorter History of Science*. Cambridge: Cambridge University Press, 1944.

Young, James Michael. "The U.S. Air Force's Long Range Detection Program and Project MOGUL," *Air Power History* 67, no. 4 (Winter 2020): 25–32.

Index